Looking Directly at Mind:
The Moonlight of Mahamudra

Bibliotheca Indo-Buddhica Series No. 224

Looking Directly at Mind : The Moonlight of Mahamudra

The Venerable Khenchen
THRANGU RINPOCHE
Geshe Lharampa

Translated by
Jules Levinson

Sri Satguru Publications
A Division of
Indian Books Centre
Delhi, India

Published by
Sri Satguru Publications,
Indological and Oriental Publishers
A Division of
Indian Books Centre
40/5, Shakti Nagar,
Delhi-110007
India

Email: ibcindia@vsnl.com
Website: http://www.indianbookscentre.com

First Indian Edition; Delhi, 2002 2013

ISBN 81-7030-748-1

Acknowledgments

We would like to thank the many people who helped make this book possible. First of all, we would like to thank Jules Levinson for translating these teachings. We would like to thank Susan Chapman and Donna McLaughlin and Peter Barth for the immense work of transcribing and editing the tapes of the retreat. We would like to thank especially Sandy Garson and Arline Mathieu who were the final editors of the manuscript. We would also like to thank Bill Lawless and Terry Lucas for helping with this book.

Note

The technical words have been italicized the first time they are used to alert the reader that they are defined in the Glossary of Terms.

We have left off the diacritical marks for the Sanskrit words in the text, but their actual spelling with diacritics may be found in the Glossary.

Tibetan words are given as they are pronounced, not spelled in Tibetan. Their actual spelling is given in the Glossary of Tibetan Terms.

We use the convention of B.C.E. (Before Current Era) for "B. C." and C.E. (Current Era) for "A. D."

These teachings were given in the five Big Bear Mahamudra Retreats in California in 1990, 1991, 1990, 1993, and 1995.

Printed at: Dynamic printers, Delhi

CONTENTS

* (Rinpoche did not cover this topic)

BOOK TWO : THE MEDITATION OF MAHAMUDRA

* (Rinpoche did not cover this topic)

Foreword

Two thousand five hundred years ago the Buddha began delivering a remarkable set of teachings. He taught that instead of relying on a god, one can attain true, permanent happiness by simply examining and working with one's own mind. This message is as true today as it was then; we are engulfed by material wealth in our modern times, yet we are not any more happy or secure. The root of this unhappiness is that our mind keeps looking outside and grasping at external things trying to achieve some measure of happiness. This is futile because to achieve any measure of stability in our life, we must look inward. Looking inward is done through meditation.

The fundamental form of meditation that is common to all schools of Buddhism is shamatha and Vipashyana meditation. Thrangu Rinpoche has given extensive teachings on this form of meditation which can be found in his book, *The Practice of Tranquillity and Insight*. This basic meditation is so important that it is also covered quite comprehensively in this book on mahamudra meditation.

There is another major kind of meditation, which is fairly specific to the vajrayana school of Buddhism, and this is *mahamudra* meditation. This meditation is the examination of the mind itself in what is called "looking directly at the mind." While this is a deceptively simple idea, it is an extremely complex and advanced form of meditation that requires years of practice to develop an extraordinarily clear and stable mind through extensive shamatha and Vipashyana practice. Mahamudra meditation and shamatha and Vipashyana practice are interlinked and complement each other.

We may ask who has practiced this mahamudra meditation? The answer is that it was most extensively practiced by a large number of ordinary and extraordinary people in India in the second through twelfth centuries. Some of their stories have been recorded under the title of *The Eighty-four Mahasiddhas* which may be found in Keith Dowman's *Masters of Enchantment*. These mahasiddhas were cobblers, weavers, arrow makers, and even kings, who carried on their ordinary life and also simultaneously practiced mahamudra meditation and achieved complete enlightenment in one lifetime. What is relevant to our age is that in the West most Buddhist practitioners lead very busy and demanding lives and do not have long periods to devote to shamatha and Vipashyana meditation, but can practice mahamudra meditation while they are making a living and raising a family.

Mahamudra meditation has been practiced in Tibet since the twelfth century, particularly by the Kagyu lineage of Tibetan Buddhism. The practice of this meditation has allowed thousands of individuals to reach enlightenment. This meditation of looking at the mind has also been practiced by Nyingma practitioners in the form of *Dzogchen* meditation, with equal results. This meditation is therefore a very powerful meditation.

In order to practice mahamudra, one has to understand it. This then leads to the question of how many of the hundreds of manuals and texts on mahamudra can one study to understand this topic properly. As Thrangu Rinpoche points out, most of these manuals are strict instructions on what to do, with little or no explanation about why one does it. This method of simply doing what one's lama says is not very compatible with the Western way of learning. Most people reading this book are well educated and have been trained to ask about the reasons for doing what one is told to do. Fortunately, Tashi Namgyal, a great scholar and meditator in the seventeenth century, wrote a detailed explanation of both the fundamental reasons behind mahamudra meditation and its practice which he called *The Moonlight of Mahamudra.* This book has been translated into English by Lobsang Lhalungpa under the name of *Mahamudra: The Quintessence of Mind and Meditation.* This book is over 400 pages long which leads to a problem because the sheer completeness and length of the book can overwhelm the practitioner wanting to understand Mahamudra.

In 1990 Thrangu Rinpoche decided to introduce mahamudra meditation to his Western students. He did this by giving a commentary on Tashi Namgyal's book in five different mahamudra retreats which were held at Big Bear Lake, in California. He also gave mahamudra teachings to the Namo Buddha Summer Seminar held in Oxford, England and Glasgow, Scotland. This was particularly fortunate because Thrangu Rinpoche holds the highest degree of Buddhist studies and was asked by the Sixteenth Karmapa, the head of the Kagyu lineage, to set up the curriculum for the lamas of the Kagyu lineage. The Kagyu lineage is the same one that Tashi Namgyal belonged to. Since Thrangu Rinpoche is not only an eminent scholar of Buddhism, but is also recognized as having the realization of the practice of mahamudra, he is well qualified to write this book. In addition, Thrangu Rinpoche is very familiar with teaching Westerners, having taught thousands of Westerners in over thirty countries in the past decade and a half.

In the first mahamudra retreat in Big Bear, Thrangu Rinpoche gave a general overview of the whole subject. This teaching is being published separately. In the following four years Thrangu Rinpoche went into great detail on the practice of mahamudra. The present book is actually a compilation of lectures given in the second and third Big Bear retreats.

In this book we do not follow the headings and chapters of the original text because this would have become too unwieldy, but we do give the page numbers in Tashi Namgyal's book so the reader can follow the book along if desired. We also included a glossary of important Sanskrit and Tibetan words relevant to mahamudra because some of these words are translated differently in other works.

Clark Johnson, Ph. D.

Chapter 1

An Introduction to the Text

MAHAMUDRA PRACTICE[1]

There are many great Buddhist traditions and of these the teachings of *mahamudra* are particularly helpful in these modern times. The reason I think that the mahamudra teachings are particularly relevant and beneficial in these times is that we find ourselves in a situation quite similar to the one in which the great practitioners of mahamudra found themselves many centuries ago. There were eighty-four great adepts[2] or *mahasiddhas* who lived in India in the second to twelfth centuries. They found themselves in a situation in which it was necessary for them to do spiritual practice in conjunction with their worldly activities. Through these teachings and practices of the tradition of mahamudra, these individuals became highly accomplished Buddhist practitioners.

For instance, *King Indrabhuti* who ruled a large kingdom was one of these eighty-four mahasiddhas. He was surrounded by great luxury and yet he received the instructions for the practice of mahamudra and practiced them while ruling his kingdom and achieved the supreme accomplishment of mahamudra, which is enlightenment in one lifetime. Similarly, the great scholar *Nagarjuna* was an extraordinarily learned person, who with his magnificent intelligence undertook the work of clarifying the teachings of the Buddhist tradition by composing many complex treatises that clearly presented the meaning of *emptiness,* a central teaching of the Buddhist tradition. However, together with these great responsibilities and extremely difficult work, he practiced the meditation of mahamudra, and through doing so, achieved the *supreme accomplishment* of mahamudra.

There were other mahasiddhas who were cobblers, arrow makers, sweepers, and even practitioners who engaged in such humble occupations as grinding sesame seeds. All of them, however, combined their practice of mahamudra with whatever activities they were engaged in. There was, for them, no contradiction between the work that they had to do and the practice of mahamudra meditation. In all cases, they were able to resolve whatever conflicts there might have been between the practice of *dharma* and their worldly activities. Thus, the tradition of mahamudra arose and flourished.

Here in the West there are many different people doing many different kinds of work and having many different kinds of thoughts. This practice of mahamudra allows them to live as they wish, to do the work that they want to do, and at the same time, without any contradiction, to practice mahamudra. It is for that reason, I feel, that we should learn to meditate on mahamudra.

One of the best things about mahamudra practice is that it is peaceful and gentle and there isn't a great danger of making terrible mistakes or creating a practice situation that can harm us. In contrast, there are some other special practices, which can certainly yield profound results if practiced well, but they also involve the danger of unwanted complications. One such practice is known as the dark retreat, which involves doing contemplative practice while staying in a room with no illumination for a month or so. If it is done properly it yields profound realization, but if it doesn't go well there is the danger of creating even greater difficulties for the person. Another example is the practice of going without food for seven or fourteen days and thereby bringing about the realization known as extracting the essence. It, too, if done well brings about profound realization, but if done incorrectly causes one to become sick and extremely unhappy.

The practice of mahamudra is free from such dangers and such complications because it is simply a matter of looking at our mind, recognizing its nature, and remaining within that recognition. The mahamudra instructions are distinctive and penetrate right to the point, and if they are followed, there is no risk to body or mind.

THE MOONLIGHT OF MAHAMUDRA

Once we decide that we should study and practice the tradition of mahamudra, there is a question of how we should approach these teachings. There are, after all, a great many texts giving instructions on the practice of mahamudra. Some of these texts are extremely vast and some are very concise. For example, the ninth Karmapa, *Wangchuk Dorje* wrote a shorter work on mahamudra called *Pointing out the Dharmakaya*, a middle length work called *Mahamudra: Illuminating the Darkness of Ignorance*, and a longer and more detailed work called *The Ocean of Definitive Meaning*. These are extraordinary texts that teach how to practice mahamudra. However, most practitioners in the West have gone to school and have been taught analytical thinking and therefore they would also like to learn the reasons for doing the practice. The text that I have selected, therefore, is *The Moonlight of Mahamudra*[3] that is known in Tibetan as *chakchen dawai ozer* and was written by the great practitioner and scholar Tashi Namgyal. This text is not only a compilation of the *quintessential instructions* of mahamudra, but also explains them in such a way that we can understand the purpose of this practice. From my own experience I have found this text to be extraordinary.

When the Sixteenth Karmapa came to America for the first time in 1974 a student of his, Mr. Shen, asked, "What text would be of great benefit to students of the West if it were translated? I will sponsor it." His Holiness Karmapa replied that *The Moonlight of Mahamudra* would be extremely beneficial for Westerners. When I heard that this book was selected, I saw this as an instance of Karmapa's remarkable enlightened mind blazing forth in utter clarity. And so, in accordance with his wish, the text has been translated by Lobsang Lhalungpa with the help of Dezhung Rinpoche. This English translation was published as *Mahamudra: The Quintessence of Mind and Meditation*. Since then I've heard that some students think that there are some problems with the translation. This may be the case, because it is difficult to translate some of the subtleties of the thought. But it seems to me that the essential points have been translated well and that they can be understood with careful reading.

It also seemed to me that if I were to explain and teach this text in a slow and careful manner over a number of years,[4] it would allow students to understand the meaning of the text. So I thought that teaching this text would allow us to get at something very essential in Buddhist practice. It also seemed to me that this must have been what the Sixteenth Karmapa had in mind when he recommended that this text be translated and studied and used as a basis for practice. Karmapa passed into *nirvana* several years ago.[5] Even though he passed away, his hope and his instruction regarding this text remains. In presenting an explanation of *The Moonlight of Mahamudra* I feel that I am offering some service to him.

The texts on the *Middle-way* (Skt. *Madhyamaka*) cover a fundamental aspect called the *Prajnaparamita* which has been explained by the great teacher Nagarjuna in his *Prajnanama-mula-madhyamaka* and by Chandrakirti in his *Entrance into the Middle Way*. These texts set forth very clearly the proper view of the way in which things exist and provide very clear explanations for an understanding of the nature of reality. However, if you want to meditate on the nature of reality, you will find that these texts don't even talk about how to meditate. The Madhyamaka texts explain the view and allow you to develop great faith and understanding of the dharma, but they don't address how you can actually meditate to gain an understanding of these views.

The *Moonlight of Mahamudra* is different in that it explains very clearly how to meditate, by developing *shamatha* or *tranquillity meditation*, and how to develop *Vipashyana* or *insight meditation*. The practices of tranquillity and insight meditation are explained very clearly; the text also shows how these meditations allow one to rest one's mind evenly to see the basic nature of reality.

The *Moonlight of Mahamudra* also describes many levels of meditation experience. If one is quite new to the practice of meditation and wants to know how to begin, this text describes how one begins. If one has practiced meditation and given birth to some results of meditation and one wishes to know how to proceed, this text talks about that also. If one has developed some genuine meditation and encounters obstacles and difficulties, this text also explains where these obstacles come from, what they are, and how to get rid of them. All these are presented very clearly. That is why the Sixteenth Karmapa said that this is the best book to translate into English for Western students.

C. Reasons to Meditate on the Nature of Mind

[6][6] When we practice meditation it is important to know the reason why we practice. There are two traditions of meditation—*analytical meditation* and *placement meditation*. The Madhyamaka or the Middle-way school has given us very extensive, clear explanations of how external things (which can also be translated as "phenomena") are actually emptiness. In analytical meditation we actually meditate on these reasons and arguments. However, it is very difficult to actually meditate on the emptiness of phenomena. In the *vajrayana* tradition of Tibet rather than meditating on the nature of external phenomena, we meditate on mind itself. The technique of mahamudra meditation is not shared with other types of meditation and is a unique, essential point of the vajrayana tradition. Tashi Namgyal who lived 400 years ago in Tibet observed that "these day there are meditators who do not understand the true nature of phenomena" and "there are those who know the true nature, but who do not practice meditation." These two systems are at cross-purposes and it is important to combine the practice of meditation with analytical understanding of the teachings.

The first Jamgon Kongtrul Rinpoche, Lodro Thaye, said that a person without the view of how to practice meditation is like a person with no hands trying to climb a mountain. On the other hand, someone who understands the view but doesn't practice is like a wealthy person who is a miser and therefore does not use his money to help himself or others. If a person has both the understanding of the view and practices this view, he or she is like a great *garuda* using both wings together to travel through space easily and freely without effort. In this way, if we are able to put the wisdom of listening to the teachings with the wisdom of meditation, we will indeed arrive at the final truth. For this reason both the explanation of the view and the explanation of the practice are taught in *The Moonlight of Mahamudra*.

The reason for teaching meditation on the true nature of the mind is that all phenomena are just mind. This means external appearances such as images, sounds, smells, tastes, and tangible objects are just mind, and internal objects such as feelings and thoughts of pleasure, pain, attachment, and anger are also just mind.

All these various experiences of mind and body come back to mind itself.

When we say that we "meditate on the mind" we are referring to meditating on the "true nature"[7] (Tib. *ngelug*) of mind which we may translate also as "the way the mind is." When we meditate in the tradition of *Dzogchen* (or "Great Perfection), we are also meditating on the mind as it is. In the *secret mantra tradition* (the vajrayana) the teacher points out to the student the nature of the mind and this is called *sem tri* in which *sem* means "mind" and *tri* means "leading someone." It is called *sem tri* in both the tradition of Dzogchen and mahamudra. This phrase means, "leading the mind" to knowing the mind as it is.

The first teaching of mahamudra is the teaching that "all phenomena are mind," or we may say "all dharmas are mind." This point comes first because the nature of the mind is most important in this teaching. In the *Mind-only* or *Chittamatra* school[8] of Buddhism the notion that everything is mind is explained in great detail. All appearances—mountains, houses, trees—are just mind and this is set forth very clearly in a set of logical arguments.

However, when it comes to practice, we aren't concerned very much whether these appearances are mind or not, because it doesn't make much difference in our meditation. When we practice mahamudra, what we are concerned with is our mind. In terms of feeling, we are concerned with pleasure and pain. We are concerned with aspects of the mind that are beneficial to us such as faith, confidence, compassion, aspiration of enlightenment for all beings, and what is harmful, such as the *disturbing emotions* (Skt. *klesha*)[9] of great attachment, hatred, the ignorance of dark obscuration, our discursive thought, and our holding onto a self. For these reasons it is the mind which is most important. If we meditate on the mind, we can understand the mind as it is. Then, with this understanding, whatever good qualities that need to be developed will be developed, and whatever negative qualities will be abandoned. Along the way all the good qualities such as faith and confidence in the Buddha, the dharma, and the *sangha*; the energy to practice (Skt. *virya*), love (Skt. *maitri*), and compassion (Skt. *karuna*) will become stronger and stronger. At the very end of this path wisdom will be unveiled, clarified, illuminated. All this just through understanding the mind as it is.

We can try to discover the nature of the mind by studying logical arguments or we can rely on the authority of the scriptures. In the scriptures, for example the *Lankavatara Sutra* says:

> *All things appear as perfect reality to the mind*
> *Apart from the mind, no reality as such exists.*
> *To perceive external reality is to see wrongly.*

In the *Samputa* tantra it says:

> *All things, external and internal,*
> *Are designated by the mind.*
> *Apart from the mind nothing else exists.*

D. PROBLEMS FROM NOT MEDITATING ON MIND

[9] Is it helpful to know the true nature of mind but not practice meditation? Well, it is somewhat helpful, but just knowing this fact is not going to allow us to abandon the various negative emotions, such as desire and hatred, to achieve complete enlightenment. Therefore, there is a great problem with not meditating on the true nature of mind. The Buddha spoke about this in the *Gandavyuha Sutra* in which he compared knowing a great deal about the dharma and not putting it into practice to a doctor who knows a great deal about medicine, but when he or she becomes sick does not take any. Similarly, if we know a lot of dharma but don't practice, it is not very beneficial.

The reason we need to practice meditation is that we have many disturbing emotions. If we do not practice, these disturbing emotions will arise in us and remain there. Mere knowledge is not in itself sufficient. The great Indian saint Shantideva spoke to this fact when he said the mind is the hub of our existence much in the same way a hub of the wheel is the central part of a wheel which holds all the other parts together. If one doesn't understand this essential point of mind, even though one wants happiness, one will not be able to achieve it.

E. BENEFITS FROM MEDITATING ON MIND

[10] *The Moonlight of Mahamudra* explains the importance of meditating on the thought that all appearances are mind by discussing the faults of not meditating in this way and then discussing the benefits of actually doing this meditation. The faults of not meditating are given by the Buddha and many learned and accomplished persons of the tradition. For example, in his *The Treasury of the Abhidharma* (Skt. *Abhidharmakosha*) *Vasubandhu* gives an example of a teller who works in a bank and spends all day counting hundreds of thousands of dollars, placing the money in this pile and then in that pile; but none of this money belongs to the teller. You have all this money, but you can never do anything with it because it isn't yours. Similarly, you can listen to all these valuable teachings and tell others about the miseries of cyclic existence or samsara and the great qualities of liberation; but if you have never actually meditated on them, they are all useless to you because you don't actually have a real understanding of them.

Many *sutras* and other teachings extol the benefits of meditation and they all more or less say the same thing, which is to say that it is far more beneficial to meditate even for one day than it is to just listen to teachings and analyze them for eons and eons. It is also far more important to meditate for a short period of time than to engage in vast virtuous and beneficial activity for a very long time. This does not mean that there is not any value or benefit or meaning in other practices. On the contrary, it is extremely beneficial to listen to the teaching of the dharma and to think about the meaning of what one has heard. However, the practice of meditation surpasses the benefit of any other type of practice that can be done.

Questions

Question: I am very much tormented by the lack of time to practice because of my work. This makes me angry at work. It really is a serious attachment problem and I want to know how to work with that.

Rinpoche: What you described is quite familiar. What you are talking about here is really more a matter of the balance between meditation and postmeditation.

By meditation I mean sitting down somewhere and drawing attention to the mind. If we have the aspiration to meditate for a long time and are busy and have other things to do, then get up and go do them while practicing postmeditation, thus making our meditation continual. Whether we are speaking with someone else or working on a particular task, we bring mindfulness and awareness to bear upon that activity so the mind is not fluttering here and there in great distraction. When we are able to bring meditation into post-meditation through this practice of mindfulness, then work and meditation cease to be contrary to one another.

If we don't combine meditation and postmeditation then meditation is one thing and work is something else; they are fighting with each other. We will feel that we can't work when we meditate and we can't meditate when we work. But if we bring this practice of awareness and non-distraction of mind into all of our actions, then these two will go together. In fact what we will find is that meditation and postmeditation begin to stimulate one another; the more we can practice meditation in our actions, the easier our meditation on the cushion will go. Then that good meditation experience will be something positive that we can easily carry back into our work. So these two begin to help one another, so that we do not have the feeling of having to flee from work, and working itself becomes a way of subduing and overcoming the disturbing emotions (Skt. *kleshas*), the wildness, dullness, lack of clarity, and instability of mind.

Question: Could you please explain the main differences between Dzogchen and mahamudra.

Rinpoche: There are differences between the lineage of transmission of these two and there are differences in the *skillful methods* (Skt. *upaya*) of these two meditations. But if we are speaking of exactly what they are, there is no difference. Both are a practice leading to recognizing mind as it is. The lineage of Dzogchen, which in Sanskrit is *mahasandhi* and means "the great completion" or "the great perfection," began with the teacher Gerab Dorje who passed it to Trisina who passed it on from teacher to student. The lineage of mahamudra, which in Sanskrit means "the great symbol" or the "the great seal," begins with Saraha and passes to Nagarjuna to Shawari and so forth. The Dzogchen which came to Tibet was mostly associated with the *Nyingma* lineage, while the lineage of mahamudra is associated mostly with the *Kagyu* lineage—with Marpa, Milarepa, Gampopa and so on. But Dzogchen and mahamudra are meditating on the mind and, as we say in the Kagyu lineage chant, "all thoughts are *dharmakaya*, as is said." That can be pointed out to us by the guru and then we meditate in terms of that. That is the way that one meditates in the tradition of mahamudra.

In the tradition of Dzogchen, one makes a distinction between mind (Tib. *sem*) and fundamental insight (Tib. *rigpa*). To elaborate: *rigpa* has the connotation of knowing and recognizing, of having understood true nature while *sem* has the connotation of not having recognized the true nature. So the technique or method of Dzogchen is separating *sem* from *rigpa* and knowing that *sem* is not the true nature of mind and coming to *rigpa,* which is this knowing or fundamental mind.

However, there is actually little difference between Dzogchen and mahamudra. For example, in *An Aspirational Prayer for Mahamudra* composed by the Third Karmapa, *Rangjung Dorje*, there is a verse that says:

It doesn't exist, even the victorious ones haven't seen it.
It is not nonexistent because it is the basis of all samsara and nirvana.
This is not a contradiction because this is the unity of the middle way.
May we realize the true nature of mind
which is free from all limitations and extremes.

There is also another aspiration prayer by Jigme Lingpa which is central to Dzogchen, called *An Aspirational Prayer for Dzogchen* and says:

It doesn't exist, even the victorious ones haven't seen it.
It is not nonexistent because it is the basis of all samsara and nirvana.
This is not a contradiction because this is the unity of the middle way.
May we realize the ground of Dzogchen.

So we see there is little difference between mahamudra and Dzogchen.

It should be noted that Rangjung Dorje was actually the teacher of the great master Longchenpa. He also wrote one of the most precious teachings of the Kagyu lineage called the *Karma Nyingthig* in which a *nyingthig* is a Dzogchen style of teaching. He composed and arranged and passed this down in the Kagyu lineage. So Rangjung Dorje was not only an author of mahamudra teachings, but also of Dzogchen teachings.

F. WHAT IS SHAMATHA AND VIPASHYANA MEDITATION?

[15] We will begin by explaining the meditation of shamatha and Vipashyana that is common to all Buddhist practices and then, in later chapters, we will discuss the meditation that is particular to mahamudra. The word covering all meditation is *samadhi* in Sanskrit. There are a great many different levels or types of samadhi described in different texts and treatises. However, no matter how many kinds of meditation there are, all of these different kinds of samadhi can be included within shamatha and Vipashyana meditation.

If our mind is continually wandering here and there, being carried away by this thought and that thought, and we are unable to rest anywhere, then it is very difficult for any spiritual growth to come about. In contrast, if our mind can be placed somewhere and rest there, then we can become accustomed to whatever is taking place in our mind. Otherwise, our mind is just like a flag waving in the wind, helplessly being blown this way and that way.

The practice of shamatha is the practice of allowing our mind to rest somewhere, to be peaceful, to be calmed in that way. However, if we were to stop there and relax with this peacefulness, that is not enough. It is important to also develop Vipashyana, often called "insight meditation," which is a clear and intense seeing. We might believe that shamatha and Vipashyana are very ordinary meditations because teachers talk about them all the time, but shamatha and Vipashyana are actually extremely important, valuable, and extraordinary meditations.

We must begin our path of meditation by bringing some steadiness to our mind. Someone could give us the *mind transmission*[10] when we just begin to meditate and point out exactly what the mind is actually like. We could have this wonderful experience and think, "Oh, now I have really given birth to a great experience. Now something fantastic has happened to my meditation." But then the next day it is not so clear and then the following day it is even a little less clear and after a year all we can think is, "Well, last year my meditation was really great." That is why we need to develop some steadiness of mind and that is why shamatha is the foundation to meditation. In the beginning of meditation it is not important whether something wonderful happens or everything is quite ordinary. We just let these experiences be and learn to focus on letting the mind be steady, firm, and still; that is, letting it come to rest.

In another example, sometimes a person new to the dharma will meet a teacher and receive the instructions for the practice of *phowa,* which is the practice of transference of consciousness out of this body and into the pure land of the Buddha. In this practice one develops a physical sign of the practice which is a very soft spot on the top of the head. One can actually feel this soft spot and think, "Oh yes, I have gotten that practice down." But a year later one might reach up there and find that the head is hard again. That is why we must begin our practice with shamatha. When we study the tradition of the *siddhas* who were highly accomplished practitioners, we find that they began with shamatha. And if we follow in the same way that they did, then we can accomplish what they did.

BOOK I

MEDITATIONS SHARED BY OTHER TRADITIONS

Table 1

Summary of the Powers, Levels, and Engagements

The Power of	Levels of Stability	Engagement
1. Hearing the teachings	1. Placement	1. Forcible mental engagement
2. Contemplating the teachings	2. Continual placement	
3. Memory of mindfulness	3. Resettling the mind 4. Intensely settled engagement	2. Interrupted mental engagement
4. Power of awareness	5. Taming the mind 6. Pacifying the mind	
5. Power of exertion	7. Thorough pacifying the mind 8. One-pointed mind	3. Uninterrupted mental engagement
6. Power of familiarity	9. Resting in equanimity	4. Spontaneous mental engagement

Chapter 2

The Shared Tradition of Shamatha and Vipashyana

BOOK I

II. THE SHARED TRADITION OF SHAMATHA AND VIPASHYANA

A. THE ROOT OF SHAMATHA AND VIPASHYANA

[17] We must first look into the root or cause of shamatha and Vipashyana to see what allows shamatha and Vipashyana to come about. There are three roots or direct causes of shamatha: discipline, hearing the teachings, and reflecting upon the teachings. What discipline (Skt. *shila*, Tib. *tsultrim*) we take up depends upon our station in life. If we have taken the vows of a monk or a nun, then we follow the discipline of the monastic orders, called the *genyan* vows. If we are working in the world and living as a householder, then we must engage in a discipline that is different. If we follow the appropriate discipline of our station in life, then we will be free from the problems, faults, and difficulties that come from not maintaining the appropriate discipline. When we listen to and think about the instructions on meditation, we will learn how to meditate. We will then be able to clear away the obstacles to meditation and will be able to develop a true understanding and confidence in meditation which will then lead to the birth of true meditation in our being. So discipline is the basic root of shamatha and Vipashyana.

To maintain discipline we also need devotion, which is a secondary cause for shamatha and Vipashyana. The Tibetan word for "devotion" is *mögu* with the syllable *mö* meaning "longing, admiration and a sense of faith" and the syllable *gu* meaning "respect." This suggests that the object of our devotion is distinctive, special, or superior so we have great longing, faith, and deep respect for it. The principle focus of our devotion is to the samadhi of mahamudra itself. The reason we have an intense longing and respect for the samadhi of mahamudra is because mahamudra can actually tame and liberate our mind from its bondage. Our devotion is also towards our *root guru* and *lineage gurus* because it is not possible to give birth to the samadhi of mahamudra without having relied wholeheartedly on our gurus.

With devotion we can give rise to mahamudra naturally and thereby receive the guru's *blessings*. To give rise to such devotion we practice *guru yoga* which helps give rise to Vipashyana. The literal meaning of the Tibetan word for "blessings" is *chin lap* or "a wave of splendor." We need the guru's blessings. We need to also accumulate merit, and we need to purify our negative deeds and obstructions that hinder our progress on the path. If we proceed in this way, we will be able to give birth to true shamatha and Vipashyana. To give rise to such devotion, in the vajrayana, we practice guru yoga.

Another indirect cause of shamatha and Vipashyana is the *accumulation of merit*. Merit is gathered by way of body, speech, mind, and our own wealth. The accumulation of merit of our body is helping others materially and also by doing physical actions of devotion such as offering prostrations to our guru, the Buddha, the dharma, and the sangha. This also includes work we do promoting the dharma. The accumulation of merit by way of speech includes doing the supplication chants and reciting mantras. It also includes offering advice that is utterly pure to help others. The accumulation of merit in terms of mind involves trying to cultivate love and compassion and *bodhichitta*, the desire to help all beings achieve enlightenment. In addition to trying to accumulate feelings and attitudes to help others, we can accumulate merit by meditating on a *yidam*, which is a deity representing an enlightened aspect of mind. A fourth way to accumulate merit is using our wealth and resources to help someone who is poor and by making offerings to the Buddha, the dharma, and the sangha to help the dharma flourish.

B. OBSTACLES TO SHAMATHA AND VIPASHYANA

[19] There is an almost limitless variety of thoughts that are obstacles to shamatha and Vipashyana. These thoughts can, however, be grouped into five different classes of obstacles.

The first group of obstacles to shamatha and Vipashyana contains two elements that appear to be completely different in their quality and content, but are the same in that they keep the mind from being able to rest. One is excitement or mental agitation, which means being so joyful and agitated about something that one's mind is completely distracted and just races along with these thoughts. The other is basic sadness or remorsefulness, in which one feels that everything has gone wrong and has not worked out and one is completely discouraged. Excitement and sadness are very different in how we experience them, but they are the same in that they prevent the mind from being able to rest in meditation.

The second group of obstacles also has two different elements. The first is a heaviness of mind and the other is falling asleep. These are different but, of course, being very heavy or dull often leads to sleep.

The third group of obstacles consists of having all sorts of doubts. This is thinking: "Is it this way or is it that way? Is it like this or is it like that?" The mind is constantly fluctuating between various possibilities and one cannot make up one's mind.

The fourth group of obstacles is the different kinds of discursive thoughts that can be classed together as attachment or desire. We feel that there is something extremely important that we must have, we are very attached to it, and we feel it is crucial to have it, so it creates a problem for practicing meditation.

The fifth group is a collection of all the thoughts of wanting to harm others. It is an attitude of revenge. We feel that others have treated us very badly and so it is necessary to get back at them by talking to them in an extremely nasty or harsh way.

REMEDIES TO THE OBSTACLES OF SHAMATHA AND VIPASHYANA

[21] By understanding the five obstacles to shamatha and Vipashyana practice, we can see how they can harm our practice. If the mind is steady, these obstacles make it unsteady; if the mind is

clear, luminous, and unobstructed, these obstacles make it dull and obstructed. If we can identify a particular obstacle, we can make use of the various antidotes to clear away these factors that hinder our practice of meditation. Not identifying obstacles is like trying to shoot an arrow without having a target. If we are going to shoot an arrow, what are we shooting at? If we can set up the target, then we can shoot the arrow and hit it. In the same way, if we want to get rid of all the obstacles to our meditation, we have to identify them to know what to do.

The first obstacle to shamatha and Vipashyana meditation is wild or excited mind. The remedy to wildness is to meditate upon impermanence. When we feel something is going very well, we become very happy and joyful and the mind is excited in that sense. But remembering that this will end (impermanence) makes us become a little bit discouraged so this serves as a remedy to the wildness or excitement of the mind.

If, on the other hand, we are feeling tremendous remorse or regret or sadness (Tib. *gyöpa*), then it is important to realize impermanence of whatever we are feeling regret and sadness about for it is done with, so there is not much point in continuing to think about it. So, if we just stop bringing it to mind, then our mind will become clear, bright, and we will be able to proceed with our meditation.

The second obstacle is heavy or dull mind (Tib. *mukpa*), which is as if the mind has becomes enveloped in darkness, it has no brilliance, and there is no joy or no delight; one simply feels completely dull. The remedy is to think about the good qualities of the Buddha, the good qualities of the dharma, and the good qualities of meditation itself. If we bring these things to mind, then they will clear away this dark, heavy state of mind and we will feel joyful. This obstacle has another element to it, which is being sleepy. When we feel sleepy and are trying to meditate, what is important is to bring to mind the sense of *luminosity*[11] (Tib. *salwa*). We actually meditate upon the sense of brilliance and when we do so, the sleepiness will subside.

The third obstacle is doubt. The remedy to doubt is to make one's mind one-pointed and to settle the matter. Instead of thinking, "Well, is it like this or is it like that; is it good or is it not so good?"

we actually settle one-pointedly and stop going back over the matter over and over again.

The fourth obstacle is the notion of continually trying to acquire. This is very negative, because even if we get what we want, we are never satisfied. No matter how much we get, we will never come to the point of saying, "Well, that is enough." Later we will always want more. There is no satisfaction from material things. If we realize this fact, then we can feel some contentment and say, "What I've got is enough, the situation is all right just as it is." Then when we feel that contentment, we are not tortured by this continual longing to acquire more and more.

The fifth obstacle is wishing to harm others. Along with that comes the notion of envy and jealousy. When we have a wish to harm someone else or have a sense of jealousy, our mind does not rest and it is not clear and steady. The remedy to such harmful attitudes towards others is love (Skt. *maitri*). It is wishing that others have happiness and that they will be free from suffering and the causes of suffering. We must realize that just as we ourselves want happiness, so others also want happiness. Just as we don't want suffering, so no one else wants to have suffering. It is also knowing that suffering really doesn't help us, so that even if others who have harmed us were to suffer terribly, it would not really help us in any way or help them either. So, wishing harm to others is just a pointless destructive act. We might think, "Yes, it is entirely fair and just and suitable for them to experience great misery because of what they have done to me." But, in fact, someone else's suffering will not help us at all. Instead we should develop kindness to others, wishing to help them whoever they might be, because there is not always justice and fairness in our world and harming others does not really level the score. And when we think about these things carefully, then bit by bit we are able to pacify that malevolent attitude of wanting to harm others.

THE REMEDIES FOR DULL AND EXCITED MIND

[23] There are many different ways to talk about the various obstructions to meditation. There is, however, one classification that is quite helpful in understanding the obstacles and the remedies for

practicing shamatha and Vipashyana. This is to divide the remedies into the remedies for heavy or sinking mind and the remedies to excited or wild mind. The heaviness of mind comes from a Tibetan word *chingwa,* which literally means "a sinking" of mind. The excited mind comes from the Tibetan *göpa* which is wildly or excitedly flying off in every direction. We can say that in terms of the five principal obstacles to meditation these two are the most important and the most problematic obstacles to our meditation.

The mind becomes heavy basically because we lose the longing and admiration for meditation. As our longing for meditation decreases, our mind becomes heavy and dull and sinks. So, the most effective remedy to this sinking is to think about the good qualities of the enlightened one and to feel great longing to become like the Buddha. As our longing and admiration for meditation—which is the pathway to enlightenment—increases, the heaviness decreases.

There are other factors that we could bring to bear in this situation such as enlivening the factor of luminosity, which is essential to *prajna*. Prajna is a word that means a very clear and sharp intelligence, not so much knowledge as a quality of knowing. If we undertake to think about the essential points of meditation or the essential points of the dharma, this lights the fire of prajna. As prajna increases, the factor of luminosity dispels the darkness and the heaviness of mind. Similarly, to arouse our joy and delight, we can remember that at last we have the opportunity to practice meditation and the dharma. This is inconceivably good fortune. Remembering that, we become joyful which leads to exertion. Exertion, then, increases the factor of luminosity of mind and as luminosity increases the heavy, dull quality of the mind is dispelled.

An excited mind is an instance of the mind being very attached to something, passionately stuck on something. The basic remedy to this attachment is remembering impermanence, and remembering that all things come to an end causes us to become discouraged and not as excited.

Another way that we can work with dull mind and excited mind is through a particular physical activity. If the mind is very dull and heavy, then we can get up and walk around, then come back and practice again. This will help to clear away the heavy feeling. And if the mind if very wild, we can do some prostrations which are hard work and will calm us down.

C. TRUE NATURE OF SHAMATHA AND VIPASHYANA

[26] We will discuss shamatha and Vipashyana by describing just what they are. To begin with, shamatha and Vipashyana are not the same thing in all Buddhist traditions. Even though the names are the same, the meaning is not. The Buddhist *Hinayana* tradition, for example, practices shamatha and Vipashyana meditation, but it is dissimilar from how shamatha and Vipashyana are practiced in the Buddhist vajrayana tradition.

In the vajrayana tradition, Vipashyana meditation is an indispensable key to abandoning the disturbing emotions and to achieving genuine happiness, the good qualities of enlightenment, and genuine wisdom. The reason understanding Vipashyana is so important is that we place a great value and importance upon external objects and the appearance of external phenomena. When we feel that external phenomena are in order, we are happy. But if external phenomena are not as we expect, we are miserable. In fact, this view of relying on the external world to attain happiness is a false view that leads only to unhappiness. Rather, the understanding of internal mind is what is most important. If we are happy, then wherever we are will appear to us to be like a palace of the buddhas. And if we don't have that happiness of mind, then even if we were living in a palace made of gold and silver, we would feel no pleasure whatsoever. Pleasure or happiness, misery or pain, the disturbing emotions or pure motivation that we experience, all goes back to our mind. That is why the mind is the most important thing to understand. If the mind is peaceful and free from fear, then we will experience our world as a peaceful, tamed, and non-threatening place.

Mind has two aspects to it: mind as it appears (Tib. *khrih lug*) and mind as it is (Tib. *ngelug*).[12] Mind as it appears is cyclic existence or samsara. When we look at samsaric mind, what we find is a lot of very coarse, stubborn, and obstinate thoughts with the false qualities of pride, envy, desire, anger, ignorance being very strong. Once these disturbing emotions dominate, our body and speech follow and we accumulate a lot of negative karma which, in turn, causes further mental anguish for us. So this is the mind as it appears.

But if we look at our mind carefully, we see that the mind is not entirely covered with disturbing emotions, that it is more than a great mass of faults. In the *sutra tradition* mind is explained as having *Buddha-essence* (Skt. *tathagatagarbha*) or Buddha-nature.[13] This Buddha-essence is the potential within ourselves that is like a seed from which all the good qualities of the Buddha can grow. It is as if we had pure gold inside of us. This essence of the enlightened one exists within us, but it is obstructed by the disturbing, distorted, and painful states of mind, such as attachment, aggression, ignorance and so forth. Because of these disturbing emotions, this Buddha-essence does not manifest. For Buddha-essence to manifest, we need to abandon all these disturbing emotions.

Upon hearing about Buddha-essence we might imagine the disturbing emotions as being external and Buddha-essence as being inside us. It is as if the disturbing emotions were extraneous and Buddha-essence was more essential. But when we examine this in terms of the experience of meditation and ask, "Where does this mind dwell? Is it outside the body or is it inside the body, or is it some place in-between? Is there some place where it dwells or exists? Does it have a form, or is it formless? If it has form, then what is its color and shape? If it doesn't have any form, then what exactly do we mean by mind?" We find there is nothing we can identify as mind and there is no place in particular where thoughts exist. There is nothing that we can point to and say, "That's mind."

There are two ways to look at our mind: either after the fact or experientially. We may look at some strong thought of attachment or aggression after it has already left, but there is no way we can ever catch hold of it. It is too late, it has already passed. When we speak of looking at our mind experientially, we mean looking at our present mind and not thinking about the future or the past. We look to see if some thought such as attachment or aggression has just occurred and ask, "What is the manner of its birth?" And if it was not born within us, we ask, "How did it get there and how did that come about?" But, when we look for the origin of thoughts, we can never find anything.

Why is it that we find nothing when we look for mind or thoughts? Is it because our mind is too small to see? No. Is it because the thoughts are so transparent that they can't be seen? No. Is it because it is too far away? No. Is it because thought is our own mind? No. The reason we can't find mind when we look for it is that mind doesn't have any nature of its own. This nonexistence is what the Buddha called emptiness (Skt. *shunyata*).

The Buddha taught about emptiness in the second turning of the *wheel of the dharma.*[14] This emptiness does not need to be verified through complicated reasoning. It is just the very nature or essence of the mind. Now peacefulness is also the nature of the mind. Similarly, the disturbing emotions are also of the nature of mind. The mind is not solid and dense like the body, but is just something that is empty of inherent existence. Because it is empty, it cannot be harmed, and does not become defective and degrade as the body does with age and illness. And because it is free from fault, one does not need to fear anything whatsoever. This peace which is the characteristic of the mind is also emptiness.

When we say the mind is empty, we do not mean it is a void in the way that space is empty. Space is indeed empty, but it does not have any ability to know, to see, or to reflect. So we speak of space as being a "dead emptiness." When we say that emptiness is the nature of mind, what we mean is that the mind is not a solid entity, and that it cannot be found anywhere, no matter where we look. Even though it cannot be found, nevertheless it has the ability to know and understand and reflect. That ability of the mind to know, to think, is what we mean when we speak of the mind's luminosity.

In the context of the sutras, we say that this luminosity is the source of all the good qualities and we give it the name of Buddha-essence. We usually say that this Buddha-essence is the union of wisdom and space, but this space is not "dead space" which is a different word in Tibetan. This "alive space" is the Tibetan word *ying* (Skt. *dhatu)* (in contrast to "dead space" or Tibetan *bem strong*) and it has the sense of spaciousness, vastness, the realm of reality. We could therefore say Buddha-essence is the union of wisdom and spaciousness. What we mean by spaciousness is emptiness, and what we mean by wisdom is the luminosity of the mind. We might think that these two are contrary to one another—the mind's emptiness and its luminosity—because the mind's emptiness means that the mind could not have the ability to know. But in fact these two are not contrary. When the mind is empty, it is luminous. And just as it is luminous and aware, so at the same time, it is entirely empty.

When we say the mind's emptiness, we do not mean that it is something that ceases or becomes nonexistent. Suppose we feel tremendous aggression towards someone else and we simply cannot bear that person. But if we look for where the thought and feeling of hatred came from, we do not find anything. Similarly, when we feel pain or sadness if we look to see where it came from and where it is now, we do not find anything at all. Nevertheless, despite our inability to find the mind, the mind is at the same time luminous. Thus, we say the mind is naturally the union of luminosity and emptiness. Resting one's mind evenly in the recognition of that is called Vipashyana.

When we practice this meditation, we have the experience of something like the sun among the clouds, in that, when the sun is shining in a cloudy sky, sometimes we see the sun very clearly and sometimes the clouds obscure and block it. Similarly, when we are meditating on the mind, upon this union of luminosity and emptiness, sometimes we see it clearly and other times it fades away. Why does it vary like this? The reason is that we do not have sufficient shamatha. To view the mind as it is requires shamatha and this is difficult for us to do because we have become accustomed to discursive thoughts and easily fall into them. To develop stability and clear vision, we need to become accustomed to non-discursive mind. And the way to do that, simply enough, is to meditate again and again and again.

D. TYPES OF SHAMATHA AND VIPASHYANA

[29] There are several classifications of shamatha and Vipashyana meditation. There are two types of shamatha—the worldly shamatha of simply resting one's mind and the shamatha that goes beyond worldly concerns and is affected by bodhichitta.

Three categories of Vipashyana were set forth by the Buddha in the *Samadhi-nirmocana* sutra. The first is Vipashyana which has arisen from *valid cognition* (Skt. *pramana*), which is analyzing the nature of phenomena through reasoning and logic. The second type of Vipashyana is the process of seeking the view, where one is looking into one's own practice, and this experience establishes what the view actually is. The third kind of Vipashyana arises from the practice of meditation. Having decisively found the view, one arrives at a Vipashyana that is called direct perception, a nonconceptual Vipashyana gained through meditation.

E. SEQUENCE OF PRACTICING SHAMATHA AND VIPASHYANA

[32] There are two different traditions concerning the sequence of practicing shamatha and Vipashyana. Most of the sutras say that one must practice and attain shamatha first and after having achieved excellent shamatha, one practices Vipashyana. For example, Shantideva said that one first practices and stabilizes shamatha and having achieved shamatha, then through Vipashyana one will be able to abandon the kleshas. Thus the sequence of shamatha first and then Vipashyana next is set forth quite clearly in *A guide to the Bodhisattva's Way of Life*. The explanation is that first one needs to make one's mind peaceful and relaxed. Then when the mind is relaxed, one can begin to develop Vipashyana to see the reality or *dharmata* of things.

The other way, belonging to the tradition of the siddhas, is that we seek meditation from within the view, seek the view from within meditation. The siddhas having understood things as they are—that is, Vipashyana, then were able to develop a very steady mind that rests in that recognition—that is, shamatha. Or the siddhas might proceed more commonly by first establishing a relaxed and stable mind and within that finding out just what's the nature of phenomena.

So whether we seek meditation in terms of the view or seek the view within meditation makes no difference. Both shamatha and Vipashyana are very important and we need to practice both. We need both because if we are trying to practice Vipashyana without having shamatha, then there will be no stability to our insight into the nature of phenomena. This is compared to a flame of a butter lamp which wavers back and forth in the wind. We cannot see very much in the light of a wavering flame. Similarly, if we try to practice shamatha without Vipashyana, we will achieve a relaxed, peaceful, happy, and steady mind, but we will not abandon the disturbing emotions from the root. If we cannot abandon these kleshas, then our wisdom or prajna cannot increase.

So, in the tradition of siddhas, we can't just say it is one way or the other. Whether we have shamatha or Vipashyana first basically depends upon what works better for that person.

F. UNION OF SHAMATHA AND VIPASHYANA

[33] We talk about developing shamatha and then developing Vipashyana even though these two are actually developed together equally. We need to develop them together because both shamatha and Vipashyana are needed to attain realization. If we have only Vipashyana, then the mind will constantly waver by sometimes seeing the reality of things clearly, and sometimes not. Sometimes our Vipashyana will be brilliant and vivid and sometimes not; sometimes our mind will be steady and sometimes not. If we don't have that kind of steadiness, it is extremely difficult to have a very vivid and clear and luminous insight that allows us to abandon the disturbing emotions.

However, if we have only shamatha, then the factor of intelligence (Skt. *prajna*) is not very strong and we will not give birth to great wisdom. Without such wisdom, we will not be able to abandon the disturbing emotions. For this reason both shamatha and Vipashyana are needed.

To sum up, usually we begin with the practice of shamatha using an object of observation that is suitable and appropriate. Very frequently it is our own breathing, but it could be any visualized object. Having developed shamatha we then need to recognize the mind as it truly is. The guru will perhaps point this out to us, and if we understand it, that is extremely good. But we also need to develop stability of mind through shamatha that allows us to meditate upon the reality that has been recognized. We must remain in that meditation for a long period of time, meditating upon the nature of mind continuously without distraction. If we can meditate that way, then we can become familiar with it. Merely knowing the mind is not enough because it is necessary to join the recognition of the mind as it truly is with the ability to meditate there for an extended period of time. When we can do both of these, it is possible to eliminate the various faults of the mind, such as the disturbing emotions, and give rise to the extraordinary good qualities such as the wisdom of the enlightened ones. It is for this reason that the union of shamatha and Vipashyana is crucial.

G. RESULTS OF SHAMATHA AND VIPASHYANA

[37] When we develop shamatha, our mind becomes peaceful and relaxed and we are able to weaken the influence of the disturbing emotions. Vipashyana is the way in which realization unfolds, which is a matter of abandoning some things and accepting others. Of course, the final goal is achieving complete enlightenment, the state of the Buddha. However, there are other good results from having developed Vipashyana because the pain and the various bad situations that we experience in our everyday life are the result of not having control over our own mind. If we achieve shamatha and Vipashyana, then our mind becomes independent, no longer under the influence of confusion and the disturbing emotions. We then have the power to create a pleasurable, happy, good, and delightful life for ourselves.

It is said that the effect or fruition of shamatha is purity of mind, that is, a mind undisturbed by false conception or emotional afflictions. The fruition of Vipashyana is knowledge (Skt. *prajna*) and pure wisdom (Skt. *jnana*). Jnana is called the *wisdom of nature of phenomena* (Tib. *ji ta ba*) and it comes about through the realization of the true nature of phenomena. This is the final wisdom at the level of complete enlightenment. When one realizes this, our intelligence or prajna increases and becomes so vast that we develop a second type of wisdom which is called the wisdom of realizing the *wisdom of the variety of phenomena* (Tib. *jit nye pa*).

Questions

Question: Rinpoche, how do we deal with the physiology of sluggishness or the physiology of pain or the physiology of exhilaration that occurs in meditation. How do we approach or utilize our mind so that the mind does not reflect that physiology.

Rinpoche: The physical feeling and mental feeling do appear to be different. In fact, the mind is powerful and if one feels the joy and enthusiasm for meditation, and has no doubt about wanting to practice meditation, then such heaviness or restlessness of the body will not pose an obstacle. If one doesn't have such a strong wish to meditate, one feels lazy and then the body will feel heavy or restless, not being able to just sit and meditate. Temporarily, body and mind appear to be very separate in that way, but in fact, the mind is dominant and is able to overcome the situation of the body. For instance Milarepa[15] had been in retreat for eighteen months, at the end of which his teacher, Marpa came to visit him and said, "Oh, you have meditating here for eighteen months, that is very good, you haven't taken a break. Why don't you take a break here and rest a little bit." And Milarepa replied that he had no need to rest, that meditation itself was rest. Now Milarepa had such a great love of practice, such great longing for meditation, he was delighted, joyful to be able to practice. With such enthusiasm for it his body posed no obstacle. Meditation itself was whatever rest he required.

Question: I am unclear how doubt differs from regret. They seem very similar.

Rinpoche: Let me try another word. Maybe a better word for regret would be to just say feeling ill at ease. You could say, for instance, that you are sitting there and meditating and thinking quite vividly about what you did yesterday. You think, "Boy, I really messed that up. That was terrible." So you keep turning it over in your mind. The other way would be if you are not thinking about it explicitly. It is just this aftertaste of the whole thing. It is something you may not be identifying in your mind, "Oh that thing I bought yesterday was a piece of junk," but you are just affected by that feeling about it anyway. So that is what I called regret, but what we may better call "ill at ease." The difference between that and doubt is that doubt is actively turning something over in one's mind, like thinking, "I don't know if this meditation is a good one to be doing, maybe I should be doing this other practice." You are all wrapped up thinking about it and sitting with an active debate with yourself about it. That is the difference between these two.

Question: How do we purify our obscurations and ill deeds?
Rinpoche: The practices that are common to the sutra tradition and the *mantra tradition* of practice say it is important to develop an attitude of remorse, of regret for what one has done. Realizing that one has done something that was harmful to one's self and probably harmful to others too should give rise to regret. While feeling this regret, not just wallowing in it, we do what are known as the *four powers of purification*. The first of these is simply recognizing that it is not good. The second is casting it out, which is called the power of banishing. This is becoming thoroughly involved in activities that are remedies which means activity that establishes the roots of what is beneficial in one's own being. The third is called the power of the basis, which means that one generates an attitude in the presence of, either literally or imaginatively, the Buddha, the dharma, the sangha, and one's root guru. This is realizing that it is not enough just to have confessed to one's self but one needs to confess the ill deeds one has engaged in to one's teacher and to the Buddha, the dharma and the sangha. Fourth, one should not think, "Oh well, I have done that, that is enough." One should generate a resolve starting from this moment on to not do that any more negative activities and to engage in whatever virtuous and beneficial activity is helpful. These four powers of purification are common to the sutra and the mantra traditions. In the mantra tradition there is the additional practice of the mantra of Vajrasattva, in which one visualizes Vajrasattva upon one's head and supplicates Vajrasattva, exposing one's ill deeds and asking for Vajrasattva to purify these ill deeds. As a result of which there is a stream of *healing nectar* or *amrita* that passes from Vajrasattva into one's own body and mind, filling up one's body and mind, and clearing away the ill deeds and obstructions. At the end of the practice one generates this firm feeling and conviction that indeed these things have been purified, and Vajrasattva melts into one's self. That's a practice that is exclusive to the vajrayana tradition.
Translator: I was explaining to Rinpoche that this notion of suppressing of emotions is something we don't like at all in our Western culture. So, if someone tells us we are supposed to suppress things, then we don't want to do that.

Rinpoche: What psychology in the West means by suppressing thoughts or suppressing emotions is very different from what we are talking about. Because we are trying here to understand the nature of the situation, it doesn't mean holding onto something without having any reason. It means understanding the reason. For instance, getting angry and exploding at someone is probably going to make things a lot worse and it won't help the situation. Instead right on the spot realizing that that's not the best way to deal with the situation, one simply endures it. So, when you understand the reason for it, then instead of your mind becoming tight, it actually becomes very relaxed. It is not a matter of holding tightly to something, it is a matter of understanding what would be the wise way to go about it that produces a real sense of relaxation. That is much different from saying don't suppress something.

Question: Could Rinpoche say something about "mind appears yet it is empty, it is empty yet it appears."

Rinpoche: The best example for describing the mind as apparent and yet empty at the same time is a dream When one dreams of an elephant, does an elephant appear to one's mind? Indeed it does. It appears very clearly and it appears very directly. Is there an elephant there? Not at all. Even though there is no elephant there, there is a very clear appearance of an elephant. So, just as this appearance dawns, at the same time it is empty. Just as it is empty, so it appears. So this appearance of an elephant in one's dream is a union of appearance and emptiness. It appears but it does not exist. It does not exist but it appears. This is the same way with all external phenomena. Not just things in our dreams: all things appear very clearly but do not exist. And even while they do not exist, nevertheless they appear very clearly. Similarly, when we say the mind does not exist, we do not mean that the continuum of the mind is severed, that the mind stops. Not at all. The mind exists, it is aware, it knows. At the same time it cannot be found, it is empty, it does not exist. And those two are simultaneous, they are not different things. If we understand this example, of the appearance of something in a dream, it is a lot easier to understand how is it that the mind appears, but does not exist and it does not exist, but appears.

Question: In your talk you said that one could use one's occupation as a way of overcoming the disturbing emotions. I was thinking that you don't always do what you want at work.

Rinpoche: It is very important to develop mindfulness and awareness in postmeditation. So, when you are working you are mindful and very aware of what you are doing. If you are writing a letter, you pay attention just to the letters you are making, not letting your mind stray to something else. Or if you are speaking to someone, you are paying attention to that conversation and not letting your mind wander off to something else. So, in that way work does not need to be detrimental to the development of mindfulness and awareness.

Mindfulness and alertness that one experiences in meditation and that one experiences in postmeditation come about through different sorts of techniques. But they are the same in terms of being mindful and aware. This is the development of shamatha in postmeditation. There is also the development of Vipashyana in postmeditation, which is to look right into the thing itself to see what it is. Whatever one is experiencing, whatever one is thinking, whatever one is feeling, one asks, "Where does this come from? Where is it?" This is difficult for a beginner, but as you become more familiar with it, it can be quite helpful.

Chapter 3

The Shared Tradition of Shamatha Meditation

III. THE SHARED TRADITION OF SHAMATHA

[39] In the last chapter we discussed the meditation of shamatha and Vipashyana as it is common to all Buddhist traditions. In this chapter we will continue explaining meditation in the common tradition, but we will concentrate on just the shamatha or the tranquillity aspect of meditation.

A. PREPARATION FOR SHAMATHA

The preparation for shamatha is explained in terms of needing to "bind the doors of the five senses" so that the mind does not scatter wildly outwards. An analogy is given to the way one should eat food. The Buddha explained that if you eat too much food you become sleepy and your mind wanders everywhere. So the Buddha instructed that one ought to divide one's stomach into three parts and fill one-third with food, one-third with drink, and one-third with air—with one's own inhalation. Then when meditating one's breathing is not noisy and one is neither sleepy nor distracted.

This sort of oral instruction with respect to meditation is given by people who have real experience of what they are speaking about. You might think that such instructions are not that important, but the truth is that when you practice meditation, such instructions are very important and very helpful.

It is important not to become distracted when developing shamatha. It is very helpful to go to an isolated place to practice because there are not many sources of distraction there. Many people lead lives that result in a lot of thoughts. In an isolated location, there is little to distract one so one's mind becomes very relaxed. If one is not able to remain in an isolated place, one can go into an isolated retreat now and then to practice and develop some experience of shamatha. Having had the experience of shamatha, one finds that going into a busy situation is not necessarily an obstacle. One can bring that experience of shamatha into one's ordinary life of many distractions and continue one's practice, increasing it further and advancing to a higher level.

B. Objects of Focus in Shamatha

[40] When developing shamatha, various sorts of objects can be observed and focused upon. There are four different classes of objects: vast or pervasive objects (Tib. *khyab pa'i dmigs pa*), the disturbing emotions, objects of learning, and elimination of the disturbing emotions.

The first class is called "pervasive objects of observation," meaning one focuses on something extremely vast that pervades all phenomena. One develops shamatha using that as the focus for one's meditation.

The second class is an array of techniques focusing on the afflictions, particularly the disturbing emotions which are called "objects of observation for purifying behavior." These are various remedies that can be meditated upon to tame a particular disturbing emotion or *klesha*. For instance, if one is dominated by desire, then it is very helpful to meditate on ugliness and to recognize the impurity of various substances in one's own body. This will reduce attachment. Or people who are dominated by hatred can meditate on love and compassion. For those dominated by ignorance, it is recommended that they meditate on the *interinterdependent origination*[16] of things. If dominated by pride and the feeling that, "I am really somebody special," one meditates on the different elements of the body, recognizing that the solid parts in the body are the earth element, the fluid parts of the body are the water element, the heat or metabolic functions are the fire element, and the moving functions of the body are the air element. Realizing that one's body, which is the basis for pride, is really just a particular aggregation of elements will allow one's pride to diminish. Thus, meditation on ugliness, on love and compassion, on interdependence, and on the composition of the body in terms of the four elements are particular remedies for each kind of problem, which weakens that disturbing emotion. When a klesha is weakened, then one's meditation becomes clearer, steadier, and more vivid.

Most of us are not dominated by a particular disturbing emotion, but have many disturbing emotions. Our main problem is that we have many different thoughts. So, for most of us it is appropriate to meditate upon the inhalation and exhalation of the breath. Meditation on the breath is the best known meditation and is the meditation that most of us do. It is not directed to any particular disturbing emotion, but to all of them, in particular to all the thoughts that we are endlessly experiencing. By meditating on the breath, our thoughts decrease. This is the practice we mostly do.

The third class of objects of meditation are "objects for learning" which enable our prajna and knowledge and education to increase. To begin with, we tend to hold onto things and be very attached to them. All sorts of problems follow because we have such strong attachment. One of the ways we develop such strong attachment is by feeling that just like these external things, which seem to be so solid and real, our body and our self as a person are also really solid and stable and steady. But, in fact, our body and our self are not solid. The Buddha gave many teachings on how we can understand the actual nature of our mental self and physical body.

The first set of learned objects is the meditation on *aggregates* or *skandhas,* a Sanskrit term meaning a "pile" or "heap." It also has a sense of being "a collection" or "an aggregation." The Buddha taught that the body is a collection of skandhas and also a collection of the *elements* (Skt. *dhatu*) of earth, water, fire, and sky. He taught about the *elements of the mind* and how all these are related by interdependent origination. Meditating upon these objects of observation develops skill and learning.

In this meditation we recognize that the psycho-physical person (the body and the self) is a collection of body and mind, not a single thing like a stone. Rather, it is just an aggregation of a lot of different things. In particular, it is the bringing together of the five aggregates of form, feeling, discrimination, composition, and consciousness. By studying our own five skandhas we see that they are just a collection of many different things that are piled together, with new things being added and other things being discarded all the time. Some things are left behind, some are discarded; some things fall apart, some come together. The psycho-physical self is not very stable at all. Recognizing this instability, we become skilled in understanding that a person has no inherent nature. When we realize that the five skandhas are without essence, our attachment to our body and mind will be greatly reduced.

The second set of objects for learning are the eighteen elements, which are composed of six types of sensory objects: visual images, sounds, smells, tastes, tangible objects and mental phenomena. The six sense organs that negotiate the relationship between consciousness and its objects are the eye, ear, nose, tongue, body, and mind or mental sense organ. The *six consciousnesses* are the eye, ear, nose, tongue, body sensations, and mental consciousness. So there are the six objects, six sense organs, and six types of consciousnesses, making eighteen in all, which describe in a thorough way the nature of our perception and the composition of our world. The reason for developing an understanding of the elements is to see the interrelationship of cause and effect and to see that when a cause occurs, an effect comes about. A knowledge of this interrelationship allows us to understand and abandon what is undesirable and unhelpful. Then the effect will simply not come about.

The third set of learned objects for learning are literally called "the doorways of perception" (Skt. *ayatana,* Tib. *kyeche*). The Tibetan word *kyeche* is often translated as "*sense fields,*" but the syllables of the Tibetan word are very meaningful here. The first syllable *kye* means "to be born" or "to be generated," and the second syllable means "to increase." These twelve sense fields are the six senses of the eye, ear, nose, tongue, body, and mental faculty together with the six consciousnesses. A sense field coming into contact with an object opens the doorway and generates sensory consciousnesses and initiates the development of mental consciousness. Studying how these consciousnesses come about enables us to see that the entire process of perception is empty: that is, it has no nature of its own.

The fourth set of learned objects is understanding inter-dependent relationships. This is a very simple: one event happens in dependence upon some other event. And following that, something else happens. So everything happens in dependence upon something else. When we understand this, we realize that everything is changeable, that good situations are not fixed as good situations, and bad situations are not fixed as bad situations. Never will something pleasant always remain that way, nor will something bad always remain bad. Things are changeable because they arise in dependence upon other phenomena. In any given situation, if you want to change it, you can change it. If phenomena had an essence or solid nature, then it would remain the same forever. However, phenomena are empty of an essence, so they are impermanent and can change.

[41] The fourth object of learning is the "objects of observation that purify behavior." There are a variety of ways or methods to abandon the disturbing emotions. The method common to Buddhist and non-Buddhist traditions is to weaken the disturbing emotions by recognizing their faulty nature and realizing that they do not benefit ourselves or others. If we are able to realize that the disturbing emotions are disturbing or harming ourselves and others, then we can realize that their absence will create peace and gentleness, which is extremely beneficial both to ourselves and others. In this way, we can think about the destructive aspect of the kleshas and the great advantages of freedom from them. If we understand this clearly, then the kleshas will naturally subside.

The uncommon way of purifying the disturbing emotions is in relation to *conventional truth* and *ultimate truth*,[17] which has two aspects to it. First is the understanding of the Four Noble Truths. One realizes that samsara is misery and that the root of samsara is the disturbing emotions, which are disturbing states of mind. One realizes that the actions that arise from such disturbing states of mind result in suffering. One understands further that by overcoming these disturbing emotions and the actions that arise from disturbing emotions, one achieves liberation, which is the cessation of suffering. The path that enables one to abandon misery and to achieve the cessation of misery is a path that realizes the nature of the Four Noble Truths. Meditating in this way one is able to abandon the kleshas in a final way.

A pure object in meditation uses the visualization of the body of a Buddha as one's object of observation. One of the benefits of visualizing a deity in front of oneself or visualizing oneself as the deity is that it facilitates meditation practice. Practicing this way gives one the blessings of those deities. From that point of view the practice of developing shamatha by taking the body of the Buddha as one's object of observation is a very special kind of practice. When practicing meditation using other objects of observation, your thoughts come and go but by the time you notice this your mind has been disturbed by thought and that thought has already come and gone and your meditation has been interrupted and disturbed. However, when you are visualizing the body of the Buddha as an object, your mind is held right to that and just as the thought itself arises, it is seen quite clearly. It can be separated into seeing one's meditation disturbed and brought back again. So from that point of view using a deity as an object is said to be very special.

When visualizing a deity in the *creation stage* (Tib. *kyerim*) stage of vajrayana practice, for some practitioners the image of visualization comes very clearly and for others it doesn't. This just depends upon the *subtle channels* (Skt. *nadi*) and *subtle energies* (Skt. *prana*) that flow in those channels within the body. Different people have different sorts of bodies. For some people this kind of practice goes wonderfully well with everything very clear. The truth is: it is not such a great quality and not terribly important. It just happens naturally for some people. For others the visualization doesn't come very clearly, but that is not really a fault because visualizing of deities is not done to establish clarity of the visualization, but rather to calm the mind and develop confidence and faith in the practice. That is the point of the practice.

OBJECT OF OBSERVATION FOR THE BEGINNER

[43] What object of observation should a new student begin with? Generally speaking, it is easier for a beginner to meditate upon an external object than upon the internal mind. In the vajrayana, there are various aspects of the creation stage of meditation. We can meditate upon a particular *yidam* such as Avalokiteshvara or Vajrasattva. Or if we are doing the *preliminary practices* (Tib. *ngöndro*), we can meditate on Vajradhara. These are all similar in this aspect of generation in that we focus upon a deity and through

the mind's focusing, we develop a quality of stability. As the resting increases, this factor becomes stronger and stronger. The other way of meditating that is common to the sutra tradition is simply holding the mind on the breath to develop stability of mind. These are the two principal objects of focus in the vajrayana tradition.

When meditating on the breath, the mind continually wanders, is continually brought back, and in this way becomes somewhat erratic. Whereas when meditating upon a deity, the mind is continually engaged and active because we meditate on the deity's face, arms, color of the body, the ornaments the deity wears, the objects the deity holds, the letters that are placed in various spots on the body, the wheel of mantra that appears in a certain spot in the deity's body. We hold our mind to these visualized aspects and in this way the mind is continuously engaged and becomes extremely stable. Thus this manner of meditation is a superior way of doing shamatha meditation.

When we are practicing meditation, we are working on the level of the sixth mental consciousness. We meditate and develop this quality of stability of resting with the object. In the development of shamatha, mindfulness and awareness are essential. When we speak about the mind, it has two aspects: mind (Tib. *sem*) and *mental factors* (Tib. *sem yung*). The mind in this case is the central awareness, the knowing quality. Mental factors are, figuratively speaking, companions that give the mind its color and flavor. What we understand as thoughts are actually these mental factors. What actually looks at the object? It is the mental factor that is called mindfulness (Tib. *drenpa*). Mindfulness is the quality of non-distraction. Without such mindfulness there can be no samadhi. When there is such mindfulness, mind does not wander and stray. If mindfulness fails, then the mind wanders. What is it that knows whether or not the mind has wandered? It is the quality of alertness (Tib. *sheshin*). This quality of alertness, which has the sense of knowing in the present, knows that the mind has wandered. These two are of great importance when one wishes to practice meditation. The great Shantideva praised their importance by saying that mindfulness and awareness should be valued by meditators more than their own lives. He said, "I place my palms together to express my respect for mindfulness and awareness and for those who have developed them."

MAINTAINING A VISUALIZED IMAGE WITH MINDFULNESS

[44] When one first practices shamatha, it is said one's mind tends to resemble a crazy elephant who runs amok and does a lot of harm whether one uses the body of a deity as the object of one's observation or holds one's attention on the inhalation and exhalation of the breath, one needs to hold one's mind to it and stay with it. How does one go about tying one's mind to the object of observation? You have an elephant, you use a rope and tie the elephant to a stake to keep it from running all over. With the mind, one uses mindfulness as one's rope and one ties this crazy mind to the object of observation.

When practicing in this way, it is essential not to hold the mind either too tightly or too loosely with the rope of mindfulness. If one tries to hold one's mind too tightly, it won't stay. When one brings it to the object of observation, it just jumps somewhere else, and when one brings it back and it jumps somewhere else again, because one is trying to tie it too tightly and it never will just stay. Similarly, if one's mindfulness is too loose, one actually forgets that one is supposed to be practicing meditation. One's mind just wanders off and never comes back at all. So, it is important to practice mindfulness without being too tight or too loose.

C. METHODS OF DEVELOPING SHAMATHA

There are four general aspects of developing shamatha: the eight impediments, the nine stages, the six powers, and the four engagements. We will begin with the most commonly used method of the nine ways of settling the mind. These nine ways can also be considered a progressive series of steps in the development of shamatha.

NINE WAYS OF RESTING THE MIND

[47] There are nine stages for resting the mind which are given in the *Ornament of Clear Realization* sutra that allow shamatha

meditation to arise. The first way of resting the mind is called placement, which is placing one's mind on a particular object. It might be a figure representing the body of the Buddha or it might be the inhalation or exhalation of the breath. It might be an external object or it might be some internal mental visualization. But whatever it is, the first step is simply to place one's mind there.

The first stage of placement is simply placing the mind on an object for a brief duration. When one is able to extend that somewhat longer, one has arrived at the second stage of continually placing. Needless to say, one's mind will continue to wander. When it wanders, one realizes through awareness that it has wandered and one brings one's mind back to the object and holds it there with mindfulness. This should be done without thinking that the mind has wandered or that this is something terrible. We should not engage in that kind of internal conversation, but simply bring the mind back, placing it again.

The third stage is called placing again. This is the notion that mind is wandering, one brings it back and this goes on and that is called settling the mind again and again. The main roadblock to this third stage is attachment to thoughts. Thoughts arise and one thinks, "Oh this is a very important thought, I have to think about this, I must be sure not to forget this." Thinking this way, the thought just comes back again and again. Instead of practicing shamatha, we just increase our attachment to thoughts. The great meditators of the past have described this particular situation with an example of how one treats a pig who has gotten into a flower garden and wants to eat all the flowers. The person in charge of the garden should be there with a stick and when the pig comes in, the person should just rap the pig's snout firmly and immediately. Then the pig will go away. However, if the person allows the pig to start eating the flowers in the garden, getting rid of the pig will be many times more difficult. Similarly, when we practice meditation and thoughts arise, we have to cut the attachment to them right at the time they appear and just severing them right then.

The fourth stage of resting the mind is called placing closely. When one meditates and develops some samadhi, there is the sense that one's mind has become larger and more vast. When thoughts arise within this vast mind, there is a sense of something very subtle and small. It might have escaped one's notice because the mind has become much larger. Something in that great space moved a little bit. And to tame the mind further, one actually constricts it somewhat by focusing and concentrating on these small things that are moving. In this way the mind becomes more stable.

The fifth stage is called taming or subduing. When one's meditation is going well, one feels joy, a lightness, enthusiasm, and relaxation. One then thinks about the extraordinary qualities of meditation, realizing that these are very beneficial for oneself and for others. Thinking about the good qualities of meditation causes the mind to rest and stabilize further and thus it is given the name of taming or subduing.

The sixth stage of resting the mind is called pacifying. One has tamed the mind somewhat in the previous stage, in response to the lightness one has felt in meditation. There is still some tendency for the mind to wander. The principal problem is that one is attached to those distractions and wanderings of the mind. That is what needs to be pacified at this particular point. The way one goes about this is to realize how beneficial it would be if one were to pacify each distraction, and how faulty such a distraction is. Recognizing the faults and disadvantages of such distraction is the way in which such distractions are naturally pacified.

The seventh stage carries this further and is called thoroughly pacified. At this stage whatever distractions and faults of the mind occur, such as attachment or discouragement, they are recognized and one applies the antidotes that are appropriate. The first six of the nine methods work mainly with the wildness of the mind and avoiding the influence of distraction. However, even if the mind is brought into an undistracted state, there can be faults with this state. These faults are mainly concerned with the obscurations of mind, and when we are under the influence of them, our mind is not clear. As discussed earlier, what helps obscurations of mind is to consider the good qualities of the Buddha, the good qualities of meditation and so on.

The eighth way of resting the mind is one-pointedness. One has proceeded in the previous stages through the power of mindfulness and awareness. Here in the eighth stage what is required is exertion, with further exertion the mind becomes quite pure. This brings one to the ninth stage, which is called placing (the mind) evenly. Because of what has been accomplished in the first eight stages, the mind simply rests evenly, naturally, and under its own power.

2. SIX POWERS

[48] The development of these nine stages for mind are paralleled by the development of what are called the six powers given in the *Stages of the Shravaka.* The first power is hearing which refers to the fact that one enters the first stage of placement, because of hearing the oral instructions of the guru on how to meditate. One hears these instructions and then brings them to one's practice and places one's mind on the object of observation. Therefore it is said that this is done through the power of listening.

One develops this further by contemplating the instructions, and this becomes the second stage of continual placement. The second power is called the power of contemplating.

The third power is mindfulness. Mindfulness is associated with the third and the fourth stages of bringing the mind to rest. Much of the power of mindfulness is that one does not forget what one has heard and contemplates during the practice of shamatha. If one's effort to practice decreases, one notices this and is able to return the mind again to the practice of shamatha. As mindfulness increases, it leads to the fourth stage of close placement.

The fourth power, awareness, is associated with the fifth and sixth stages of taming and pacifying the mind. It is through the power of awareness that one is able to understand the good qualities of meditative stabilization and the faults of one's mind being distracted. Therefore, one practices the fifth and sixth stage through the power of awareness.

The fifth power is called power of effort or exertion. This is associated with the seventh and eighth stages of thoroughly pacifying the mind and making the mind one-pointed. It is through effort that one is able to dispel the faults of heaviness and obscuration of mind. With the mind free of these thoughts one passes to the ninth stage which is a state of equipoise and this is associated with the sixth power, the power of familiarity.

4. FOUR MENTAL APPLICATIONS

[49] The development of the nine stages of the mind coming to rest is also paralleled by the four mental applications or engagements. The first application is called forcibly engaging and is related with the first two stages. In these stages you have to force your mind on an object of observation.

The second mental engagement is called interrupted engaging and is related to the third, fourth, fifth, sixth, and seventh levels of the mind coming to rest. At this stage your practice is still interrupted by various thoughts and you have to continually bring the mind back.

The third engagement is called uninterrupted engaging. This is related to the eighth stage of mind settling, because at this level mindfulness and awareness have come to maturity and the mind does not wander and therefore stays with the object uninterruptedly.

The fourth application is called spontaneous engaging and is related to the ninth stage of settling the mind. In this stage one does not need to apply any sort of methods or antidotes whatsoever. The mind simply rests in a state of equipoise.

Questions

Question: Rinpoche said that if one feels pain or is discouraged or feels sadness to look where it came from. When I look into those places I find external causes, like a marriage that just ended, or a doctor saying that there is a disease. And those causes don't seem to disappear, they just seem recur. It becomes very difficult for me to meditate under these conditions.

Rinpoche: There is a distinction between the conditions of the relative world and the mahamudra practice of looking directly into the object itself. It is exactly as you say, of course, there are various things we experience in our mind and body that arise in dependence upon various external conditions. There is no question about it. There is a sequence and a connection between them. But that is not what we are talking about here. At this point we are talking about the painful feeling itself which we feel. We are trying to look right into that pain itself and ask where did it come from? Was it down here and then it came up there? Or was up here and then it went down there? What happened?

We also ask these same questions with an illness. Of course, there are various situations and causes for illness. But what we are talking about is the actual feeling of pain. If I pinch my hand hard, it hurts. What is that pain? Where is that feeling and where does it come from? We are looking right at it and not trying to trace its interdependent origination. We are just trying to look at the feeling itself right straight in the face. It is not something that exists inherently. So where does it come from? We are trying to find out what the nature of the pain actually is. So there is a distinction between the whole complex and network of the relative world and mahamudra practice, in which we are trying to look right at the thing itself. Mahamudra practice does not deny that there is a relative chain of cause and effect.

Question: Rinpoche, could you give some examples of those pervasive objects of meditation?

Rinpoche: This refers principally to meditating without having any particular point of reference or support such as the visualization of a Buddha. Meditation with visualization causes the mind to become narrowed. In meditation without having a particular basis the mind becomes extremely relaxed and very vast. This is called pervasive meditation. The notion of pervasive here is that nothing is excluded, it pervades everything.

Question: Could you say in the fourth stage of placing closely that when there is a lot of space and then the small thoughts occur, you just decide you are not interested in those so they just dissolve.

Rinpoche: The little thoughts that arise at this point are talked about as the movement of thought from below, because there is the sense that something small is living somewhere below one's self. It just tends to rise up somehow. To bring the mind to complete development of shamatha, these thoughts need to be stopped. The way they are stopped is through focusing on them and it has nothing to do with them in particular. It is just that they serve as a message that one needs to focus and concentrate more upon the object of meditation.

Question: Rinpoche said that yidam practice in the vajrayana is superior to attention to the breath because your mind doesn't wander. My mind wanders in visualizations, so how does one work with wandering mind in yidam practice?

Rinpoche: Meditating upon the breath or upon some visualized object is a way of developing one-pointedness of mind. It is a very good way to proceed and does bring about one-pointedness of mind. However, it is somewhat boring. When you meditate upon the deity, there are all sorts of things to look at. There is the face, the hands, the various ornaments, the clothing, and what is held and it is terribly interesting. So there is always a sense of something fresh and new going on. From that point of view it increases the quality of stability greatly.

Chapter 4

The Shared Tradition of Vipashyana Meditation

IV. THE SHARED TRADITION OF VIPASHYANA

A. THE TYPES OF VIPASHYANA

[51] There are three types of Vipashyana: worldly Vipashyana, the Hinayana Vipashyana, and the mahayana Vipashyana. Vipashyana is made up of the Sanskrit syllable *pashyana* which means "see" and the syllable *vi* which means "intensely." When *vi* was translated in Tibetan as *lha,* it carried the sense of "beyond" or "surpassing." Thus the Tibetan word for Vipashyana is *lhag tong*, meaning "insight" which is not seen by ordinary persons. Therefore one passes beyond what ordinary people see. Now, this is the meaning of the first type of Vipashyana, worldly Vipashyana. One can cultivate the four levels of concentration of the *form realms* and the four levels of absorption of the *formless realms*. When one does this, one begins to understand that the lower levels are relatively coarse and agitated in comparison to the higher levels which are less coarse and more peaceful. That is sort of special insight that one achieves with worldly Vipashyana.

Passing beyond worldly Vipashyana is the Hinayana Vipashyana, which is understanding the Four Noble Truths (the truth of suffering, the origin of suffering, the cessation of suffering, and the eight-fold path of liberation) that were taught by Buddha, and meditating on them. So this level of Vipashyana involves actually meditating on the Four Noble Truths and developing the understanding of egolessness which is to say, seeing that conceptual consciousness, "I," does not exist. This is called seeing the selflessness of persons.

The third type of Vipashyana is the mahayana Vipashyana. Meditation on this is done in terms of meditating on the two truths: conventional truth and absolute truth. In addition to seeing the non-existence of self, one also realizes the non-existence of a self in phenomena. One realizes that phenomena have a lack of inherent existence, that phenomena are like illusions or dreams and have the nature of emptiness.

One determines the true nature of phenomena through a path of reasoning and analysis. If one understands the nature of phenomena by way of reasoning, settling in that manner, one has taken up the practice of mahamudra. The study and understanding that one has acquired previously will greatly help facilitate and make much easier one's practice of mahamudra.

VIPASHYANA OF THE SUTRA PATH

The Vipashyana discussed in this chapter is not the Vipashyana of mahamudra, but the Vipashyana that is common to the sutra and mantra traditions.

In the sutra path one proceeds by examining and analyzing phenomena, using reasoning. One recognizes that all phenomena lack any true existence and that all appearances are merely interdependently related and arise without any inherent nature. They are empty yet apparent, apparent yet empty. This is understood inferentially and one develops certainty about this understanding by meditating upon what one has understood. Then through gradual familiarization one develops direct realization, which sees the true nature of phenomena (Skt. *dharmata*) in a direct manner. The realization at this point is stable and firm. However, getting to this point takes a very long time.

On the inferential path one uses knowledge (Skt. *prajna*), not wisdom (Skt. *jnana*), as path. One develops a certainty about emptiness, and this knowledge is in the realm of mind (Skt. *chitta*) as opposed to wisdom (Skt. *jnana*). One becomes familiar with this knowledge over a long period of time, with the sutras speaking of practice that goes on for eon upon eon during which one accumulates vast stores of merit, purifies all ill deeds and obscurations, and listens again and again to the teachings of the dharma. Gradually, one comes to realization.

VIPASHYANA OF THE MAHAMUDRA PATH

The path of mahamudra is different in that one proceeds using the instructions concerning the nature of mind that are given by one's guru. This is called taking direct perception or direct experience as the path. With the blessings of the guru, the nature of mind is pointed out and one is introduced to that and sees it directly. This process is a rapid path. In the tradition of the vajrayana and particularly that of mahamudra, we speak about achieving the state of realization or the union with Vajradhara in one lifetime, with one body. When we are talking about realization of mind as it is, there is no difference between the sutra or the mahamudra path. In either case, it is dharmata, reality as it is, that is realized. In both cases it is realization of the mind itself. The only difference is in the speed of this realization.

B. VIPASHYANA IN DIFFERENT BUDDHISTS SCHOOLS

[53] The Buddha gave teachings in three stages called the turnings of the wheel of dharma. The first turning was for the sake of arousing confidence and aspiration for new practitioners. To do this he taught the Four Noble Truths of suffering, its origin, its cessation, and the path. This first turning of the wheel of dharma is called the Hinayana teachings, which are extensively practiced by the Theravadins.

In the second or intermediate turning of the wheel of dharma, transcendent knowledge (Skt. *Prajnaparamita*) was fully and carefully explained. These were the teachings which included the explanation of emptiness of self and emptiness of phenomena. In the final turning of the wheel of dharma the Buddha taught the definitive meaning. The intermediate and final turning of the wheel of dharma are largely identical in meaning. However, there is a difference in the manner of instruction and the way in which reality (Skt. *dharmata*) is described. In the intermediate turning emptiness (Skt. *shunyata*) was emphasized. In the final turning, the Buddha taught that wisdom pervades this emptiness, in this way teaching about Buddha-essence or Buddha-nature.

Different traditions of commentary arose clarifying various aspects of the Buddha's teachings. The principal exponent and commentator for the final turning of the wheel of dharma was Asanga. The principal person to clarify and expound on the intermediate turning of the wheel of dharma was Nagarjuna. These two traditions of commentary flourished, leading to the tradition of the Middle-way or the Madhyamaka school. Later, by analyzing these positions carefully, two different traditions of Madhyamaka developed: the Rangtong (or "empty of itself") tradition and the Shentong (or "empty of other") tradition. By all these teachings, great confidence was aroused in students that indeed emptiness is the nature of all phenomena and that all sentient beings possess Buddha-essence.

ALL PHENOMENA ARE MIND

How then does one practice the teaching that all phenomena are nothing more than one's mind? Considered this way, objects appear to be external phenomena but are nothing more than appearances to one's own mind. They do not truly exist. Nagarjuna presented logical arguments with a demonstration that phenomena are neither single nor multiple to prove his point. For instance, when we think "my body," it suggests we believe that there is a single thing that we refer to. In fact it isn't one thing. Because "my body" refers to my head, my right hand, my left hand, my right leg, my left leg, and so forth. There is no body that is separate from those parts. Nor are any of those parts "my body." Rather my head is my head, my hand is my hand, and so on. Therefore this so-called "body" doesn't exist.

Now suppose we look at one of the parts. What about "my head" for example. Well, my head is composed of my eyes, my ears, my nose, my tongue, my teeth, and so my "head" is just a designated category for the collection of these many different parts. We can continue this sort of analysis to ever subtler levels until we finally reach the smallest of particles. However the more finely we analyze, we always find more substances that are a gathering together of many different things, rather than something that is a truly single thing. Even the smallest particle such as an atom that serves as a building block for everything else will have an eastern quarter, a southern quarter, a western quarter, and a northern quarter. Even the smallest particle is a collection of these different quarters. So we can never prove the true nature of external phenomena.

What then about internal phenomena, that is, the mind? Well, there two methods of reasoning that demonstrated that appearances are merely mind. The first one is called "the certainty of simultaneous observation." For example, a glass full of water appears to my mind. However, the glass that appears and the eye consciousness perceiving that appearance are always together. They come together and happen at the same time. There is no such thing as a glass that isn't appearing to a consciousness and there is no such thing as a consciousness observing something when there isn't anything there to observe. Rather object and subject only happen simultaneously.

The second reasoning is called "luminous and knowing" which is to say that the only way to demonstrate that anything exists is to show that it has appeared to someone's consciousness. Except for objects that are perceived in my eye or ear or nose or tongue or body consciousness or in somebody else's consciousness, there aren't any phenomena whose existence that can be proved. These two logical arguments show that all phenomena are merely appearances, that is to say, that all phenomena are merely mind.

Nagarjuna made the logical arguments about phenomena not being either truly one or truly many as a way to demonstrate that phenomena lack any nature of their own. He also explained how conventional phenomena or appearances exist. That is to say that even though phenomena ultimately lack existence, nevertheless through interinterdependent origination there are conventional appearances. For instance, even if the body is no more than a collection of parts, this aggregation of the head, the arms, the legs, and so on do appear in the mind. Similarly, even though the head is nothing more than a collection of its parts, nevertheless there is an appearance of head. Thus ultimately phenomena are empty of any true nature; but on the relative level there are appearances because of interinterdependent origination.[18] Thus this sort of reasoning was made to explain the true nature of phenomena. The Buddha also spoke about the question of single and multiple in terms of a chariot.[19] Now, if you examine a chariot and analyze what exactly a chariot is, you find it has two wheels, an axle, and a carriage. But if you ask, "Is this wheel the chariot?" No, it is not the chariot, it is a wheel. Is this other wheel the chariot? No, it is not the chariot, it is the other wheel. Well, is the axle the chariot? No, the axle is not the chariot, it is the axle. Is the carriage the chariot? No, that is the carriage in which the person rides. Is there something separate from the chariot that is the chariot? No, there isn't anything separate from these pieces that is the chariot because the chariot is made up of them. A similar argument can be made with our own body and mind. There is no self separate from body and mind, nor are the various components of the body and mind, the self. This is because they are multiple. You may ask: Are all these collective parts of body and mind you? No. Then you may ask: is there something separate from them that is me? The answer is also, No.

In this way the Buddha taught the inherent non-existence of self. The Buddha also taught that there are lifetimes prior to the present birth and that there will be lifetimes subsequent to our present lifetime. It sometimes seems that these two teachings contradict one another because if there is no self, how could there have been former or future lifetimes. If there is no self to accumulate actions and experience the fruition of these actions, then there is no way for rebirth to happen. However, reincarnation does take place merely in terms of the continuum of the mind. One might argue that the continuum of mind is the self. But in fact that is not so, because the self is something other than the continuum of the mind. The continuum of the mind has the nature of cessation and then birth, cessation and then birth, and so on. Something comes to life and then it ceases. Then something else is born and then it ceases. That is what we mean by the continuum of mind. Consider, for instance, the mind of a young child, the mind of an adolescent, and the mind of an aged person. These three stages of a person's life are connected by the continuum of mind, connecting the mind of the child to the mind of the adolescent to the mind of an aged person. But they are not similar. For instance, the games that fascinate and delight a young child are not very interesting to an adult and the work that is very interesting to an adult is not anything that a child enjoys. So, in their character, the mind of a child and the mind of the old person are extremely different. As a mere continuum one can say they are the same, but that is all.

THE STORY OF ASANGA

Let us discuss the story of the great master Asanga. In the fourth century C.E. a fire broke out and did a great deal of damage to the library at the famous monastic university at Nalanda. It burned many of the Buddhist treatises and, in particular, it burned a great number of the texts of the Abhidharma. At that time there was a nun who was an emanation of a *bodhisattva*, named Tsawai Tsultrim, which means "clear unobstructed discipline." She was upset that these teachings had been destroyed and felt very strongly that it would be important to restore and strengthen the teachings of the Abhidharma so that they would not disappear. She felt that she was not able to do so herself and therefore gave up her vows as a nun and gave birth to two sons. The tradition in that part of the world at that time was that a son would take up the work of his father. So at a certain point her sons asked her what work their father did so they could follow in that occupation. She replied to them, "I did not bring you into this world for that purpose. I gave birth to you for another reason. You must exert yourselves for the sustenance and extension of the teachings of the Abhidharma." So the elder of her two sons, Asanga, performed the practice of *Maitreya* and the younger son, *Vasubandhu*, became a student of a Kashmiri teacher, named Zangpo in Tibetan, who was very learned and received from him the teachings of the Hinayana Abhidharma. So in that way they were able to do a great deal of benefit for the Hinayana and mahayana Abhidharma teachings. Asanga practiced for twelve years seeking to meet face to face with Maitreya, who was in the *sambhogakaya* realm of *Tushita*. At the end of that time he did meet directly with Maitreya. He went with Maitreya to the Tushita realm and received what have come to be known as the five treatises of Maitreya. In addition to those five treatises, Asanga composed his own commentaries on them. His younger brother, Vasubandhu, also composed what have come to be known as the twenty sets of doctrines of Maitreya, all of which are concerned with demonstrating that phenomena are nothing more than appearances of mind and that the nature of phenomena is emptiness.

The traditions of Nagarjuna's Middle-way and of Asanga's *Mind-only school* passed to Tibet and initiated a systematic study of the teachings of the intermediate and the final turning of the wheel of dharma. The Rangtong and Shentong schools allowed students to develop correct understanding by listening to expositions of the dharma and thinking about them very carefully. This allowed them to gain an understanding in which they could have great confidence that emptiness indeed is the nature of phenomena and that wisdom is the nature of the emptiness.

By studying, students developed a true skill and sharpness of knowledge about the Middle-way and the *Prajnaparamita*. When it came to meditation, these students practiced bringing their direct experience to the path through mahamudra and Dzogchen meditation. In this way they achieved the fruition that they sought and achieved great spiritual accomplishment. They combined the study of the second turning teachings of emptiness and Buddha-nature together with the practice of bringing direct experience onto the path. This allowed them to proceed in an effective, steady, and unerring manner. This is the Vipashyana that is common to the sutra and the vajrayana tradition.

C. THE GENERAL MEDITATION ON EGOLESSNESS OF SELF

[54] The sutras speak about non-self or egolessness of self (Skt. *anatman*, Tib. *dakme*). To elaborate, there are two non-selves: the *egolessness of the person* and the *egolessness of dharmas* or phenomena. We will first speak about the egolessness of persons. We all have disturbing emotions which need to be eliminated. If we simply think, "Okay I am not going to give rise to disturbing emotions anymore," the disturbing emotions still arise because we believe in and hold onto self, which is the basis of these disturbing emotions. For instance, hatred arises when someone harms us and we then think they harmed "me." Desire arises by thinking "I" need that. Jealousy arises because we think that some condition or honor should be "mine." Pride arises because of the thought "I" am better than that person. Ignorance is a very cloudy state of mind, but

basically it is thinking "I" that gives rise to the five kleshas and also not seeing things as they are.

[56] To abandon the disturbing emotions, we require a method that would allow us to do so. Whenever we think "me" or "mine" there is some object in reference to which we are thinking "I" or "me." Sometimes "I" refers to the body and sometimes it refers to the mind. We take that self to be real, something that actually exists.

As we saw previously, there is no such thing as a self. Instead there are merely the five aggregates of form, feeling, discrimination, formation, and consciousness that are gathered together. If we understand this completely, we realize that there is no self. Through realizing the nonexistence of self, the disturbing emotions which depend upon that notion of self are destroyed. Therefore, we must meditate upon the egolessness of the person.

There are two aspects to the way we conceive of the self. One of them is to just think "I." The other is to think "mine," or that which belongs to me. Between those two, the thinking "I" is the principal one, but the thinking "mine" is somewhat easier to understand. There are various kinds of things that we believe belong to us, sometimes very small things like maybe a bowl or an article of clothing. We might just think, "that is mine." We might also think of something larger than that as mine, such as one's house, a friend, or even one's country. We might think that everything from California to New York is "my" country, even though it obviously is not.

There is a good reason for realizing that this conception of mine leads to a lot of pain. For instance, suppose we go into a restaurant and sit down and across the way a waiter drops a glass which falls to the ground and breaks. We then think, "Too bad, somebody broke a glass." But if my own glass were to fall on the ground and break and all the water spill out, it would be a rather different matter because that is "mine." That would be very upsetting and I would have a very painful feeling. There is no way in which a glass is distinguished by its color or its shape or any inherent properties that would make it mine; it is just a glass. There is nothing about that water that is different from other water to make it my water. It is just water. Consequently, having become very confused, we feel a great deal of pain when "my" glass breaks. And that unhappiness, that displeasure is a feeling that comes from thinking "mine."

It is helpful to look at the various objects that serve as a basis for this notion of mine. It might be one's body, thinking of everything from the top of your head down to the soles of your feet as being "my" body. You identify with your mind, thinking that mind is "me" and the body is "mine." Or, it might be the other way around. You might think the body is "me" and the mind is "mine." You might locate yourself somewhere in the upper part of your body and regard your feet as "my" feet. Or you might regard your head as "mine" and the rest of your body as "me." Or you might regard your skin as "my skin" so that "I" am inside and "my" skin is something that belongs to me but it is out there somewhere.

So there are all these different ways in which we think about ego and it is continually shifting. First, it goes with one object then with some other object: the feet, the head, the skin, the inside, the outside. This continual shifting of ego points out that there isn't such a thing as "me" or "mine." Nevertheless, we still think that there is some "me" that exists.

Neither the body nor the mind constitutes a self. Neither of them is me. There is no such me. There are just the aggregates. We tend to regard them as one solid thing, but in fact "me" is just a great many things gathered together that can be classified in these five groups called the five aggregates. When we understand this and gain real confidence in our understanding, this leads us to the realization of selflessness. Realizing that egolessness of self, we pass to a nonconceptual, direct realization of it.

Sometimes when we get a sense of the nonexistence of the self, we feel afraid. There is no need to feel afraid. If the self existed, then someone could harm us and there would be a reason to be afraid. But if that self does not really exist, then there is nothing for someone to harm. Therefore, we have no need to be afraid. Realizing that the self does not exist causes great courage to come about and then fear simply disappears.

D. GENERAL MEDITATION ON EGOLESSNESS OF PHENOMENA

[64] The second kind of non-self is the egolessness of external things such as trees, rocks, and mountains—which we call

"phenomena." This egolessness of phenomena is also called the "non-self of dharmas." Dharma has many meanings but in this particular context it means all appearances of the world which includes our thoughts and feelings. We usually believe that these phenomena are unchangeable, that they are solid and permanent. However, phenomena are not really like this. The Buddha taught in many places that phenomena are empty, for example, by teaching on the sixteen kinds of emptiness. The *Prajnaparamita* sutra, the *Heart* sutra says, "There is no eye, no ear, there is no sound, there are no forms" and so on. This is the way the Buddha indicated that all phenomena lack the inherent existence; that is, they do not have any real nature that is their very own.

One has to carefully follow a path of reason and analysis that leads one to realize that all dharmas are emptiness. In the sutras the Buddha gave the logical arguments that enable one to realize that all dharmas are emptiness. The sutras briefly gave a reason and these grounds were then elaborated and explained clearly and fully by great masters such as Nagarjuna who composed treatises clearly giving many reasons for emptiness. From these many arguments, one that is easy to understand is the reason called "freedom from being either one or many," or "freedom from being either single or multiple." These arguments will be given below to give the reader an idea of how they go.

THE INTERDEPENDENCE OF PHENOMENA

There are also the logical arguments explaining interdependent relationship showing that one thing arises in dependence upon something else and that arises in dependence upon something else again and so on. As a result without depending upon something else, things do not come into existence. So things don't have a solid reality of their own because they are always relying upon other things to exist. Nevertheless, the eye consciousness sees visual images and the ear consciousness hears sounds and so on; so we wonder how it is that these things are empty. Doesn't saying they are empty mean that they don't really exist?

Let us consider the reasoning of interdependence with a simple example. If one looks at a two-inch and four-inch stick of incense, everyone would say that the two-inch one is the short one; and the other one is the long one. If you had a hundred people they would all agree that the two-inch is the short one and that the four-inch one is the long one. Now we bring out a six-inch stick of incense and put it next to the four-inch one and take away the two-inch one. The one that was long is now short and the other one is long. Everyone who looks at it would say that the four-inch stick is the short one, that the six-inch stick is the long one. This example illustrates that objects don't have an inherent "shortness" or "longness" but this quality is dependent upon other conditions. So, it is always in relation to something else that something is either short or long. The stick's inherent nature is not long or short. That is the way it is with all things. Whatever nature they seem to have is only a quality that depends upon other things.

What we have discovered about the interdependence of long and short applies to many other things. It is not true only of long and short, but also of beautiful and ugly, good and bad, big and small, and so on. We can't look at something and just say it is good. In comparison to one thing it is good, in comparison to something else, it is bad. If we gathered a hundred people together and every last one of them would look at it and identify it as good. They would say it is very good, at the same time, that goodness that they see coexists with this emptiness. And so, it appears quite good, and at the same time it is empty of that. In this way emptiness and appearance coexist. There is no question that whatever appears at that very moment is empty of that. So, a piece of incense appears long at one time and the same piece of incense also appears short at another time. Just when it is short, at the same moment it is long. These two coexist. This indicates the way in which all things are empty yet apparent, apparent yet empty. These two exist together.

THE ARGUMENT OF SINGLE AND MULTIPLE

The above argument of interdependence applies to relative categories such as long and short, good and bad. But we might think that there are some things that are not comparisons, like the substance of the incense stick itself. We might think, "Well there are things that don't exist in terms of their dependent relationship upon something else." But, let us now consider an example of a hand. If I hold out my hand, it does the work of a hand; we see it with our eyes as a solid, single object of a hand. But if we examine more closely, we find that it is designated as hand through the gathering together of many different things. For instance, is the thumb the hand? No, that is the thumb. Is the index finger the hand? No, that is the index finger. And so on, with third, fourth, and fifth fingers. Is the palm the hand? No, that is the palm of the hand. Is the skin the hand? No, that is the skin. We can go on with the flesh, bone, nails, the blood, and so on.

If we look for something that is the hand, we don't find a hand. What we find are all these different things that when arranged in a certain way are seen as a hand and can function as a hand. That is another example of the unity of appearance and emptiness—the interdependence of many different things gathered together. We see a hand and we think "hand." At the same time hand is in reality empty of being a hand. We might think, "Okay, the hand doesn't exist, but what about an individual finger." We carry out the analysis in the same way. What is the finger? Is the first joint a finger? No, that is the first joint of the finger. Is the second joint a finger? No. What about the third? No, there is really no finger there, rather there are different pieces that are put together and it's the interdependence of these pieces being gathered together that makes it be seen as a finger.

This is true of whatever one looks at. Everything is a collection of many different things that are heaped together and designated as something depending on how they have been gathered together. They do not exist as substantial selves. One can apply this reasoning to one's feet, or any part of one's body. Then one can apply this to all external phenomena, which are things that are gathered together, the way skandhas are. We give those phenomena the name of composites. The Tibetan word for composite is *duje* and what it means is that it is made of many things being gathered together. Since all that we consider as phenomena are in fact composites, they are apparent yet empty; empty yet apparent.

[64] Mental consciousness is also a composite of the eye consciousness, the ear consciousness, etc. Mental consciousness also

has many different moments to it: past, present, and future. It is newly born in every moment. There is nothing that has existed from the past up to now and will continue to exist into the future. There is no mental consciousness that has any duration. This emptiness is the absence of true existence and we call this *dharmadhatu*. It is not a voidness that is like space because space is nothingness; it cannot be made into anything; it does not change; it cannot give rise to good qualities. The dharmadhatu is nothing whatsoever, but appears as everything through the interdependent relationship of phenomena. Through this interdependent relationship all relative phenomena appear. This emptiness that we call dharmadhatu is the suitability for anything whatsoever to appear. And when it appears, the thing that appears does not exist; it is empty. It is empty, but it appears. The emptiness is not separate from the appearance. It is the appearance itself that is emptiness.

Not realizing this emptiness of appearance, we become confused. In such confusion we revert to attachment. So the root of that attachment is our not having realized emptiness. We cling to the objects of attachment, objects of hatred, of ignorance, pride, and envy. But in fact, those objects do not exist, they are peace, they are purity. To overcome our attachment we meditate upon that emptiness and realize that indeed the nature of all phenomena is dharmadhatu which is nothing in itself, but which appears as everything, which is the nature of all things, the way things are. Understanding this and resting our mind there evenly is called the view of mahamudra.

Even though we practice mahamudra meditation, it is very necessary to understand the view that is common to the sutra and mantra traditions. This is because when we meditate, we develop experiences that we might think are good and experiences that we think will lead us astray. By understanding the view common to the sutra and vajrayana traditions, we can evaluate that experience. If we reach such realization developed through analysis leading to a very certain understanding of the way in which things exist, then that inferential realization is extremely helpful and beneficial. We can then determine if our experiences are the same as that taught in the sutras and commentaries (Skt. *shastras)*. We can see if it is similar or dissimilar to experiences of others. If it is not similar, then we can see that we have done something different and haven't realized the view of emptiness. If, on the other hand, our experience within the practice of mahamudra is in accord with the meaning set out in these teachings common to the sutra and mantra tradition, then we can say that our experience is just like that of the Buddha. When we have some inner confidence in our experience and a certain understanding that is in accordance with the Vipashyana common to sutra and mantra, then this is very important.

Some people say that listening to the teachings can obstruct our meditation practice. If we have heard a lot about emptiness or luminosity then when we sit down to meditate, it is quite possible that we might fabricate some sort of emptiness or luminosity with our mind. In fact, it could be something that has been fabricated by our mind and this will obstruct the reality that we would like to realize. Rather we must rest evenly in just whatever experience we have, placing our confidence in that rather than something made up that seems better. One must not to meditate upon emptiness or luminosity using conceptual mind because it will merely be fabricated. It is not a matter of taking something that is not empty and making it empty. Nor is it taking something that has no luminosity and making it into luminosity. From that point of view Maitreya said that there is nothing to be cleared away and nothing to be constructed. By constructed he meant that one does not have to manufacture good qualities. Rather one is realizing things that are authentic and genuine and correct just as they are. One sees the genuine as the genuine and then chooses liberation. One is not creating something that didn't exist before nor is one making up an emptiness or luminosity that wasn't there. Rather, one is simply introduced to the way things are.

Questions

Question: Rinpoche, could you please explain why the egolessness of self always seems to be taught before egolessness of dharmas. Because for myself it seems that it is much easier to experience interdependent origination than to understand how the skandhas work.

Rinpoche: When the Buddha taught, there were a great many other traditions and teachers of dharma who all spoke about emptiness. However, they did not understand the nonexistence of the self. If one does not understand the emptiness of the person, then one cannot understand the emptiness of dharmas properly. For that reason the Buddha taught about impermanence, emptiness of persons and so forth. Once one understands a person lacks a self, then one can proceed to understand the nonexistence of dharmas.

From another point of view, the main thing to be abandoned are the disturbing emotions. To abandon the disturbing emotions one must understand the nonexistence of the self. If one can realize this, then the disturbing emotions will automatically disappear. When one has cleared away the disturbing emotions, then one can go further to eliminate the obscurations of knowledge which is understanding the emptiness of all phenomena.

Question: Could you briefly explain how it is that earth, water, fire, and wind are the nature of emptiness.

Rinpoche: Earth, water, fire, and wind are explained in the Buddhist text known as *The Treasury of the Abhidharma* by Vasubandhu. The four elements described in the Abhidharma and as they are generally understood are not the same thing. Earth in the Abhidharma is explained as that which is hard and has the quality of solidity. Water is fluid and has the quality of moistening. Wind has the quality of motion. And fire has the quality of ripening. It is not quite the same as when we say the earth is this solid thing we live on and water is like a body of water, fire burns, and wind blows things back and forth. The earth, for example, appears in this world as very solid yet even though it appears to be very large, it is a composite of many very small particles. Whatever we look at is composed of many, many, many particles like many grains of sand. So earth exists as all these individual separate things, not as one thing. From this point of view the earth is not truly existent. It is something that is not free from being either single or multiple; it is an interdependent relationship. In a similar way one can analyze anything big or small, and with reasoning demonstrate that it is empty.

Question: I think where I am getting confused is the example of the hand. My understanding is that if you really took it down, you end up with the elements of earth, air, fire, and water.

Rinpoche: Yes, what you say is true. If you analyze this thoroughly you come down to earth, water, fire, and air. When you analyze the hand what it comes down to is that which is solid, that which is moistened, that which is ripening, and that which is moving. The parts of the hand that are hard and obstructing is the earth element of the hand and there are a good many of these little particles. The water element of the hand causes its cohesion. During the life of a person, the hand changes a lot from childhood to youth to maturity to old age. What causes it to change is the fire element. Then you can move your hand around and that is the air or wind element. So *The Treasury of the Abhidharma* talks about a mass of eight tiny particles. It is said in the smallest element an atom is composed of eight particles. These eight particles are earth, water, fire, wind, visible form, smell, taste, and tangibility which are the qualities and properties of the smallest physical thing, which we could call an atom. And without those you don't have anything at all.

Question: I have a feeling this word "emptiness" causes a lot of problems for us Westerners. When I hear emptiness, it means nothing. Does not empty of intrinsic nature mean beyond the duality of subject and object?

Rinpoche: Yes. The definition of the words doesn't matter a lot. The point is to overcome one's strong fixation on conceptualization. When it is said that things are empty, it means that things do not exist in the way they seem to exist. It is one's fixation on them that must be overturned. As I said before, emptiness does not mean a blank emptiness or space. It is not a dead emptiness. It is an emptiness that is the suitability for everything to appear. It is the possibility for anything whatsoever to happen.

In the impure state of sentient beings, what is meant by emptiness is that dharmata, the reality that is beyond the confusion of samsara, is the nature of samsara and nirvana. In the pure state of enlightened beings emptiness means *jnana*, or wisdom, of the buddhas. In the impure state one speaks about the inseparability of appearance and emptiness. In the pure state one speaks of the inseparability of luminosity and emptiness which are the *five wisdoms* of a Buddha. These wisdoms are entirely ungraspable, yet they do appear. The nature of their appearance is non-dual, yet these five wisdoms do appear. It is the union of dharmata and emptiness or spaciousness or the union of wisdom (Skt. *jnana*) and spaciousness.

The union of appearance and emptiness seems contradictory in that when there is appearance, one does not see dharmata. One might think that dharmata would cancel appearance but, in fact, these two are not contradictory to one another. Appearance and dharmata coexist and are inseparable.

When we speak about luminosity and emptiness, we say these two coexist, are simultaneous and do not contradict other one.

Question: I don't understand why we would, for example, ask to be born in the buddha paradise of *Dewachen* in the *Chenrezig* practice if everything is actually empty.

Rinpoche: You need to make a distinction between the conventional truth and ultimate truth. You need to make a distinction between things as they appear and things as they are. Things as they appear is what we mean by the conventional truth. Things as they are is what we mean by the ultimate truth. Ultimately there is no self, but relatively we do indeed perceive the self as a solid object and it appears that way to us. The five aggregates that make up our continuum of body and mind do appear. In this context there are former lifetimes and later lifetimes with a continuity from a former lifetime to a later lifetime. All that does appear even if ultimately it does not exist.

It is helpful to think of the example of a dream. Suppose we were asleep and dreaming of a tiger and became afraid that the tiger was about to bite us and we would be very frightened. Now suppose someone who has clairvoyant powers comes along and sees that we are dreaming of a tiger and are very afraid. Rather than laughing, this person feels compassion and wakes us up and says, "Don't be afraid, the tiger is just a dream." It is just like this with all the things that we experience in former and later lifetimes. Birth and death, the five skandhas, the karma that is accumulated from good and bad deeds certainly has a cause which leads to a result. All of these things are happening to us and that is the way things appear. If none of these appearances were going on, then it wouldn't be necessary to practice the path. But since it does appear, it is necessary to get help because we have not realized the ultimate nature of things. And because we have not realized the ultimate nature of phenomena, there are these appearances.

In the context of the practice, that prayer is made in the context of conventional truth because we have not realized the ultimate truth of how things really are.

Chapter 5

Eliminating Doubts Concerning Vipashyana Meditation

V. ELIMINATING DOUBTS CONCERNING VIPASHYANA

A. ANALYTIC AND PLACEMENT MEDITATION

[70] Let us continue our discussion of Vipashyana. Vipashyana can be viewed in terms of four aspects: view, meditation, action, and fruition. First of all, view serves as the ground and we arrive at the view by listening to the teachings and reflecting upon what we have heard. With this we know what we should meditate upon. However, the view alone is not sufficient. It needs to be joined by action so that our understanding and experience are increased. Together these three—view, meditation, and action—bring us to the fruition of Vipashyana. The question now is how do we sustain the view in meditation.

The siddhas have described the practice of sustaining the view in meditation in many different ways. We could say the view in meditation is basically a discussion of the merits of analytical meditation (Tib. *je gom*) and placement meditation (Tib. *jo gom*). Analytical meditation is the meditation of the *pandita* who is a great scholar. In analytical meditation one only investigates and analyzes and that is the style of this meditation. On the other hand, there is placement meditation of the *kusula*, who is a very simple person who allows his or her mind to rest in equanimity without doing any investigation and analysis.

B. THE ANALYTICAL METHODS OF VIPASHYANA

[72] There are some who say that when one practices shamatha, shamatha is only placement meditation and analyzing meditation

will only harm the practice of shamatha. They also say that Vipashyana is just analytical meditation and so there is no practice of placing and resting the mind within Vipashyana. Tashi Namgyal, however, does not believe this is correct and those who say this have not had much experience in meditation. He goes on to say that in general shamatha is a placement meditation in which the mind is placed and rests there. However, when one is practicing shamatha, one continues to look into it to see how it is going, being mindful of the shamatha itself. "Is it going well? Is it not going well?" or "Which antidote needs to be applied?" and so forth. That checking of one's mind as one practices is analysis. So, shamatha meditation is not just placing the mind and resting, but also involves analytical meditation.

If Vipashyana were only analytical meditation, then it would not be authentic. If we only analyzed and never placed the mind and allowed it to rest upon what we have understood, then Vipashyana would not lead us to abandon the kleshas and we would not develop a definite and certain understanding. So, there is also placement meditation within Vipashyana. If we look at it this way, we can see that both shamatha and Vipashyana involve both analytical and placement meditation. Having said that much, it is then fair to say that shamatha is mainly a matter of placing the mind doing only some analysis. And Vipashyana is mainly a matter of analyzing and placing the mind a little.

C. PRACTICE OF ANALYTICAL AND PLACEMENT MEDITATION

[75] When we speak about the view, meditation, and action, Vipashyana concerns the view. There is one view that we must listen[20] to many explanations of the scriptures and analyze them very carefully with reasoning so that we can develop a very clear and definite understanding of emptiness and the interdependent relationship of phenomena. Having developed such a clear understanding, we then place our mind in an even meditative state of the nature of phenomena, without analysis. If we do not alternate analysis with resting the mind, then our Vipashyana will degenerate and just become shamatha. Tashi Namgyal, however, states that this

method of meditation is not correct. He says that this analysis of *valid cognition* (Skt. *sema*) is not the same as seeing phenomena directly as they are. Rather this information is what appears to one's mind that has been created by one's mind and it is not genuine, authentic meditation. Does this valid cognition help? Yes, but it is not genuine meditation itself. Tashi Namgyal says we should listen to the instructions and think about them and analyze what we have heard. We do it in the manner of showing the race track to a horse. If we want a horse to follow a certain course, the first thing we do is to show the track to the horse so the horse knows where to go. That is the purpose of hearing the teachings and reflecting upon them. It is a matter of being shown the way to go so that we can go correctly and we develop the prajna to achieve certainty and confidence. At the same time, the prajna that arises from hearing and contemplating the teachings is not sufficient. We require the prajna that arises from meditation. We meditate upon the dharmata that exists right with things themselves.

The lama Gotsanpa explained that analytical meditation and placement meditation ultimately have the same destination. However, the path of placement meditation proceeds more quickly. Therefore, even the great learned persons have ultimately relied upon the path of placement meditation as their principal practice. So the great gurus of the lineage, such as Naropa and Maitripa, who were extremely learned, depended mainly on the quintessential instructions and meditated by settling the mind in equipoise. So we need to listen to and think about the various teachings on the true nature of phenomena but when it comes to practice, we need to depend upon the quintessential instructions of the siddhas and meditate in that manner.

The Moonlight of Mahamudra suggests that there are three incorrect views and then refutes these views. The first incorrect view is that when one practices shamatha, one does not need to perform any analysis and when one practices Vipashyana, one does not need to place the mind in equipoise. However, in shamatha one needs to investigate and analyze to determine how to clear away the afflictions, distractions, and thoughts that have arisen. One needs to employ the various methods for bringing the mind to a state of rest and that involves analysis of one's meditation. Similarly, in

Vipashyana even though one emphasizes the development of prajna, one must also set the mind in a state of equipoise to do this. Therefore the practice of shamatha involves both analytical and placement meditation and the practice of Vipashyana also involves both analytical and placement meditation.

However, with beginning meditators, the main problem tends to be wildness of mind, so that just focusing upon shamatha practice of calming the mind will help settle the mind's wildness. When one's shamatha practice is going well, one can then work with the obstacles of heaviness of mind, working with these through investigation and analysis.

A second incorrect view is the procedure of alternating back and forth between shamatha and Vipashyana. One practices the methods for calming the mind and then having done so, one turns to developing certainty with regard to the view. But this is not such a good way to proceed because if one does, so then one's shamatha and one's Vipashyana oppose each another. It is better to find the view and then to settle into equipoise within the view.

A third incorrect view was suggested by the Sakya Pandita who said mahamudra meditation of Gampopa was basically the meditation taught by the Chinese master Hashang Mahayana who is best known for his famous debate with Kamalashila in Tibet. Briefly, Hashang taught that the way to practice meditation was to simply abandon all notions of good or bad and just not to think about anything at all.[21] However, the practice of mahamudra that was taught by Gampopa and the meditation taught by Hashang Mahayana are not at all alike.

D. MEDITATION ON MIND ITSELF

[77] The discussion of the main body of the practice of the view has two parts. The first is an analysis of other traditions and the second is setting forth our own tradition. There is a great deal of material on other's traditions in the text and I will leave this aside to discuss the view itself.

When we speak about dharmata or things as they really are, we are speaking about absence of the confusion and mistaken appearances that ordinary people experience most of the time. When we talk about the mind itself (Tib. *sem ne*) and mind as it is, what we mean is the inseparability of luminosity and emptiness. There are a variety of ways for describing what mind is trying to realize. It is important to recognize just what this is. If we just meditate without having identified dharmata, then while meditation is beneficial and will make us more peaceful, gradually causing us to understand the view, meditation alone will not cut the root of the disturbing emotions, and we will not abandon what must be done to reach enlightenment. Therefore, we need to find out just what dharmata is and rest our mind there. Having found the mind itself as it is, we meditate upon dharmata not covered up by anything else. When we meditate on external phenomena, dharmata is covered and hidden underneath those things. But when we meditate on the mind itself, we are meditating on the naked form of emptiness itself. And that is what we mean when we talk about bringing direct perception to the path. It is meditation upon the mind itself.

Questions

Question: Rinpoche, you said that when we attain the equanimity of mind, we will see the world as a safe place. How do we combine the equanimity of mind with the need to have discrimination and avoid dangers.

Rinpoche: What you have described is certainly true of the relative world, the world of conventional truth or *kundzop* which comes about through the interdependent relationship of one thing to another due to the latencies that have been established with your own mind. For instance, if you put your hand in a fire, it will indeed burn your hand. If you just think to yourself, "Oh, it is just emptiness" that is not going to help very much. The reason it doesn't help very much is not because emptiness is not the nature of the fire or your hand. It is because you have not realized that emptiness. Because you have not realized the emptiness, the nature of phenomena, if you put your hand in the fire, it will be burnt or if you drink polluted water, you will get sick.

What I was talking about was really about feelings that you experience in your mind, by pointing out that it doesn't necessarily have to depend upon what is going on in the outer world. For instance, having tremendous wealth does not guarantee that you are going to feel good and happy. And people who are poor are not necessarily miserable. There is no necessary correlation. If you are happy mentally, then it doesn't matter whether you have or don't have a lot of things.

As you say, at this point the world is not entirely safe. This comes about because we have not realized the reality of this world, we have not realized dharmata. And so we live in the world of the relative, the world of kundzop. Not having realized the reality of phenomena, we have to deal with the relative world. We live in the relative world because we have not understood the mind as it is and we have not actualized the mind's deep nature and have not arrived at that final wisdom. Because we have not achieved such *siddhi* and actualized such ultimate wisdom, we are not able to change things right away.

Question: Could you explain the relationship between alternation of shamatha and Vipashyana and wildness and heaviness of mind?

Rinpoche: Dullness and wildness of mind are problems for the practice of shamatha. They are also problems that one experiences when one practices Vipashyana. So if one is practicing shamatha and heaviness of mind occurs, then various methods such as encouraging oneself and remembering that *sugatagarbha* exists, thinking of the good qualities of a Buddha and so forth, should be practiced at that time. If wildness is the principal problem in one's shamatha practice, then one should think about impermanence, the suffering of samsara, and generate some discouragement about all the things one is getting excited about. Realizing that samsara is entirely futile should pacify one's wildness. Similarly, when one is practicing Vipashyana and one has actualized this true nature of mind, one could have the wildness come into one's meditation. If wildness begins to afflict one's meditation of Vipashyana, one should look right into that wildness to see just what it is. And similarly if heaviness and obscurations come into one's practice of Vipashyana, then one looks right into its nature.

Question: In the discussion of internal phenomena and the two logical arguments concerning the operation of one's own mind, could Rinpoche describe the difference between the first and second. Also isn't the argument that separate objects establish in one's consciousness the same question that if a tree falls in the forest and there is no one around to hear.

Rinpoche: First of all several people have asked about what actually is the difference between the two arguments. Although these two logical arguments were originally given in a sutra by the Buddha, the main place where these arguments are set forth is in the treatises on valid cognition composed by Dharmakirti. This logical argument is just called the sign of the clear and knowing and this one principle covers both arguments. What is being presented is that all sorts of appearances arise, but never in the absence of mind. That is to say the appearances appear only in the perspective of mind. So if this quality of luminosity and awareness isn't present, then there are no appearances. That's the main point being made. The second reasoning about the simultaneity is a branch of the first logical argument. It is not a distinct point but elaborates this point further by pointing out that within that arising of appearances for the perspective of an observing consciousness, they always happen simultaneously. They always happen together because it is a meeting of appearance in the mind. It takes two things to meet. If there is no mind there, there is nothing to meet. So that is the relation of the two.

The second point about if a tree falls and nobody hears it then was there any sound? This previous argument is about mind only and is made in the context of *alaya consciousness*. A lot of people have translated that as "universal consciousness" or compared it to Jung's collective unconsciousness, but that is wrong. The alaya consciousness is something that exists within the continuum of each person and is like the repository for latencies or traces of whatever experience one has had, instead of universal consciousness in what I will translate as the "mind-basis-of-all." I call this the mind-basis-of-all because on the one hand it is a mental entity of consciousness as well as the basis of all the other consciousnesses that one experiences. Also the appearances of phenomena to one's own consciousnesses both arise from predispositions that are established with one's own mind. So this alaya consciousness gives rise to the six consciousnesses or the eye, ear, nose, tongue, body, and mind consciousnesses. They arise from predispositions or latencies that are come from one's own alaya consciousness and then various phenomena appear to those consciousnesses. Those appearances also arise from that same predisposition of dormancy with one's own alaya consciousness. Now that applies to this thing about trees falling in the forest. There is some basis for this: there has to be some latency in one's own mind that could enable this to take place. Yet at that time since there is no one there, there is no sound that is being perceived by anybody's ear consciousness. Nevertheless, there must be predispositions within the alaya consciousness of various people for that sound to occur. Even if at the time there is no manifestation of sound.

Question: I am a doctor. Many people coming to me have a memory that is causing great pain that may have happened a long time ago such as neglect or abuse from a parent, relationship loss, a divorce. This event becomes a memory and they go to the psychologist and say, "I have this memory and my whole life is not working because of this memory." So they work and work for years on one memory and still nothing is really gained. My question is how to help people who have persistent memory causing emotional pain that eventually becomes physical pain?

Rinpoche: Yes, it does happen as you describe that through the power of various predispositions or latencies there is a lot of distress in one's mind and then that becomes distress in one's body. So naturally having those predispositions lead to a situation of difficulty and anxiety.

Well, what can one do? We talk about the precious human birth that is endowed with freedom from bad conditions and engendered with good conditions. It can be very helpful to think about the significance of such an opportunity. One has the capacity to do almost anything. But we don't recognize this or we don't remember that we actually have that precious human birth. Our heads begin to spin and we don't know that is the situation. So we begin to think that there is this something that we have to have. And if we don't have it, then we become very discouraged. Whatever that thing is. What we are doing is not noticing the tremendous range of options, the great variety of paths that are open to us. Instead we focus on some narrow thing and let our minds be drawn in and captivated by that. So I think that what is very helpful is remembering all those other things that are open to us. We let our mind become vast and very spacious. Furthermore, the past is over and done with. Whatever has happened either helpful or not helpful, there isn't too much that can be done about it right now. So I don't think there is a whole lot of benefit in dwelling upon the past.

Question: Could you explain interdependent origination more?

Rinpoche: The argument of interdependent origination is the reasoning of the dependence of one thing on some other thing by showing that there is nothing that can set itself up without dependence on something else. For instance, when you are standing here, this is here, that over there is there. But if you go to the other side of the room then what was "here" is not "there." You can look at that from many points of view and you can apply it to many to different situations. What it means is that there is no certainty of something being here or there, it just depends upon where you happen to be looking at it from. In the end what is demonstrated is that there is no such thing as here or there because they just depend upon each other. So, this is the feature of interdependent origination. It is a reasoning that demonstrates emptiness.

The other logical argument establishes that appearances are just appearances of mind. For instance, yesterday you saw a patch of blue and you remember that. When you remember the blue, you don't just remember blue, you also remember the scene of blue, you remember the knower apprehending blue and the qualities associated with the experience of seeing the blue. This shows that whenever you remember something, you remember both what you saw and what you saw it with. It shows that these two are inextricably tied together and what appeared to be an appearance of something external to the perceiving consciousness was not actually something external to that consciousness but of the same entity as the perceiving consciousness. So principally what is being demonstrated in the case of dependent arising is how one thing depends upon another for its identity and thereby demonstrate emptiness. Principally what is being taught in the case of this simultaneity is how the apprehended object and the apprehended subject occur only together, thereby demonstrating that what seem to be external appearances are really just appearances of the mind.

BOOK II

THE MEDITATION OF MAHAMUDRA

The Lineage of Mahamudra

The Close Lineage

Tilopa (988-1069 C.E.)
An emanation of Chakrasamvara who received mahamudra teachings from a number of dakinis.

Naropa (1016-1100 C.E.)
An abbot at Nalanda University who left and became Tilopa's student.

Marpa (1012-1097 C.E)
A Tibetan who came to India three times and studied under Naropa and Maitripa.

Milarepa (1040-1123 C.E.)
Received teachings from Marpa and thoroughly practiced the mahamudra and the practice of the six yogas of Naropa.

Gampopa (1079-1153 C.E.)
Received mahamudra teachings from Milarepa and also combined these with Kadampa analytical teachings of Atisha. Set up first Kagyu monastery.

Dusum Khyenpa (1110-1193 C.E.)
The first Karmapa who took Gampopa's teachings of mahamudra and founded the Karma Kagyu lineage.

Karma Pakshi (1206-1283 C.E.)
The Second Karmapa who was known for his practice and ablity to perform miracles.

Rangjung Dorje (1284-1339 C.E.)
The Third Karmapa who was a great scholar who wrote many treatises on meditation.

Each Karmapa passed down the mahamudra teachings right up to Thrangu Rinpoche who was asked to set up the monastic college in Rumtek by the 16th Karmapa.

Chapter 6

The Origins of Mahamudra

VI. THE ORIGINS OF MAHAMUDRA

Up to this point we have been discussing the stages of shamatha and Vipashyana common to the sutra and mantra path. Now we are going to speak about the practices which are specific to mahamudra (called the "uncommon practice").

A. THE DEFINITION OF MAHAMUDRA

[92] To begin with we need, first of all, to have confidence in mahamudra. For this confidence to arise there must be causes, such as knowing the extraordinary, good qualities of mahamudra. These can be illustrated with the various synonyms for mahamudra. The Sanskrit term *mahamudra* has the first syllable of *maha* which has the meaning of "vast," "very large" and "pervading everything." It means not just pervading some things, but pervading both outer and inner phenomena. For that reason *maha* means very large. The syllable *mudra* principally means "seal" in terms of a king placing his seal on a document so that nothing passes out of its sphere. An equivalent now would be a signature. If someone places his or her signature on something, then everyone knows that it is the speech and the activity of that person. mahamudra then is the seal for all phenomena and it is the dharmata, the reality, of all things. There are no objects that pass beyond mahamudra. There is nothing outside it because it is the reality of everything. Thus, mahamudra has the meaning of a great seal.

If we were to translate mahamudra directly in Tibetan, we would translate *maha* as *chenpo* and *mudra* as *gya*. The Tibetan translators, however, added a syllable of *chak*. This syllable is an honorific term and indicates that mahamudra is not an ordinary object, but something worthy of respect. *Chak* is also the honorific word for "hand" so in this context one would use the word *chak* when one speaks about the hand of a guru or a king who is able to benefit people. Instead of using the ordinary Tibetan which is *lagpa,* one uses an honorific word *chak*. It indicates that person's activities and qualities are not like the activities and qualities of others, principally indicating purity. The choice of the word for a hand is important because a guru sometimes bestows an empowerment by just touching a person with his or her hand. Just the touch of the lama's hand bestows blessing. Similarly, an accomplished person composes Buddhist treatises by hand to help purify the continuum of being of ordinary people. Also, the work of a person in the position of authority such as a king is with the hands, to clear away obstacles. Thus, the word *chak* is used to indicate the transformation of something from an impure state to a pure state. *Chak* also indicates something that has capacity, potency, and ability. In the context of mahamudra, it indicates that through mahamudra one is able to discard all impurities such as the kleshas, so that one's being becomes pure and all good qualities increase and expand.

There are many different names for mahamudra. In the context of the Middle-way or Madhyamaka school it is called the ultimate, it is called suchness. This school also speaks of unsurpassable wisdom. In the context of the Dzogchen school, it is called *Kuntozangpo* which means "all good" or in Sanskrit *Samantabhadra*. In the context of fruition it is called dharmakaya. Even though there are many names for mahamudra there is no difference in the meaning of them; the meaning of all these is the same.

To summarize, Maitripa said in the *Yogasapta*, "What is mahamudra? It passes beyond the mind of ordinary people, it is luminous, it is without conceptuality, and it is like space."

THE TYPES OF MAHAMUDRA

[95] The nature of mahamudra is that it pervades everything: external things, internal mind, ourselves, others. At the same time it cannot be identified and labeled. There are three kinds of mahamudra: ground mahamudra, path mahamudra, and fruition mahamudra. Whether we realize ground mahamudra or not, it is the

nature of all phenomena. It is not that if we realize it, it is created and if we do not realize it, it doesn't exist. mahamudra is there from the very beginning. The only difference is whether or not we have realized it. Even when we have not realized it, it is still there.

From the point of view of experience, ground mahamudra is mind as it is. From the point of view that ground mahamudra pervades everything, it is reality, things as they are. It pervades all sentient beings. Sometimes it is called the jewel of the mind, sometimes it is called tathagatagarbha, Buddha-essence. Whether we are suffering or doing well, the ground mahamudra is no different because it pervades all sentient beings in precisely the same way.

However, there is a difference at the relative level in that someone may temporarily be unable to realize ground mahamudra due to adverse circumstances or obstacles. These adverse circumstances need to be overcome, and their confusion needs to be corrected. We need to purify our understanding, get use to it, make it extremely clear. It is the guru who introduces us to that mahamudra. We recognize it, meditate upon it, and become familiar with it. This, then, is path mahamudra. Path mahamudra is not any different from ground mahamudra except in terms of mahamudra becoming more and more clear.

The benefit of path mahamudra is that it brings us to fruition mahamudra. When we have realized mahamudra completely, realized it continually, realizing every factor of it brilliantly and lucidity, that is fruition mahamudra. Maitreya in the *Uttaratantra* spoke about this in terms of three different situations. The first is called impure referring to the state of sentient beings, which is the occasion of ground mahamudra. The second is called impure and pure, referring to having realized mahamudra somewhat and this is path mahamudra. The third is called is extremely and thoroughly pure. That is the occasion of having realized mahamudra completely, which is fruition mahamudra.

THE IMPORTANCE OF MAHAMUDRA

[96] The problem of not understanding mahamudra is set forth for the purpose of arising confidence in mahamudra. In *A Guide to the Bodhisattva's Way of Life,* Shantideva discussed the six different

branches of *perfections* (Skt. *paramitas*) of generosity, discipline, patience, exertion, and so forth. Then he said that the subduer (meaning the Buddha) taught all of these branches for the sake of prajna. Prajna, in this context, is the name for the wisdom (Skt. *jnana*) that realizes things as they are. Shantideva then went on to say that although we might do many hundreds of thousands of other practices such as recitation of mantra, all of them are simply methods for realizing mahamudra. If we do not realize mahamudra, then even though all those other practices are beneficial in terms of bringing one to the point of being able to realize mahamudra we will not be able to achieve the final fruition. However, if we realize mahamudra, then we will achieve that fruition. The text in the *Mahamudra Subtledrop* then cites the tantra of the Buddha that says if one realizes this, then one will become Vajrasattva:

He who does not understand Mahamudra
Is not a realized one, however illuminated.
He will not achieve supreme fulfillment
Without perfectly understanding
The essence of mahamudra.

So, to achieve final state, one must understand mahamudra. That then is the great benefit of knowing mahamudra and the great fault of not understanding it.

B. ORIGIN OF MAHAMUDRA IN THE SUTRAS

[97] Mahamudra was spoken about by the Buddha in various sutras and was described as being very profound and special. The Buddha described mahamudra in various sutras sometimes calling it mahamudra and sometimes not. But whatever name the Buddha used, the meaning was the same, referring to phenomena as being naturally pure and sealed as primordially liberated. That was how mahamudra was spoken about in the sutras.

C. ORIGIN OF MAHAMUDRA IN THE TANTRAS

In the vajrayana there are four sets of tantras with the first three being called the lower tantras. These are the *kriya tantra*, *carya tantra*, and the *yoga tantra* or in English action tantra, performance tantra and union tantra respectively. The higher tantras are those tantras in the *anuttarayoga* tantra or the unsurpassable yoga tantras. There are four different sets of tantras: *kriyatantra* or action tantra, *caryatantra* or performance tantra, *yogatantra* or union tantra, and the *anuttarayogatantra* or unsurpassable yoga tantra. Mahamudra is taught in all four of these sets of tantras, in particular, in the unsurpassable yoga tantras which are the main texts of the vajrayana. Mahamudra is taught in each and every tantra of that class. Mahamudra in the lower tantras is spoken of as being the "hand seal," just as one seals something closed by sealing it with one's hand. The point is that the true nature of phenomena is indicated in that way. Mahamudra is also sometimes spoken of in terms of the *four seals* or four mudras. These four are the *samaya* seal, the wisdom seal, the action seal, and the great seal. In Sanskrit it would be the *samayamudra*, the *jnanamudra*, the *karmamudra*, and the mahamudra (or *dharmamudra*). In the anuttarayoga tantra, there are three internal divisions: the father tantras, the mother tantras, and the non-dual tantras. The mahamudra is taught in all of these subdivisions. In particular there is the extraordinary uncommon presentation that is given in the *Wheel of Time* (Skt. *Kalachakra*) *Tantra* which belongs to the non-dual section of the highest yoga tantras. In the context of that Kalachakra tantra, it was spoken of as "the emptiness possessing the supreme of all aspects," indicating that it is the basis of all phenomena. It is also called "the supreme unchanging bliss" because upon realizing it, one passes beyond changeable samsara and arrives at unchanging bliss.

So mahamudra was taught in the sutras and tantras. It was also taught in a tantra not included in the above four tantras called *Mahamudra Subtledrop* tantra. In this particular context, "subtle drops" (Skt. *bindu*, Tib. *tigle*) means "without change." This tantra belongs to the various treatises contained in the *spiritual songs* (Skt. *doha*) of Saraha. Saraha composed three cycles of dohas: the king doha, the queen doha, and the citizen's doha. The bindu tantra also contains the eight treasuries of dohas by Tilopa, Naropa, and Maitripa.

So, it is taught in all of the tantra sets, especially in the fourth and highest set of tantras. Mahamudra is specifically taught in the *Wheel of Time* and the *Mahamudra Subtledrop* tantra.

ELIMINATING MISTAKEN PERCEPTIONS

[105] Some scholars have criticized mahamudra and attempted to refute it by saying that it is mistaken because there are some who give instructions and practice the meditation of mahamudra but do not really understand what they are doing. If one practices in an incorrect away, then there is a danger. Thus, the criticism is of those who use the name mahamudra without understanding its meaning. For instance, the Sakya Pandita has said that meditating upon mahamudra would probably lead one to take rebirth as an animal and in the formless realm. Now this statement is really made for those who have an incorrect understanding to discard their misunderstanding.

At the same time it is necessary to reply to that statement because there are some who, without recognizing its intent, will simply take it to mean that mahamudra is a useless meditation. So, there is a real purpose in making a reply that clears up this confusion. Therefore we can see that both the refutation and the reply to that refutation have a purpose.

D. THE SUTRAS AND TANTRAS IN MAHAMUDRA

[109] The text then discusses the way in which the profound meaning of all the sutras and tantras is included within the mahamudra. For instance, in the second turning of the wheel of dharma emptiness that is realized with transcendent knowledge is included within mahamudra. The Buddha-essence that is taught in the third turning is also included within mahamudra. And the quintessential instructions of the completion stage of the vajrayana are included within mahamudra.

If we understand mahamudra, we will see how all of these are included within it. Gampopa said that there are three different paths with their nature being the same, but the practice as being different. These are taking inference as the path, taking blessing as the path, and taking direct experience as the path. Taking inference as the path refers to, for instance, the various reasons that are set forth in the Madhyamaka showing all things as being neither single nor multiple. Taking blessings as the path refers to, for instance, meditation upon the body of a deity or the practices involving the subtle channels and subtle energies (Skt. *nadi* and *prana*). Taking direct perception as the path is mahamudra. It is pointed out to us, we recognize it, we become accustomed to it, and we take direct experience as the path.

One could also classify all the different paths into the paths that abandon the ground, paths that transform the ground, and paths that recognize the ground. The first path of abandoning the ground is the vehicle of transcendent action of the sutra vehicle in which some things are recognized as something to be abandoned and others are understood to be remedies for those things that ought to be discarded. The second path of transformation of the ground refers to the practices of the vajrayana in which one purifies one's body and mind by meditating on one's own body being a deity. One's body is thus transformed into the body of the deity—into something pure. One's mind is transformed from discursiveness into wisdom. The third path of understanding the ground is mahamudra. Whatever the ground is, one knows that one does not need to abandon it nor does one need to transform it. Rather, one knows it as it is. When one knows the ground as it is, then all appearances are recognized as the magical display of the mind. Thus, in terms of what we have talked about so far, we could say that mahamudra is a matter of using direct perception as the path. This can also be called the quick path.

E. The Good Qualities of Mahamudra

Since the teaching of the mahamudra is extraordinary, the lineage of transmission of this teaching must also be extraordinary and distinctive. The text describes the lineage of transmission by first explaining the way in which the Buddha came to India and turned the wheel of dharma so that the dharma flourished and spread both the dharma and the teaching of mahamudra.

DISTANT LINEAGE OF MAHAMUDRA

[116] There are a number of stories recounted in the text about people in India who had very unusual experiences and high realization of the practice of mahamudra in India. The Buddha taught mahamudra in the tantras that are known as *Mahamudra Subtledrop* tantra, with the word bindu having the sense of "essence." He taught it also in the *Glorious Unblemished Tantra* and the Buddha also taught mahamudra in the *Thoroughly Abiding Tantra*. The Buddha gave the mahamudra teachings near the end of his life. After the Buddha's passing away, the great bodhisattvas Manjughosa and Avalokiteshvara gave these teachings to Saraha.

When Buddha taught mahamudra to those bodhisattvas, he said that in the future there would be great bodhisattvas who would practice and propagate this teaching. In particular there would be Saraha and Nagarjuna who would receive, practice, and propagate this teaching. Later it came to pass that the great bodhisattva Manjushri appeared as a bodhisattva named Lodro Rinchen ("precious intelligence") and the great bodhisattva Avalokiteshvara appeared as a bodhisattva named Dewa Gönpo ("protector of happiness"). These two bodhisattvas gave the mahamudra teachings to Saraha and he achieved immediate liberation. In this way Saraha became a *siddha* or accomplished person. He passed this teaching to Nagarjuna who, prior to meeting with Saraha, was a great learned *pandita* or scholar. After meeting with Saraha, he became a great adept, actualized mahamudra and lived as a siddha. Nagarjuna passed the lineage of quintessential oral instructions on how to practice mahamudra to Shavari. Maitripa, having heard the name Shavari and his tradition of oral instructions, was greatly inspired and with profound faith he immediately went to southern India to meet with Shavari. He underwent tremendous difficulties and hardships on his journey to and in meeting with Shavari. He eventually succeeded in meeting him and received all the mahamudra instructions in their complete form. He went to central India where he disseminated these teachings to others. This lineage is known as the "long lineage" of mahamudra.

Saraha then served as the source through which the mahamudra spread and flourished in India. Saraha gave these teachings to

Nagarjuna, who gave them to a great many highly qualified and accomplished students. Among them was one particularly highly accomplished student named Shavari who achieved siddhi. Shavari then not only received the teachings directly from Saraha, but met face to face with the bodhisattvas Devaputra Ratnamati and Devaputra Sukhanatha, who were emanations of Manjughosa and Avalokiteshvara respectively. He met them in a visionary manner and received the mahamudra teachings directly from them. Shavari thus received the transmission of mahamudra from those two and also from Saraha whom he met face to face. This transmission is known as the distant lineage of mahamudra.

THE CLOSE LINEAGE

[116] There is also a close lineage of mahamudra that begins with Tilopa who received the teachings of mahamudra from Vajradhara. The Buddha has three bodies: the dharmakaya, the sambhogakaya, and the nirmanakaya. The Buddha Shakyamuni was a nirmanakaya, or emanation body. He was called the supreme emanation body in that he gave the teaching to achieve enlightenment, turned the wheel of dharma, demonstrated the way of passing into nirvana, and so forth. After his death that particular supreme emanation body no longer existed. However, his mind continued, and his mind is of the nature of wisdom or the wisdom dharmakaya. That wisdom knows the nature of all phenomena and the full variety of phenomena, is endowed with qualities such as compassion and so forth. This wisdom dharmakaya did not pass into nirvana, but remained, so that fortunate students are still able to meet with it. In that way, it is called the "vajra dharmakaya" in which "vajra" means unchangeable. This dharmakaya also appears in the form of the sambhogakaya. In the sambhogakaya, the Buddha appears like the Vajradhara that is depicted on the scroll paintings or thangkas with a dark blue body, one face, two arms, and wearing the customary ornaments. That is the appearance of the dharmakaya when it appears in the sambhogakaya. It is possible for students with ability and good fortune to meet with that sambhogakaya. There is, however, no difference whatsoever between that sambhogakaya and the nirmanakaya Buddha who appeared in this world.

Tilopa met directly with the sambhogakaya Vajradhara and received from him the instructions on mahamudra and thereby achieved utterly remarkable realization. He then took Naropa as his student, bestowed blessings upon him, cared for him, and under his tutelage Naropa endured great hardship and in the end manifested realization. So that is the origins of the close or proximate lineage of mahamudra. In India these students were for the most part the eighty-four mahasiddhas who practiced mahamudra and achieved fruition.

The main disciple of Tilopa was the great pandita, Naropa. Naropa received a prophecy from Chakrasamvara and the *dakinis* that he must go to the eastern portion of India and meet Tilopa. Enduring great hardships he traveled there and met with Tilopa and with great hardships he studied with him. However, in the end he received instructions on mahamudra and was able to practice and realize mahamudra where upon he became a siddha. Then he began to gather students himself, including Maitripa who was said to be a student equal to himself.

From the time the Buddha appeared in India until the time his doctrine disappeared from India, it spread widely and vastly. From among the many teachings that were given and the many people who accomplished great things, the best among them were those who achieved realization because of mahamudra. Such people as Saraha, Nagarjuna, Shavari, Maitripa, Tilopa, Marpa, and many others. They received profound realization from the practice of mahamudra. What were the instructions that they gave to their students? It was these instructions on mahamudra. Thus from among the many oral instructions, teachings, and doctrines that spread under the banner of the Buddha throughout India, the best among them, the highest among them, was mahamudra.

THE LINEAGE IN TIBET

[119] The teaching of mahamudra then spread in Tibet, through the teaching of the vajrayana and the oral instructions of mahamudra. The first Tibetan to receive the mahamudra teachings was Marpa the translator who went to India in the 12th century C.E. and took Naropa and Maitripa as his principal gurus. He remained in India for

a long time and received the teachings of the vajrayana and also those of mahamudra. He not only received these teachings but also practiced them and he achieved realization. He gave these teachings to Milarepa who then gave them to Gampopa.

These three teachers, Marpa, Milarepa and Gampopa illustrate three different ways in which to practice mahamudra and achieve realization. This shows that a person of any station in life is able to practice mahamudra. Marpa owned a house, he had a wife, wealth and possessions of all sorts, a circle of students and with this situation achieved great realization. Milarepa practiced the lifestyle of yogi leading a very simple life without wealth, a home, practicing in solitary places and achieving complete enlightenment in one lifetime. Gampopa, on the other hand, practiced mahamudra as a monk and manifested great realization, meditated upon mahamudra, and achieved realization and was able to greatly further the welfare of sentient beings. This shows then that each of these lifestyles is quite capable of practicing mahamudra and achieving realization. It is suitable to live as a householder or to live a simple life or be a monk or nun. Each is a completely appropriate way to practice mahamudra and achieve realization.

The teaching of mahamudra as it was practiced in India was a very profound dharma indeed, but it was practiced in a superior way in Tibet. One might believe that in this degenerate time that the teaching of mahamudra has declined and has been corrupted and consequently, even if one were to practice, one would not be able to achieve the result. However, there is no reason to have such doubt. The Buddha spoke about this in two different sutras: the *King of Meditation* sutra and the *White Lotus of Compassion* sutra.

While teaching the *King of Meditation* sutra which is about mahamudra, the Buddha said that in the future the teachings would decline and be corrupted and asked, "Who among you will preserve this teaching, propagate it, and cause it to flourish?" At this point a young monk whose name was Candraprabha (or "young moon") said, "I will do that. In the future I will propagate this teaching." The Buddha replied, "Yes it is just as you say: in the future in a Northern land you will take birth as the monk with the name of Vimalapradha and you will propagate this teaching of the *King of Meditation* sutra and will cause it to flourish and increase.

In the *White Lotus of Compassion* sutra, the Buddha said that in the future a monk named Jivaka would insure that the practice of meditation survived in an unbroken and unstained way. So, in accordance with that prediction, it came to pass that a boy who was named Jivaka was born in Tibet. He was known as Gampopa and gathered around him many students, gave these central teachings, and since that time the lineage has continued with gurus transmitting it from one generation to the next. The students have continued to meditate and achieve realization. And in that way the teaching of the mahamudra has not declined or degenerated.

There is no reason why people now cannot achieve the result from practicing this teaching. If one has great exertion and great devotion and great confidence, then there is no reason why one cannot achieve the same realization that Marpa or Milarepa or Gampopa did.

THE LINEAGE HOLDERS OF MAHAMUDRA

In the lectures on mahamudra that I have been presenting to you,[22] you have heard the names of a lot of different lamas whose spiritual songs and treatises are cited by the author of the text that we are reading. You've heard about Gampopa and Gomtsul and Gomchung and Hamatruba and so forth. For those of you who have been around for a while, you've heard of these people before. But for the newer students, it presents the problem of wondering who in the world these people are. So I thought I would tell you a little bit of the story of the lineage of mahamudra so you will have a sense of who we're talking about.

We trace the lineage of mahamudra back to the great Indian siddhas Naropa and Maitripa. It was Maitripa who gave the teachings on mahamudra to the Tibetan translator Marpa, who went to India three times to receive instructions on the Buddha-dharma, and in particular, to receive the complete instructions on mahamudra. Later, in Tibet Marpa gave these instructions to Milarepa, and Milarepa, having practiced and accomplished them, gave them to his student Gampopa.

The lineage of mahamudra has been passed down from teacher to student very carefully. Gampopa spread these teachings widely with his activity being extraordinary, far-reaching, and of great benefit to sentient beings. This was foreseen by Milarepa who at one point said to Gampopa, "You should go to the mountain called Phaglagambo, because I feel that if you go there, it will bring about a great benefit for sentient beings and the Buddhist teaching." After Gampopa departed for that mountain, Milarepa said to his other students, "I had a dream and in this dream, a wild vulture flew into the sky and landed upon the peak of a mountain. This vulture was surrounded by many beautiful white swans who were so numerous that they completely filled the sky." Milarepa explained that this dream mean that Gampopa was the vulture, and that the white swans were the hundreds and hundreds of students who would gather around him and would benefit from him. So Milarepa concluded by saying, "Although I myself am very poor, I see a great wealth of benefit for sentient beings coming about through the activity of my student Gampopa."

Following the instructions of his guru, Gampopa went to the mountain known as Phaglagambo and began to teach the dharma there. He attracted a huge flock of great meditators, said to number about 800, who came there to hear him teach the dharma and to practice in accordance with his instructions. There were, as you can see, a great many accomplished meditators who came to study with him and to further their practice and realization. The Kagyu teachings are said to be made up of the four greater and eight lesser lineages. Some say that the greater schools were better than the lesser schools, but that is incorrect. The four "greater" refer to those who were the direct disciples of Gampopa. Among those four are included the great master Pamotruba. The eight "lesser" refers to the eight lineages that came from the eight students of Pamotruba who became founders and authors of lineages themselves.

Gampopa's great accomplishment is rooted in a promise that he made many lifetimes previously at the time of the Buddha. At that time, there was a student in the Buddha's retinue whose name was Chanjukumara (Tib. *Daweishinnu*) or in English "youthful moon." At that time, the Buddha was teaching the *King of Meditation* sutra.[23] After the Buddha had taught this sutra, he asked the assembled students, "Who among you will take the responsibility for propagating this teaching in the future?" The Bodhisattva Chanjukumara stood up and said, "I will do so." Chanjukumara took a vow to propagate this teaching in the future. Because of the profundity of the teaching on meditation itself and the accomplishment of Gampopa, those students who have followed in his lineage have been excellent meditators. They have been able to generate meditation that has soaked their being and become very powerful, very stable, and a very truly extraordinary meditation.

Gampopa taught the dharma at Phaglagombo, and eventually passed into nirvana. His principal student was a relative of his, Gomtsul (his full name was Gom Tsulchim Nimbo). Because he had spent so much time with Gampopa, and had received his teachings completely, and thus possessed a large treasury of quintessential instructions, he wrote down many of these instructions, and became an important teacher. Thus in this text, you will see many citations from this teacher Gomtsul.

When Gomtsul passed into nirvana, the succession of this lineage passed to a cousin who held the seat of Phaglagambo. He had met both Gampopa and had studied for many years with Gomtsul and thus was the direct student of both of them. He too came to possess a great treasury of quintessential instructions, which he passed on to future generations. He is referred to in this text by the name Gomchung.

The three men from Kham, as they are known, were the other principal students of Gampopa. The one whose enlightened activity was the most significant is the teacher known as Pamotruba. He had eight accomplished students, each of whom became the founders of a lineage in their own right, those lineages then becoming known as the eight lesser lineages of the Dakpo Kagyu. Pamotruba is known by a variety of names: his full name Pamotruba and sometimes just as Patru. He was also known as Dorje Jelbo or "Vajra kin," and sometimes as just Dorjel. He too had a great treasury of quintessential instructions to impart and the text cites his teachings on many occasions.

Among the eight students of Pamotruba, the one whose enlightened activity was the vastest was a student whose name was Lingjerepa. He was the founder of one of the four major lineages of the Kagyu known as the Drukpa Kagyu. The text cites his teachings on many occasions, as he was a very powerful propagator for the teachings of mahamudra. Sometimes it refers to him by his full name, Lingjerepa; sometimes just as Lingre. Lingjerepa's principal student was a highly accomplished meditator whose name was Fumbajarrei, who did a great work in propagating the teachings of the Drukpa Kagyu. He was a supreme teacher, and the text refers to him many times as Fumbajarrei, and sometimes just as Jarrei.

All of these teachers studied earnestly and listened well. They received the teachings of mahamudra. They meditated in accordance with the way in which they had been instructed diligently and with exertion and with great intelligence. Having accomplished these teachings, they then passed them on to their own students. Sometimes in the texts of one teacher, a certain instruction might not be very clear, and so the instructions of another teacher are cited. For instance, you might find something that Gampopa said that sounds very intriguing and interesting, but it's not exactly clear what he meant, and so you have to refer to teachings that were given by one of his students—perhaps Gomtsul or Pamotruba—where the meaning of Gampopa's words is clarified. This brings about some real benefit for students. Or maybe, there's a passage in the teachings of one of these great gurus that is extremely appropriate and beneficial to the practice and experience that students have. And, for that reason, that teacher's words will be cited by Tashi Namgyal, the author of the text that we are studying.

Questions

Question: Rinpoche, you talk about mahamudra as cutting the root of the disturbing emotions and developing the good qualities. Could you speak further about how mahamudra practice develops good qualities? My mind tends to think that those good qualities are imputed as the nature of the mind, that compassion is the nature of mind.

Rinpoche: We talk about what is to be abandoned and what is to be realized. Disturbing emotions are to be abandoned and through realization wisdom increases and expands. The reason why wisdom increases is that the capacity for such wisdom exists in the dharmata of mind. The Buddha's wisdom is described in various ways. Sometimes it is enumerated as five, sometimes as four, sometimes as two wisdoms of the Buddha. The Buddha's wisdoms are twofold:

the wisdom of the nature of phenomena and the wisdom of the variety of phenomena. The first of these two realizes dharmata directly. The latter understands all conventional appearances of phenomena. When one sees dharmata directly, one sees that all conventional appearances exist within dharmata. When one realizes that completely and clearly, dharmata dawns and one sees it clearly. It is seeing lucidly which is the knowledge of the way in which all things exist. Seeing dharmata directly leads one to have that wisdom of the full extent and variety of phenomena, conventional appearance (Tib. *kundzop*) which causes the good qualities to increase and expand. In particular, a very special compassion is generated. From one's own experience one knows that the disturbing emotions can be abandoned and that wisdom can be expanded. One also knows that this dharmata, this mind itself, exists in all sentient beings, who are as limitless as space. It exists within each and every sentient being, without any degeneration whatsoever. However, through the misfortune of not having realized dharmata, sentient beings continue to wander in samsara unable to realize it and as a result experience great suffering. It is not necessary that sentient beings need to experience suffering. It happens only because they have not been able to realize the way things are. One also knows the methods for preventing suffering and in this way compassion arises effortlessly. Thus one speaks of emptiness that has compassion as its essence. If one realizes that emptiness, then very strong compassion arises.

Question: You said that mahamudra is taking direct perception as path. Also, you said that mahamudra was the path of blessing of faith and longing devotion. Could you explain the relationship of devotion to mahamudra practice?

Rinpoche: I spoke about three different divisions of paths. They were taking inference as the path, taking blessing as the path, and taking direct experience as the path. The second of those, the taking of blessing as path, is the meditation upon yidam deities and the practice of guru yoga and the practices of subtle channels and drops. The third means being introduced directly to the mind as it is. These latter two are not incompatible with one another. The introduction to mahamudra is the pointing out of one's mind. It is not something distant, it is one's own mind. It is just that which exists within one's self. One looks and realizes it and in that way one's mind is pointed out. At the same time, there might be a particular place for blessing in that there are some very fortunate people who are able to realize this suddenly. But there are others who do not have such good fortune and are not able to realize it right off. What is the root cause of one's being able to realize mahamudra in such a manner? Through having faith and confidence, one is able to give birth to such realization by feeling that there is utterly no mistake, one has no doubt whatsoever about it. This leads back into one's faith and devotion. With such faith, it can be pointed out to one straight off. But if one has a little bit of doubt, then that doubt binds one's mind. Even though mahamudra is not so subtle that it would be very difficult to realize and because it exists in oneself, if one has the misfortune of not having one's mind pointed out, realization does not arise. So, realization depends upon receiving blessing from the guru and upon one's own faith, confidence, devotion, and exertion.

Question: I have two questions. One is that I am slightly confused about names. Were there two Maitripas? One that went to the south of India who is also this great student of Naropa?

Rinpoche: He was involved in two different lineages, but it is the same person. There is the long lineage that goes from Saraha to Nagarjuna to Shavari to Maitripa. In that lineage he received the teachings from Shavari. Then he is also associated with this close or near lineage which is from Tilopa to Naropa to Marpa to Maitripa. It is the same person.

Question: It is also said that the Dzogchen teachings are the greatest teachings and have the greatest practitioners with the greatest realizations. I am wondering are these essentially the same teachings?

Rinpoche: In terms of true nature of phenomena or *ngelug*, the Dzogchen teachings are said to be leading in terms of the mind. The mahamudra teachings are also said to be leading in terms of the mind. So it is the same words. As for the meditation there isn't much difference. There is, however, a slight difference in terms of the method with which they are associated and they are taught in different tantras. There are the Dzogchen tantras and there are mahamudra tantras. But as far as the meditation itself, they are mostly the same. Some people say they have the great fortune to practice Dzogchen teachings, some people have the great fortune to practice mahamudra and each says their teachings are very special and the highest teachings. It is like some people like rice and some people like wheat.

Question: Could you say something else about what exactly is Vajradhara. Are you saying there are two kinds: dharmakaya Vajradhara and sambhogakaya Vajradhara?

Rinpoche: A vajra has five points on it. The five points indicate the five wisdoms. It is called vajra because it is unchangeable. Vajradhara means the one who holds the vajra. That is to say, one who holds those wisdoms in an unchanging manner. When one talks about holding this, it indicates their existence. The dharmakaya Vajradhara is the wisdom mind of the Buddha. When we practice the path, the main result of our practice is the dharmakaya. However, this dharmakaya has no form and an ordinary person is not able to meet with this wisdom, this mind of the Buddha, this dharmakaya. Therefore, if there were no other form in which the Buddha appeared, there would be no purpose in Buddha's having achieved enlightenment because the purpose of achieving enlightenment is to help others. If you can't communicate with others, then you can not help them. So, there is another expression of these five wisdoms. It is in terms of the character of the Buddha's mind, wisdom and his knowledge, tender love, and potency. However, for ordinary people to meet with the Buddha, the Buddha must display a form body. So, the dharmakaya emanates two types of form bodies. There is the pure form body and the impure form body. The sambhogakaya is the pure body form and the great bodhisattvas and adepts are able to meet with it and receive teaching from it. The impure form body is the nirmanakaya or emanation body. From among many types of emanation bodies, the one that showed the way of achieving liberation and enlightenment and gave these teaching is called the supreme nirmanakaya or supreme emanation body. An example of this is the Buddha Shakyamuni. There were other buddhas in former times who were emanations of the dharmakaya. In the realm of the sambhogakaya there are a great many buddhas such as Amitabha, Amoghasiddhi, Vajrapani and so forth. So the sambhogakaya Vajradhara is one of these sambhogakaya emanations.

Question: How did the teachings of mahamudra come from Gampopa?

Rinpoche: The transmission is called the golden rosary of the lineage of command. In that lineage we have Gampopa giving the teachings to Dusum Khyenpa, the first Karmapa. Then Dusum Khyenpa passed it along the Kagyu lineage. We could talk about the extensive lama lineage listing each person or if we wanted to just abbreviate the matter we could say it comes from the sixteenth Gyalwa Karmapa. Although there have been sixteen Karmapas with a great many manifestations, the mind of the Karmapa has always been the same. Some of you have met the sixteenth Gyalwa Karmapa, so as far as the teachings of mahamudra are concerned, we all depend upon the sixteenth Gyalwa Karmapa, Rangjung Rigpa Dorje.

Chapter 7

The Preparatory Practices of Mahamudra

VII. THE PREPARATORY PRACTICES OF MAHAMUDRA

A. ENTERING THE PATH OF MAHAMUDRA

[121] In order to enter into the dharma we must engage in hearing, contemplation, and meditation. Moreover, we need to rely upon a *spiritual friend* who teaches us meditation and the dharma. A good spiritual friend should be a person about whom we think highly and someone who can teach the genuine authoritative path of dharma. Since we are dealing with human beings, it is difficult to find someone who has eliminated 100 percent of all faults and has developed 100 percent of the good qualities. But we must seek someone whom we regard as being capable of teaching the authentic path and teaching it well.

After we find a good spiritual friend, we must engage in discipline which is the basis of all good qualities. If we can engage in the discipline of a person who has renounced the world, such as a monk or nun, that is very good. But this is not absolutely necessary to do because in the past there have been householders who have practiced successfully. In the Kagyu tradition, for instance, there are the examples of Marpa, Milarepa, and Gampopa, each representing a householder, a yogi who was neither a householder nor a monk but practiced *chagchow* which means "free from action," and Gampopa who was a monk. So, we have these three important persons in our lineage who were examples of householders, monks, and yogis and all of them were able to practice successfully and attain the highest realization.

THE TREATISES

It has been said that one must train with discipline (Skt. *shila*, Tib. *tsultrim*). Tsultrim means that one must engage in the decent and proper ways of doing things, giving up the improper ways of doing things. In the path of hearing we must listen to what was said by the Buddha and practice it to its completion. Within the teachings of the Buddha there is the Hinayana, mahayana, and the vajrayana, which comprises an enormous amount of literature. This was condensed into the treatises (Skt. *shastra)* which were composed by the great Buddhist scholars of India. The Tibetans have tended to rely upon these treatises more than on the many different sutras and tantras spoken by the Buddha himself. Some have thought this rather strange because, after all, the scholars of these treatises were not at the same level as the Buddha. They also didn't always agree with each other. One may think this is a problem, but actually there is a very good reason for relying mainly upon the treatises. The reason is that the Buddha taught individuals in accordance with their own situation and own abilities. If someone would come to him and say "What is this emptiness you have been talking about?" the Buddha would explain, "Well emptiness is such and such and it is like this and it is like that." Another person might come to him and say, "Why is it that one should not kill people?" And the Buddha would answer, "The reason for not killing people is such and such." So the Buddha taught different individuals on different occasions according to their own abilities and understanding. This then makes it very difficult to understand everything the Buddha taught in a single consistent body of teaching.

So the scholars in the Indian Buddhist tradition gathered together all the teachings the Buddha gave on a particular subject on many different occasions and to many different people. These learned persons analyzed and organized these teachings, put them together so that people such as ourselves could study these treatises and see how the dharma was organized and the reasons for giving one teaching on one occasion and another teaching on another occasion. This allowed for the understanding of the whole range of teachings which are so vast that one individual could never study them all. But by reading these treatises one can then understand the meaning of the words of the Buddha.

thought that was pretty strange. But I looked into it and it seems to me that what this comes down to is that one's mind wanders. It is like this: when one does shamatha practice one is able to pay attention—one doesn't have any physical work and one is just sitting there and tending to one's mind. However, when one does prostrations or mantras, there is physical work for the body and speech. There is a feeling that goes along with the practice and the mind tends to become distracted. So once the mind has wavered, one begins to think and then one does the next prostration and one thinks about it some more. And then one does the third prostration and by that time one is pretty well worked up and becomes very angry or whatever. So, that is why I think that the important thing is even if you do only a few prostrations, stay with it and do not let your mind wander off to something else.

The vajrayana has very special oral instructions that enable a person to achieve complete enlightenment in one lifetime. However, to achieve enlightenment in one lifetime requires exertion. We may think, "To practice the dharma I must achieve Buddhahood in this very lifetime with this very body, and if I don't, everything I have done will have simply been a total waste of time." To think this would be a mistake. Making the exertion that leads to achieving complete enlightenment is, of course, a wonderful thing. However, if we cannot exert ourselves to that degree, but are able to practice well and over a longer period of time achieve complete enlightenment, that is also very good. Even if we can practice a little bit, that is extremely good fortune and one should not think that this is a waste of time. However much practice one can do is extremely good and meaningful; even the tiniest bit of practice is a marvelous thing.

The Buddha said if one is not able to practice very much and doesn't have much faith, this is beneficial. If one's faith is such that one can put one's two hands together and feel tremendous devotion, this is wonderful. Someone asked the Buddha, "If the most you can do is just put one hand up in devotion, would there be any benefit to that?" Buddha replied that it was beneficial and there is definitely fruition from that. Even if one has no faith and just sticks up one's hand in the air that is also good.[25]

Questions

Question: When you were talking about fruition mahamudra, you said that compassion arises effortlessly out of emptiness and one knows the skillful methods to help people. Could you please say more about how those skillful methods arise out of emptiness?
Rinpoche: The 23rd verse of the *Aspirational Prayer for Mahamudra* by the Third Karmapa, Rangjung Dorje says:

> *The energy of unbearable compassion is unceasing,*
> *Yet when one feels compassion,*
> *it is nakedly clear that it is free from any nature.*
> *May we meditate day and night inseparable*
> *From this unity, the supreme unerring path.*

Therefore, compassion is not opposed to emptiness in any way. Because of emptiness, we have compassion and are able to help others from suffering. Take the example of a person who is dreaming of a tiger and is very frightened and someone with clairvoyance comes along and sees that the person is dreaming of a tiger. This person knows the method for preventing that person from the suffering and that is simply to shake them until they wake up. It is because of the emptiness of the tiger that it is possible to protect somebody from it. If it were not empty, but real, then the tiger would eat the person with the clairvoyance, too. It is because of emptiness that there is no tiger and because of this that we are able to help others.

Chapter 8

Shamatha Meditation in Mahamudra

VIII. THE MEDITATION OF MAHAMUDRA

A. DIFFERENTIATING MAHAMUDRA MEDITATION FROM OTHER MEDITATIONS

[143] The teachings on mahamudra spread widely in Tibet along with the teachings of the word of the Buddha, the commentaries by the successive Indian masters, and the oral instructions of many accomplished people. There arose many different lineages of mahamudra in Tibet. However, among these an especially distinguished one came from Gampopa. Gampopa gave the oral instructions on mahamudra to his students; they practiced meditation in accordance with these instructions; their experience and their realization became perfected and the lineage continued in this way from teacher to student in an unbroken manner until today. In that way the lineage from Gampopa has become especially distinguished.

If we meditate upon the oral instructions, then great benefit will come about. In the *Moonlight of Mahamudra* Tashi Namgyal mentions that some people have said that even though these instructions are very profound and were beneficial in the past, they are ineffective in our degenerate times. So even if we practice mahamudra, it won't help anymore. This belief is wrong. The truth is if we practice, there will be benefit from it. It is said this path of mahamudra involves great realization and accomplishment with little difficulty. In the past, many people practiced it and became mahasiddhas. If we practice as they did, then we also can become accomplished and achieve the fruition.

SUDDEN AND GRADUAL REALIZERS

[144] Gampopa taught two different traditions of meditation in accordance with two different types of people. There are some people called sudden realizers, who are able to generate realization very suddenly. Then there are others who must proceed gradually, stage by stage. To the sudden realizers Gampopa taught the view initially and from within the view proceeded into meditation. To the gradual realizers he had them first develop experience with meditation and then led them into the view. Among gradual realizers there are two subtypes: those whose mind is extremely wild and those whose mind is extremely unclear. To those with wildness he taught Vipashyana initially. To those with a lack of clarity of mind he taught shamatha first. Nevertheless, the procedure followed in the *Moonlight of Mahamudra* is starting with shamatha and then proceeding to Vipashyana.

B. MAHAMUDRA SHAMATHA MEDITATION

1. MASTERING SHAMATHA MEDITATION

[146] Previously shamatha was explained in relationship to the sutras and the shastras. Now the text discusses shamatha from the point of view of actual practice of mahamudra. We begin with a variety of applications that are appropriate to shamatha. For a beginner, everything that was said about shamatha before is appropriate and applicable here. In particular it is beneficial for the beginner to go to an isolated place and practice there, because there will not be a lot of commotion in the daytime and not a lot of noise from people talking at night. If one finds such a place, then one can practice in a very relaxed and quiet way. And the advice given here is that one should practice for brief sessions and do a great many of them.

2. THE POSTURE IN MAHAMUDRA MEDITATION

[147] One should employ the *Seven Points of Vairocana*. One sits on a comfortable cushion and assumes the vajra (full-lotus) posture with both legs crossed, putting one foot on the opposite thigh. Or if that is uncomfortable, one can have the legs loosely crossed, one in front of the other. It is said that on this particular point it really doesn't make

any difference. The posture of the mind is more important. Basically the mind is very relaxed. The hands can be placed with the thumbs touching one another below the navel. One can also follow a particular instruction that is a feature of the Karma Kagyu lineage from a text called *Pointing Out the Three Kayas* by the third Karmapa, Rangjung Dorje. This position is called the "pressing down the earth" posture with the palms resting on the thighs. It doesn't make much difference which of these two are used; either one is fine. The most important thing is that the body is straight, that the vertebrae are straightened and lengthened. The throat is slightly curved and the tongue is placed just behind the front teeth on the upper palate. The eyes are turned down toward the tip of the nose. These are the first six features of this posture. The seventh is that the shoulders should be extended or straightened and slightly stretched, not so as to be rigid, but so as to be upright with the chest opened and relaxed. If one is able to sit in this way, then the body will be very relaxed and as a result so will the mind be relaxed.

3. OBJECTS OF OBSERVATION IN MAHAMUDRA

[149] From the beginning of time we are accustomed to the mind being very unstable and wandering all over the place. So, when we begin meditation it can be very helpful to use an external object on which the mind can rest as a medium to establish stability. There are two kinds of external objects of observation: impure and pure objects. Impure objects would be like a small stone or a piece of wood. Pure objects would be a small statue of the Buddha.

In meditation we hold our mind on the object not too lightly because this tension will cause a great deal of discursive thought. Rather, the instructions are to simply not wander and not to forget the object. We do not engage in any analysis of the object by thinking about its shape, or color, etc. Without analyzing and investigating, we simply observe the object in a very relaxed way without wandering to something else and forgetting the object. And again, it is recommended that we do this for brief sessions, but in many sessions.

If we use an internal object, we would visualize the form of a Buddha, which is very beautiful, ornamented with the thirty-two principal marks. Meditation upon the figures of deities is extremely important in the vajrayana tradition and is known as the generation stage. Sometimes we meditate upon the deity Avalokiteshvara, sometimes upon the deity Vajradhara and so on. There are a great many different deities upon whom to meditate. We usually visualize the deity's abode, which is the mandala. Sometimes we imagine these things as very large, sometimes we imagine them as being so small that they fit into our heart. There are reasons for visualizing things in different ways and in great detail: trains our awareness, bringing forth agility and dexterity, the energy of awareness.

Awareness in visualization can change very rapidly. Resting in tranquillity on an internal object is gaining mastery over this moving awareness. Sometimes we imagine a mantra wheel that is spinning; sometimes moving slowly, sometimes moving very rapidly. At this point of visualization, we are not just concerned with the mind resting but how the mind can be still and stable while consciousness is moving.

It is not that one's shamatha becomes like the stage of completion. Rather, the mind becomes very stable and peaceful. For instance, if one meditates upon a mantra garland, one concentrates first on the different syllables to be visualized one by one and then one visualizes them starting to turn following one another. It is not like watching material things go around in a circle. It is something one is doing completely with one's mind. When you can do that, it brings about a very stable and very relaxed mind. When you get used to doing this, the shamatha will become a very good shamatha.

But, we are looking ahead to how meditation upon a deity brings about the blessings of the yidam, of the buddhas and bodhisattvas, and how those blessings may help achieve the common and supreme siddhis. So if we cultivate tranquillity meditation in this way, it brings about a very special sort of shamatha.

THE RESTING MIND

[152] For a beginner to achieve an excellent shamatha is rather difficult because the mind tends to wander. For that reason, mindfulness and alertness are extremely important. If one's mind has various thoughts, one is aware of those thoughts and with

mindfulness one can return one's mind to the object of observation in a relaxed way. Mind can be divided into consciousness and mental factors. In this case, mindfulness is regarded as a mental factor which is a perceiving subject, with the mind being its object. In other words, mindfulness is looking at the mind to see whether or not it has wandered. The Tibetan word for "mind" is *sem*, with the Sanskrit word being *chitta*. The Tibetan word for "mental factors" is *sem yung* which literally means "arising from the mind" or "arising with the mind." Mind or *sem* has six consciousnesses; sometimes one speaks about eight consciousnesses.[26] The six are the eye, the ear, the nose, the tongue, the body sensations, and the mental consciousnesses. These consciousnesses know their objects individually so that eye consciousness sees visible forms, ear consciousness hears sounds, nose consciousness experiences smells, and so on with mental consciousness being where many different thoughts appear and are integrated. The mental factors occur with those main consciousnesses.

There are several types of mental factors. Some are always there and always accompany each consciousness. Others exist sometimes, but not other times. Mental factors that always accompany the mind are pleasure and pain. Sometimes the feeling is strong, sometimes it is weak, but the feeling accompanies every consciousness. Similarly, discrimination is a mental factor that knows what things are and recognizes the details of things. This consciousness accompanies all the six consciousnesses because every consciousness has some quality of discrimination. The mental factors that occasionally appear are, for instance, mindfulness, awareness, faith, and confidence. These are said to be beneficial mental factors and when they accompany the mind, the mind is a favorable mind. Not being permanent, sometimes they are there and sometimes not. There are also mental factors that are not beneficial such as passion, aggression, envy, or the wish to harm. When these negative factors accompany the mind, then that mind is not favorable.

The mental factor of mindfulness (Tib. *trenpa*) keeps one from forgetting the object. As long as mindfulness is present, one does not forget the object, and when mindfulness is absent, one does forget the object. If one then places one's mind back on the object, thinking, "I am not going to let my mind wander again," with the absence of mindfulness, the mind will again fall under the influence of other things. So it is important that mindfulness be there all the time to keep the mind from wandering.

Along with mindfulness, alertness (Tib. *seshin*) is also very important, since it brings the mind back. Mindfulness is a mental factor that looks at the mind itself to see whether or not the mind is staying with the object. This allows the mind to rest within a state of relaxation. Mindfulness then serves as a guardian of that state. The nature of the relationship between mindfulness and alertness is that if mindfulness is present, it brings alertness along with it. And if mindfulness is absent, then alertness doesn't happen either. So it is very important to develop these both and not lose them.

PROTECTING THE MIND

Protecting mind from the disturbing emotions and discursive thought can be compared to protecting oneself from thieves. Thieves will know not to attack a strong, powerful, well-disciplined and attentive person. Rather they will attack someone who is sloppy and lazy and weak. Mindfulness and awareness make one strong, attentive, and well-disciplined. With these one cannot be robbed by distrubing emotions and discursive thought. Someone who lacks mindfulness and awareness is the one who will be plundered. What is stolen are the roots of beneficial factors that exist within one's mind. With mindfulness and awareness, the disturbing emotions will have no hope of being able to rob you and will just give up.

DEVELOPING SHAMATHA USING BREATHING

[154] One can hold one's mind to the movement of prana in two ways: counting the breath and by a special breathing exercise called the fullness of prana. Counting the breath is just the ordinary way of meditating in shamatha in which one counts one's in- and out-breath. The fullness of the prana can be done in two different ways. One is called vase breathing, which is extending the abdomen and holding the breath there. If that is not sufficient, then there is a further way of holding the mind to the fullness of breath which is called vajra repetition. This vajra repetition involves coordinating the motion of the breathing with the mantra syllables OM AH HUM. As the wind or breath comes in OM is said. As the wind is held briefly inside AH

is said. As the wind exits, HUM is said. So one is dividing the cycle of the breath into three parts and correlating each part of it with OM AH HUM.

VASE BREATHING

[155] It might be helpful to talk now about a practice that we have not gone into great detail about before, which is the development of shamatha through the mind's being held to the subtle wind as it fills the body. This is the practice known as *vase breathing.* This practice is very helpful sometimes, because it can help to clarify your mind if it is not clear and it can help to stabilize your mind if it is not stable. It should be noted that there is another practice of vase breathing that is more harsh or rough, using a very forceful inhalation and exhalation. The purpose of the practice of vase breathing in mahamudra practice, however, is different. It does not involve forceful breathing for the purpose of clearing out the subtle channels in the body. This practice is better done from the point of view of allowing the mind to rest, so it is a very relaxed and gentle. When the breath comes into the body, it is done gently and when it leaves the body, that is also done gently.

We begin with three cycles of dispelling stale breath: the breath is brought into the body very quietly, without making any noise as we do so. When the body is filled with the breath, it is expelled in a very gentle manner again not making any noise. As we expel the breath we extend our fingers and hands that are resting on our thighs.

On the first cycle of this practice, we sense that sickness and discomfort of every sort is leaving our body. The breath is brought in again and allowed to leave in the same way. In this second cycle there is a sense that harmful spirits, or *dons,* are leaving the body. In the third cycle there is a sense that any other obstructions to our practice are leaving our body and we become free from them.

Then the breath is brought into the body and is brought down to a point below the navel and the body is filled in this way. There, below our navel is a sense that the breath is contained as if we were closing a container or vase in which the air or wind is held the breath. It is somewhat pressed down from above, and somewhat pressed up from below and just held there very gently without any sense of strain. And when it becomes stressful, we allow it to leave the body, very gently without making any noise.

Holding the breath in this way is a means for pacifying or taming the mind and developing the mindfulness. That is what is meant by the term "shamatha of being filled with wind," meaning being filled with prana.[27]

When we practice shamatha in this way, the main point is that the wind is held below the navel, and the upper part of our body is just left alone, as it normally is. We don't attend to it particularly and especially we don't constrict it in any way. It is just left very relaxed and spacious, clear, more or less as it always is, without paying particular attention to it. If we intensify our experience in the upper part of the body, then it might create some discomfort in our lungs or our heart or wherever. But in this practice we only attend to the wind below the navel without doing anything in particular about the areas where we ordinarily breath.

When we breathe ordinarily we neither inhale or exhale fully. So when we begin this practice it is good to exhale completely, and we do that only for the first vase breath. We might do vase breathing five or six times, but we exhale completely only for the first time. When we expel the air for the vase breath, we expel it completely. The breath is held between the inhalation and exhalation. We draw it in below the navel and put a ceiling above it, and draw in the lower wind, closing it off, like the *empowerment vase* with a bulging belly. We do vase breathing when we are experiencing a very dull mind—when it is sleepy, dark, dull. When this is experienced very strongly, or when the mind is wild, we can do vase breathing two, three or four times, as much as we like.

In summary, I explained some of the ways in which the mind can be brought to a state of rest in shamatha and the different sorts of objects upon which to focus upon when we are practicing the shamatha meditation. With external objects, we focus on impure and pure objects. With internal objects of observation, we set our mind upon the movement of the breath in a variety of different ways. The reason for proceeding from external to internal objects is that from the beginning of time we have been accustomed to our mind's wandering by focusing on external objects. Because of this, it is difficult for us to set our mind in a state of resting evenly and smoothly. We therefore first use the support of an external object to enable the mind to rest. After having gotten used to that, we make use of the breath, turning the mind inward somewhat. This enables the mind to rest using the breath as an object of observation.

4. MEDITATION WITHOUT A REFERENCE POINT

[159] The next step is to set the mind in a state of rest without even using the breath. When we do this, the posture is the same as described before but one does not focus the mind on anything at all. One does not think about the past, future, or stop to analyze present events. One simply sets the mind in a relaxed way. For a beginner this is not easy to do; however, as one grows more accustomed to it, the mind is able to rest without resting on any object.

Meditation with an object is called "observation that possesses a sign." Now we will speak of observation of focus without signs. There are two principal points here: first, the way in which one searches for shamatha free from faults; the second, the way in which one sustains the resting of mind. The first is primarily a discussion of tightening the mind on the one hand and loosening the mind on the other. In the earlier discussion of the common stages of shamatha, we talked about the mind sinking and the mind becoming wild as the two principal kinds of obstacles in shamatha. In the quintessential instructions on mahamudra, we talk about the mind being either too tight or too loose, too focused or too relaxed, rather than about the mind sinking or becoming wild. The advice given is that if the mind is not luminous, not clear, not vivid, then one needs to tighten or concentrate more. And if it is too bright, too vivid, too luminous, too clear, then one needs to relax it somewhat. An example from the great master of mahamudra, Saraha, is that it was the custom of the day, especially for the Brahmin to wear clothing that was woven out of cotton thread. Saraha said that when you weave this thread, if you make it too tight, it will snap; but if you make it too loose, then it won't hold together. Saraha said it is like that when you practice meditation. If you make it too tight, that won't be very good; but if you make it too loose, that won't work well either. Rather, you have to set your mind in a way that is a balance between being too focused and too relaxed, making it very even, equal, and smooth. If you do it that way, your meditation will be a very comfortable, delightful, and pleasant meditation.

It is important to know when to tighten the mind and when to loosen it. We need to tighten our mind when the mind has become extremely loose, lethargic, and dull. At this point we obviously need to concentrate, tighten, to focus. However, our mind might stay with the object of meditation, but that meditation is not very clear; it becomes too gentle or too soft. It is easy to mistake this for good shamatha but it, in fact, is not good shamatha. Even this sort of subtly unclear state of mind needs to be purified by tightening the mind by making our mindfulness become very strong, very clear, and very bright. There is a sense of lifting both body and mind. This is the kind of mindfulness that is required when our shamatha practice is too relaxed. The problem with a loose mind is that it is slightly unclear and various sorts of appearances begin to dawn. We then think, "Oh, I am having a meditation experience. This must be a sign that I am beginning to have a profound experience showing that my meditation is going well." But it is not. That's the problem.

So this is about how we would bring about the factor of clarity when the mind becomes dull. Sometimes the factor of clarity becomes excessive, sparking many, many different discursive thoughts, and we can't get back to shamatha. At this point it is necessary to relax. As Saraha said, "When the mind is very active in discursive thought and we try to bind it at that point, it will just scatter to the ten directions." The ten directions is the Buddhist way of saying everywhere. If it is already that way and we try to tighten it more, it just explodes. But Saraha said at this point we need to relax by letting your mind proceed the way a camel does. A camel moves in a very steady and relaxed way.

A more modern example would be a cat. If you have a cat and you lock it in a room and shut the doors and windows, the cat just freaks out, running everywhere. But, if you open the door and the window, then the cat looks around for awhile and then goes asleep. In that way your mind too can become very relaxed. Tightening or concentrating the mind when it is appropriate to do so and relaxing it when it is appropriate allows you to develop a shamatha in which the mind rests comfortably, in a very even way. At this point, it is very important not to let mindfulness degenerate. It is important that mindfulness be strong so that the mind is relaxed, yet bright and one-pointed.

As discussed in the sutras and shastras, there is a distinction between mindfulness and alertness. However, in the quintessential instructions of mahamudra, there is a great deal of instruction about mindfulness and only a little about alertness. The reason for this is that awareness accompanies mindfulness. If one has mindfulness, then one will also have awareness. If one does not have mindfulness, one will not have awareness. From this point of view the two are very similar so Tashi Namgyal omits the discussion of awareness but does emphasize repeatedly the importance and necessity of mindfulness.

[160] The most important thing in meditation is understanding how to concentrate and how to relax. When our mind is heavy, obscured, dark, then concentration is important. When our mind is wild then relaxation is important.

When practicing meditation, clear mindfulness may come along but later we might find that our mindfulness decreases and then, we are not observing the object of observation. At that point, a very strong heaviness and dullness of mind has come about, with no clarity in our meditation. Some may think that this is very good shamatha practice, but it is not. If this heaviness is not cleared away, then good meditation doesn't happen.

How do we clear away such heaviness of mind? It is important to heighten the clarity and brilliance of our mind. Sitting up straight, raising our gaze somewhat, expanding the perspective of our mind by making our perception vast and spacious will make the heaviness of mind pass. Sometimes we are unable to clear away this heaviness and dullness. Then it is necessary to strengthen our mind with real concentration. What may be very effective to do is just to leave off the session and then come back to it. As we sit down and concentrate, that will help to clear away the heaviness and dullness.

Sometimes we experience great desire or longing in our practice and sometimes we experience regret thinking about things that we have not done very well. We think, "I didn't do this, I made a mistake there," and feel regret about it. Sometimes we feel angry thinking about something someone has done to us and we wish harm to that person in return. So wildness, desire, regret, and anger are certainly distinct from one another, but from this point of view, they are all the same in that they are excitement of mind. What we need to do at this point is to relax. In terms of our body, we could just loosen up our posture somewhat. In terms of our mind, we must drop all thoughts about how well the meditation is going or how it should go. We just let our mind be very spacious as if we were resting.

Sometimes we encounter discursiveness in our meditation. There are two ways to go about dealing with discursiveness that don't work very well. One of them is to chase after your thoughts, one right after the other getting completely involved in them. Then one thought comes, then another, another, and another. The other way is trying to stomp on it. Just stop it cold. That doesn't work very well either. What is recommended at this point is a very subtle kind of mindfulness. It is just a light touch. You bring in your mindfulness, but not with forceful concentration, but with a light touch.

In the same way we should go about dealing with wildness. But it has a little mindfulness in it. To tie things or just bind them up doesn't help. The great Saraha gave the example that if we try to get a camel to calm down by tying it to a very short rope, that is not going to work and the camel will to continually want to go. What we should do instead is to untie him and let him be. He will wander around a little, then he will settle down. It is similar with our mind. If we try to tie it up, that is not going to do. Rather if we just relax then some stability will come.

Therefore, a good understanding of when it is appropriate to concentrate and when it is appropriate to relax is what is necessary for our meditation to go well. If we can understand and practice this well, then our meditation will be both clear and stable.

5. SUSTAINING RESTING OF MIND

[166] Sustaining the resting of the mind is related to the importance of having a great longing for meditation. In the beginning, one tends to have a great longing to practice meditation. Then if one tries to practice for lengthy periods, one's enthusiasm tends to decrease. When one's enthusiasm decreases, one's longing decreases, and one's aspiration declines, reducing one's exertion and practice altogether. The antidote to this is to think about the extraordinary qualities of meditation and their benefits. We need to realize that if one develops meditation or samdadhi, good qualities will come from it. And if one does not develop meditation, then those good qualities will not appear. It is a matter of understanding the relationship

between meditation and the qualities that are developed through practice. If one understands that, then one will have great aspiration to practice meditation. Such aspiration will lead to exertion. Exertion develops what is known as *chin lap* in Tibetan meaning "thoroughly processed." This is a state of being supple and flexible and pliant. When one reaches this stage of being thoroughly processed, one is able to enter into meditation easily. So, it is important to think about the reasons for practicing meditation and to understand the benefits of developing meditation. If one does so, then it becomes far easier to meditate and one meditates with joy and with delight. If one does not do so then meditation tends to be rather difficult. So, that is the way in which one has to practice it.

6. STAGES OF A SETTLED MIND

[169] There are three kinds of stages that appear after our meditation has developed. The first is like a stream that is crashing down a narrow ravine. When we initially begin to practice meditation, we have the sense of having lots and lots of thoughts. We feel that previously our mind was not dull and wild and now it has become extremely wild. Actually that is not so; it is just that we have never bothered to look at our mind before. As we begin to take possession of the situation, we just begin to recognize what was occurring all along. Now we have the sense that sometimes the mind is very heavy and dull, and sometimes it is very wild with many thoughts. Seeing that is not bad, but is a very good quality like recognizing an enemy as an enemy. The second stage is like all these mountain streams opening out into a great wide river. The river flows along smoothly and gently. The third stage is the point at which the river spills into the ocean. At this point things are very smooth, gentle, spacious, vast. This is dwelling, resting very smoothly without much fluctuation.

7. THE IMPORTANCE OF DEVELOPING SHAMATHA

[173] Put very simply, if we do not develop shamatha then the good qualities that can come about through the full development of the path will never be realized. We need to develop a shamatha that is steady, one-pointed, and that rests very evenly. If we do not do so,

then such good qualities will not be born in ourself. Even if we have Vipashyana, in the absence of shamatha, this Vipashyana will not have the strength to abandon the disturbing emotions. So we need a genuine shamatha and if we develop that, then our Vipashyana can become potent. And with a potent Vipashyana, everything that is to be abandoned can be abandoned and all the good qualities that are to be realized can be realized.

This can be summed up in that if we don't have good shamatha and we sit for an hour, then our mind will wander and we won't actually be there for that hour. But if we have well developed shamatha and we sit for an hour that shamatha will definitely be something of great importance.

I would just like to say that I see how all of you place a great value on meditation, you pay attention in general, you regard the dharma as something important, you have a great longing for it. Also, you put a great deal of energy into listening to the teachings. And the questions that you have asked are questions that arise from the experience of practicing meditation. So, I would like to say that this has made me extremely happy. When I was on my way here in the airplane it was difficult for me because I sat there thinking I really don't know whether I am going to be able to help people or not. I was bothered by this. Then when I arrived here and could see that you have a great interest in meditation and that you meditate very well and ask questions which have arisen from genuine experience of meditation, I felt extremely gratified. Now I am very happy about this. I want to thank you very much for your kindness, and say now I don't feel there are any problems at all.

Questions

Question: Rinpoche, you had pinched your hand and talked about how, if you really looked at pain, it was empty. Later you talked about the necessity of looking directly into experience. I am wondering if you just look at emotions or do you experience them? Western psychology would say that you need to experience the emotion and then you can experience the energy underneath it. If not, Western psychology would say it was suppression or denial. So,

I am wondering how the mahamudra model of working with feelings relates to this Western psychological model?

Rinpoche: There is much that is similar between meditation and Western psychology and there is also something that seems to be significantly different. It is certainly true that one needs to know what one is experiencing. One needs to experience it. But there is a difference between merely experiencing it and looking right at the nature of it. The Tibetan word for nature is *ngowo*. The distinction between experiencing something and looking at its nature is different, because when one looks right at the nature of it, there is nothing that can be found. In contrast, merely experiencing something, one does experience it, whatever it is. But what is entailed in "looking right at its nature," "experiencing its actual nature," is that the thing that was experienced or the perceiving, experiencing mind and the whole environment of the experience are ungraspable and cannot be identified as anything whatsoever. One's mind cannot be found, the feeling that was being felt cannot be identified. The ground of the experience cannot be found either. This is very different from just saying, "I experienced that pain or event." There is a real purpose to taking the experience a further step by examining its nature, because it causes one to understand the thing fully and correctly. When one knows what its actual features and characteristics are, in this case, the fact that it cannot be found and identified, then one realizes that it can not actually harm either. Then one's mind becomes very peaceful and joyful and one experiences pleasure. Whether one is talking about pain in the mind or in the body, if one looks for and tries to see what it's actual nature is. Then one realizes that one doesn't have to get rid of it because its nature is emptiness. In this sense, there is nothing that is unbearable.

Question: It seems like sometimes the word "look" is understood in English as a totally intellectual process, but I have a sense that it is much more an experience in Tibetan.

Rinpoche: In Tibetan when one speaks about investigating and analyzing with prajna, one doesn't talk about "looking" with that type of mind. One talks about thinking, reflecting, and contemplating. When we say "look," we mean like when you look at something with your eye, just direct experience without conception. So, probably it is the same thing what you are meaning in English when we talk about experience.

Question: Rinpoche, you said that when we do yidam practice, we receive blessings, the supreme and ordinary siddhis. You also said that if we cultivate shamatha in this way, that it brings about a very special sort of shamatha. My question is: How is it different from common shamatha?

Rinpoche: It is not that one's shamatha becomes like the completion stage of meditation. Rather it is that the mind becomes very stable and peaceful. For instance, if one meditates upon a mantra garland one concentrates first on the different syllables to be visualized one by one and then one visualizes them starting to turn, following one another. It is not like watching material things go around in a circle. It is something you are doing completely with your mind. When you can do that, it brings about a very stable and very relaxed mind. So when you get used to doing this, the shamatha is a very good shamatha.

The mind should be being protected from disturbing emotions and discursive thought that are compared to thieves. Thieves will know not to attack a strong, powerful, well-disciplined, and attentive person. Rather they will attack someone who is sloppy and lazy and weak. So, mindfulness and awareness make one strong and attentive and well-disciplined. With these one cannot be robbed by disturbing emotions and discursive thought. Someone who has no such mindfulness and awareness is the one who will be plundered. What is stolen is the roots of beneficial force that exists within one's mind. If one has such mindfulness and awareness, then those disturbing emotions will have no hope of being able to rob you and will just give up.

Mindfulness is regarded as impermanent, as a temporary, rather than a permanent mental factor. But, suppose you were to sit down and practice meditation for an hour and exert yourself, develop good mindfulness, then when you got up, you didn't have such mindfulness. That is all right, because gradually you get used to it and as you get used to it, you become familiar with it, and then it doesn't take such effort to have mindfulness. It will arise effortlessly of its own force.

Question: I lose my mindfulness after I have had it. But I also see that I become more familiar with mindfulness and that is beneficial.

Rinpoche: No, it doesn't just disappear. When you cultivate qualities such as faith, devotion, and prajna, they become more and more stable and clear. They don't just suddenly disappear one day. You can think about it in comparison to the way you go to school and develop prajna. You go year after year and you develop knowledge and intelligence. You don't just suddenly wake up one day and find they are gone. When you go to school, you are developing prajna. When you practice meditation you are developing mindfulness and awareness. In the same way that when you go to school to train your prajna and it doesn't just suddenly disappear. So, when you are trained in meditation and develop your mindfulness, you don't just wake up to find that your mindfulness has just completely disappeared. Sometimes if you have been in some real hardship and are quite tired, it is difficult to maintain mindfulness. But as you meditate more and become more familiar with the good qualities and benefits of meditation, then it is easier for that mindfulness to remain. If you think about the discussion of the nine stages of resting the mind and what was presented in terms of pacifying the mind and taming the mind, the fifth and sixth stages, look back at those. You will see some notions about how mindfulness becomes very steady.

Question: I have heard that one must complete ngöndro practice before going into a three-year retreat and then that it is not necessary. Which is correct.

Rinpoche: Generally, the ngöndro practice is done within the three-year retreat. So if you have completed it before hand that is very good. If you haven't then you will do it in retreat.

Question: I was wondering if the alaya consciousness is what is reborn from one lifetime to the next?

Rinpoche: Where would one look for this alaya consciousness? Alaya consciousness is a name that is designated to the factor of clarity of the mind. It is not a coarse type of knowing. The factor of clarity appears as well as being called this alaya consciousness. So, I would not say that is what is going from one lifetime to another. What goes from one lifetime to another is the continuum of the six collections of the six consciousnesses.

Question: Would that continuum be the seventh consciousness?

Rinpoche: No. The *seventh consciousness* is the seventh consciousness. The six consciousnesses are the continuum of the six consciousnesses. The seventh consciousness refers to this conception of self which is unbroken, uninterrupted. This seventh klesha consciousness pervades all the consciousness and is always there. But the six consciousnesses and the continuum of the six consciousnesses are not the seventh consciousness nor the eighth consciousness.

Question: Is it that thinking self in relation to the appearance that we are talking about when we say perception of self.

Rinpoche: There are two different types of conception of self. There is the notion of self that relates to the sixth consciousness and there is the concept of self which relates to the seventh consciousness. With the sixth consciousness thinking "I" comes and goes because the sixth consciousness is involved with the other five sensory consciousnesses. Sometimes you are thinking "I" and sometimes you are not. But whether you are or aren't thinking of "I" at the level of the sixth consciousness, there is always the notion of I at the seventh consciousness, but it is something very subtle. Whether you are going somewhere or sitting down or asleep, the continuum of that I is never severed. It just goes on at a very subtle level in seventh consciousness. It is not in this manifest form of thinking "I," but with this very subtle conception of self.

Question: Many people endure some deep psychological wounds at some point in their lives and often approach the dharma in the hope that it will clear such things up. When one talks about clearing away secret obstructions, predispositions lying deep within the alaya consciousness perhaps, is that a case of doing something about these deep scars in the mind from traumatic experiences of one sort or another?

Translator: I think that traumatic experience is what we call *kunzin*, these sorts of deep wounds. Kunzin literally says holding onto anger.

Rinpoche: The remedy is to develop a lot of compassion which is to say, when another person has harmed one, the person that did so has done this out of ignorance and obscuration. It is a mistake that ordinary people make. If it were some highly accomplished person who inflicted such a wound upon another that would really be a deplorable thing. But it isn't, it is an ordinary person, someone who is confused. This is just the way things are with ordinary people. As Shantideva said, "If you stick your hand in the fire and get burned, you can't really complain about the fire that burned you, for the nature of fire is to burn things." So it is similar with ordinary people, they make mistakes and hurt others out of confusion. The best thing to do is to develop love and compassion for these people.

Question: Could Rinpoche give an example of a secret obstacle as opposed to an ordinary obstacle?

Rinpoche: "External obstacles" refers to what we normally mean by obstacles we encounter in daily life. "Internal obstacles" refers to disturbing emotions in one's own mind. But, secret obstacles have to do with the practice of getting into the true nature of mind. For instance, the practices of the subtle channels, the subtle energies or winds, and subtle drops. The obstacles that prevent one from doing that sort of practice are what we mean when we speak of secret obstacles.

Chapter 9

Vipashyana Meditation in Mahamudra

C. MAHAMUDRA VIPASHYANA MEDITATION

[175] This section on the meditation of mahamudra is divided into two major parts. One is concerned with the practice of shamatha. The second concerns "insight" or Vipashyana. Vipashyana is the Sanskrit word and *lhagtong* is the Tibetan word with *lhag* meaning "surpassing" and *tong* meaning "to see." There are six main sections to this chapter on Vipashyana of the mahamudra.

1. REASONS FOR PRACTICING VIPASHYANA

[175] The discussion of Vipashyana begins by giving the reasons it is necessary to practice this. When one practices shamatha, one learns to let one's mind rest or dwell in peace, then one's mind becomes relaxed and peaceful. Delusion lessens. However, it is necessary to go further, and do Vipashyana.

It's not as if there were really a large difference between shamatha and Vipashyana. It is a slight shift. When one practices shamatha, one's mind naturally rests in a state that is free from a great deal of thought and conceptuality and in which kleshas are reduced. However, when one practices shamatha, delusion (Skt. *klesha*) is not eradicated from the root. With Vipashyana, the mind takes on the aspect of realizing selflessness. The quality of luminosity is enhanced and the mind's lack of any inherent nature is realized. One realizes the way the mind actually exists, and through realizing in this luminous state and emptiness that is the mind's nature, the practitioner is able to abandon all delusion from the very root. So it is not sufficient to meditate only in shamatha and to rest there exclusively. In the teachings on Vipashyana methods for realizing the mind's actual nature are given.

This explanation that I've given on the need for the practice of Vipashyana is illustrated in a story of the life of the Buddha. As you know, the Buddha wanted to emerge from the ocean of misery that is known as samsara. Having aroused this renunciation the Buddha left his kingdom and went to the forest to learn meditation and achieve liberation. He met with two Brahmin sages, Rimpoor and Lhagje; and learned from them the practice of shamatha. His mind became quite peaceful but after a while, he realized that this peaceful state was not enlightenment. Having understood that, he realized that he would have to go further. The Buddha found a way to achieve this realization that is called knowledge that realizes selflessness in the sutra tradition (Tib. *da me dog pe sherab*), and which means the wisdom of Vipashyana in the tradition of mantra (Tib. *fan tong yeshe*). Achieving Vipashyana, he was able to reach Buddhahood.

2. HOW ONE BEGINS VIPASHYANA PRACTICE

[176] After presenting the reason why one must meditate upon the Vipashyana aspect of mahamudra, the text then explains how one actually does it. First of all, one must listen a lot to the instructions on mahamudra. Then, one must think about what one has heard until one has understood it properly. This gives rise to what is called "the pure view" that arises from hearing and thinking about the teachings. It is the initial stage of entering into the Vipashyana aspect of mahamudra and is common to both to the sutra tradition and to the mantra (vajrayana) tradition.

One begins by listening (or studying) to the teachings and contemplating about what one has heard. This is very valuable, but it leads only to conceptual understanding. Next we have to meditate upon what we have learned to realize it completely. We meditate using mahamudra meditation in our *practice lineage* (Tib. *drup ju*). To learn how to meditate directly on mind, one must rely upon the guru's blessing which are a kind of potency or power. We must rely upon the blessing that has come down through the lineage gurus to our own root guru. Through these blessings of the root and lineage gurus, we can definitely develop the view of mahamudra. To develop these blessings we practice guru yoga.

The *Hevajra Tantra* says, "No one else can explain this." When it says no one else, it means no one other than a lama, who has experienced mahamudra. With mahamudra it's necessary to rely upon someone who has deep experience and real skill in the mahamudra. With this person's instruction and one's own merit, it's possible to give rise to the realization. So we have to rely upon an extraordinary being who is a truly experienced guru and when we do, the blessings of this lineage can enter us helping us to meditate upon mahamudra. It is for that reason that we listen to teachings, supplicates the guru, and practice the meditation of guru yoga.

3. THE TYPES OF VIPASHYANA MEDITATION

[178] We begin by studying Vipashyana as it is described in the sutras. There are many different ways of categorizing the practice of Vipashyana. We could talk about four ways of practicing Vipashyana, or three different ways to Vipashyana, and so on. However, we can actually boil this down to relating Vipashyana to the two aspects of egolessness: the egolessness of self and the egolessness of phenomena. These two types of egolessness were described very clearly by two great Indian masters Nagarjuna and Asanga in their texts upon the Middle-way or Madhyamaka. In these treatises they explained very clearly and precisely just how external phenomena do not inherently exist. From a reasoned and analytical approach Nagarjuna and Asanga were able to demonstrate quite clearly just how it is that phenomena lack the inherent existence. Thus, they demonstrated that phenomena are empty, which is to say they do not really exist. In Tibet, these teachings of Nagarjuna and Asanga were studied quite extensively, but when it came to the actual practice of meditation, these teachings weren't used. As Tashi Namgyal says, as far as meditation is concerned, this way of practice does exist in the Tibetan tradition.

Rely on the analytic approach to the emptiness of phenomena, helps us to begin to understand emptiness. This is a good way to go about understanding emptiness, but it's very difficult to generate real experience of emptiness. So, the Tibetan tradition has followed the instructions handed down through the lineage which begins with the great Saraha instead. He passed this understanding down to his student Shavari who eventually passed it down to the great master Tilopa. In these instructions we do not look at external things to try to discover whether or not they exist, rather we look directly at the mind and meditate upon its true nature. This approach is not a conceptual approach, but it's taking direct perception as the path.

When we practice the meditation of mahamudra, we are not looking at external things. Rather, we are looking at our own mind, and cutting through all of our hesitations and misconceptions about the mind and decisively understanding the mind's nature. When we discover the mind's nature, we discover that emptiness is the mind's way of being. When we understand the lack of inherent existence is the nature of our mind, we can easily understand that the lack of inherent existence of external phenomena. Thus, this approach makes it quite easy to give rise to genuine experience and realization and is therefore a superior way of proceeding. This approach is very much in accord with the instructions for realizing emptiness that are given in texts such as the *Stages of Meditation* composed by the great Indian master Kamalashila and the *Quintessential Instructions on the Middle Way*, given by the great Indian master Atisha.

4. The Main Meditation of Vipashyana

(a). Why One Achieves Insight

[179] By looking at the mind itself, we can realize the mind's true nature. When we have realized the mind's true nature, we can abandon all delusion. By abandoning all delusion, wisdom and the good qualities of mind will arise. This point is indicated in the spiritual songs and advice given by the siddhas or accomplished ones of the mahamudra tradition. For instance, there is a passage of Saraha which says, "When mind has been bound, one is bound; when just that is released, there is no doubt." Which is to say, bondage comes about by way of the mind, and freedom comes about by way of the mind. Similarly, Tilopa said, "For example, when the branches and leaves of a tree spread, if the single root is cut, 10,000 or even 100,000 leaves will dry up. Cutting the root of mind—samsara—is like that, too." In other words, if you cut the root of a tree with many leaves and branches, then it doesn't matter how many leaves there are; all of them will dry up. It is the same way in samsara. There are innumerable kinds of suffering. But if the single root of that suffering is cut, all of that suffering will be pacified.

Similarly, the great Shantideva said: "If you do not know the mind, this will become the cause of all suffering. If you know the mind, and protect the mind this is the supreme of uncontrived action." Which is to say, if you do not understand the mind's nature, you will not be able to abandon suffering. If you understand the mind's nature, then you can achieve happiness and abandon suffering. That is why it is vital to know the mind's nature and to protect it. When we speak about uncontrived conduct, we are talking about the conduct for the purpose of familiarizing with and guarding one's mind through recognizing its nature and then acting on the basis of that nature.

Some people criticize this practice of meditating on the mind's nature saying that meditation upon emptiness is the essence of the dharma, not meditating upon the mind's nature. They also find fault with the assertion that the mind is primordially pure or the mind is a *Buddha-field*. They say if that were the case, then sentient beings would already be buddhas and no effort would be required to achieve enlightenment. However, those who criticize the practice tradition are a little mistaken because they think emptiness is something good and the mind is something bad. So they have really not understood the mind's nature. The reason they are confused is that the nature of phenomena and nature of mind is precisely the same. Thus, if you meditate upon the mind's nature, you will naturally realize emptiness.

In the sutras of the Buddha and the treatises composed by his followers, emptiness is discussed widely. However, when it comes to meditation, it's not possible to meditate upon the emptiness of external phenomena readily. We can't do that directly so we have to look at mind and cut through its confusion. Having seen the nature of the mind, we can meditate upon that. Thus, in the tradition of mahamudra, we talk about *semchi* means "leading or pointing out the mind." These are instructions directly pointing at the mind's true nature, not only in the tradition of mahamudra, but also in the tradition of Dzogchen.

(b). THE SUTRAS ON THE MIND'S TRUE NATURE

[183] It is well known that in the sutras the Buddha said many times that it is important to meditate upon the mind's true nature. The Buddha said this again and again, and so this notion of meditating upon the mind's true nature was not made up later by those who were involved with the Kagyu lineage. Similarly, the text makes it

clear by citing from many different treatises and commentaries written by different scholars and sages over the ages, that one must meditate upon the mind's true nature. Finally, there are passages drawn from the sayings and spiritual songs of the siddhas of the mahamudra tradition in India, which again emphasize the importance of meditating upon the mind's true nature. All of these taken together, point out very clearly that this approach to meditation and realization is not just made up, but was dependent upon the sutras and shastras.

(C). STAGES OF VIPASHYANA MEDITATION

[184] There are two different types of meditation: analytical meditation and placement meditation. Placement meditation refers to the practice of shamatha. In shamatha the mind is placed within a state that is free from a great deal of thinking, that is peaceful, and in which the mind is not under the power of a lot of thinking. For that reason, the practice of shamatha is referred to as a placement meditation. However, Vipashyana meditation is a type of analytical meditation. At any given session of Vipashyana meditation, one first begins with shamatha, resting briefly in the meditative equipoise of shamatha. Then one gives rise to what in Tibetan is called *gsal gnarh*. The first syllable *gsal* means "clear" or "luminous" and "brilliant" and the second syllable *gnarh* meaning "a tightening of the mind." Putting these two together gives the sense of brilliant sharpness that is not relaxed. It's that sharpness of the mind, this cutting quality of the mind, that gives rise to insight and that leads to what is called *soso rang dge yeshe*, meaning "the wisdom of individual realization," or "the wisdom of discriminating awareness." This awareness is not a loose, relaxed state of mind, but a brilliantly clear with a sense of tautness to it. This is what arises in the process of looking directly at the mind.

We begin initially to look for the nature of the mind in the same way we discover the egolessness of the self, as taught in the sutra tradition. There are two types of egolessness taught in the sutra tradition: the egolessness of self and the egolessness of phenomena. When one looks for the personal self, the "I" or "me" doesn't find anything. In this way one discovers the non-existence of the self. In the same way, when one looks for the mind by asking is it in the head or is it in the body or is it outside the body, etc., one finds it is nowhere to be found.

To do this practice, we keep our eyes open according to the great master Saraha who says the yogin does not close his or her eyes. Not closing the eyes really means staring wide-eyed, without even blinking and meditate. Some people have difficulties meditating with their eyes open and if this is the case, well perhaps it doesn't make all that much difference. However, in this tradition of mahamudra practice, it says to keep one's eyes open, and if one meditates in that way, it is a better way to meditate.

Saraha also says: "The Brahmins look up; the peaceful hearers look down; the vajra eyes look directly." Many nonBuddhist traditions of contemplative practice raise their gaze and look up contemplating a deity feeling that this deity lives somewhere in the sky when they meditate. The shravakas or accomplished Hinayana practitioners look down so as not to give rise to thought, particularly the disturbing emotions. They feel that if they were to look up, they would see lots of things and start thinking about them arousing passion, aggression, envy, and so forth. Where the Theravada tradition of Buddhism is practiced, the monks go on their rounds of begging food from the laity by walking with their eyes on the ground in front of them. The third category of vajra eyes refers to the practitioners of mahamudra, of the vajrayana tradition. "The vajra eyes look directly," means that they don't look up or down; they just look straight ahead. And when they're looking out that way, what exactly are they looking at? They're looking at their own mind.

HOW WE LOOK AT MIND

Thus, we begin with the practice of shamatha, and then as the session continues, we look for the mind while in shamatha. So, do we look out for our mind, or do we look in for our mind? The text raises this question and answers it by saying, whichever way you feel comfortable with it. You may have the sense that you're in here somewhere and your mind is over there or that you're here. So it feels that you are looking out for your mind. But, you might have the sense that you are on the outside and your mind is on the inside. Then, you feel you want to look in for your mind. Either way is fine, but when you look, you look nakedly. "Nakedly" means you do not look in the matter of cognitive investigation, but you look directly: "Where is it?" and "What is it?"

If mind exists, then you ought to be able to find the thing. You ought to be able to say, "Well, this is what it is." So you start looking for it. One of the ways to look for it is to see whether or not it has a shape. Is it round? Is it square? Is it in the shape of a mountain? Does it have the shape of a human being? If you can't come up with a shape for it, but you still feel, "this is my mind, it's something." Then ask, "if it exists, it ought to have a color." So, Is it white? Is it red? Is it black?

External things have colors and shapes; but does you mind have a color? Moreover, mind ought to be somewhere. Where does it dwell? Is it outside somewhere? Probably not and you think that your mind dwells within your body. So you look through your body starting at the top of your head and going down. Is it in my head? Is it in my arms? Is it in my heart? You look through your body completely, from the top of your head to the soles of your feet. Whatever part of the body it might be, can you find your mind somewhere in there? Well, No, it's not like that. Maybe it pervades throughout the body. If that's the way it seems to you, then you look.

What do we mean when we talk about mind? What is it that we think this mind is? Well, mind is that which sees and hears and knows and remembers. If something happened in the past and you can think about that now, then that's what the mind is; it remembers things and knows different things. After you've begun to do some of this investigation, you might ask the question, "Don't we think about things? Don't we remember things?" Well, of course, we do. But then the question is, "Where is that mind that is remembering these things and thinking about them?" That's what you have to look for. You look for that mind that knows. Can't the mind see colors and shapes and so on? Of course, but where is that mind that is seeing colors and shapes? What about hearing sounds?" Of course we hear sounds; but where is the mind that is hearing those sounds? You're looking for the mind that sees and hears and knows and remembers, but you don't find it. The non-finding of the mind is called emptiness. That non-finding of the mind is the mind's lack of inherent existence, the lack of any nature of its own.[28]

We think that our mind exists, but despite this our mind cannot be found. This is why the Buddha said that "form is empty; emptiness is form; form is no other than emptiness" and so forth in the *Heart* sutra. We go through, for instance, the five aggregates from which all the different elements of body and mind can be grouped, and the *Heart* sutra says: "form does not exist, feeling does not exist, discrimination does not exist, mental formations do not exist, and consciousnesses do not exist." Thus the Buddha says very clearly that the body and the mind do not truly exist—which at this point is what we are discovering. We are looking for the mind, but we do not find it anywhere. Can we not find mind because it is too small? Is it because the mind is to brilliant, clear, or radiant that's just too overwhelming to see? No, that's not why. Is it because the mind is hidden behind something else? Of course not, it's our own mind. The reason we don't find our mind is because the mind is empty.

We look for our mind and we don't find anything. The mind is not to be found and therefore it is empty. What is the nature of its emptiness? Is it an emptiness like the blankness in space? No, it's not like that. For instance, we remember things and know things, however, we cannot find the mind that knows and remembers and sees. It is something that knows but the knower is not to be found. In the *Heart* sutra the Buddha said "form is empty," and then he went on to say "emptiness is form." This can also be applied to each of the other five aggregates that make up the body and mind of a person. Just as the Buddha said, "form is empty, emptiness is form," we can also say, "consciousnesses are empty, emptiness is also the consciousnesses." That is to say, while being form, form is empty; while being empty, it is also form. These two happen simultaneously so we speak about the union of appearance and emptiness in regard to visual images and the union of luminosity and emptiness in regard to consciousnesses or mind. The inseparability of appearance and emptiness means appearing forms are empty; while empty, they do appear. Similarly, while consciousness is empty, at the same time it is luminous. This union of luminosity and emptiness is exactly what we discovered when we look for the mind above.

In the *Heart* sutra after it says that "form is emptiness, emptiness also is form," it then goes on to say, "emptiness is no other than form, form is no other than emptiness." That same point is to be made in regard to the mind: mind is empty and emptiness is also mind. Emptiness is no other than the mind and the mind is no other than emptiness. When it says "not other than," it means, you won't find them in separate places. It's not possible to put the form over here and its emptiness somewhere else. The emptiness of the mind and the mind itself are one. There is no mind that is not emptiness in terms of its very nature. You won't find a mind that is not empty in the sense that we have been discussing this emptiness.

However, it's necessary not to understand this intellectually, but to actually experience of this. It isn't quite good enough to say, "Well, I think it's like this." You have to tighten the matter up or as the text says the mind analyzes itself in the manner of "rock meeting bone." When you look at mind with this directness and intensity, you find the luminous empty nature of mind, which is the non-finding of mind within awareness, and then you rest within that. Then it is no longer a theory that the mind is empty; you know that the mind is empty. You meditate within that luminosity and emptiness in a manner called *phyam gnas pa* in Tibetan which means "smoothly and evenly." This means you stay there steadily and don't waver but rest there smoothly with a sense of comfort and doing it for a while. It's not just scattered, but resting fully within that.

(d). SUTRA DESCRIPTIONS OF MEDITATING ON THE MIND

[186] In the next section of the text, many more passages are cited from the Buddha's teachings showing the importance of meditating upon the nature of mind, the way to meditate upon the nature of mind, and what is seen and not seen when one meditates upon the nature of mind. It's an exhortation to actually do this, not to have just some sort of vague understanding of it. But it's something we actually have to do. In particular, what becomes apparent in looking at this is that we have had the good fortune to encounter the tradition of quintessential instructions. In the sutra tradition, it takes eon upon eon of accumulating merit in order to strengthen and empower the mind to the point that it can actually realize emptiness. However, in the tradition of quintessential instructions, there is the direct introduction to the nature of mind. That's something of extraordinary value and importance.

(e). HOW TO DETERMINE THE NATURE OF MIND

[190] When we look properly, relying upon the quintessential instructions that have been passed through this Kagyu lineage, what kind of experience arises? The mind has no shape whatsoever. It does not have any shape because it is not a thing. Similarly, it has no color because it is not a thing. Anything that's a form has a shape and a color. So, once we've understood that the mind has no shape and no color, we discover the mind is not a form. Does the mind dwell somewhere? We see that the mind does not dwell outside the body, inside the body, or somewhere in between those two. The reason why it doesn't dwell anywhere is that there is nothing to dwell. Once there is no mind that stays somewhere, then there is nowhere that it dwells. Similarly, the mind cannot be identified as anything. It cannot be said to exist in a certain way, nor can it be said to be non-existent. If it were an existent phenomenon, you could show the way in which it exists. If you could identify the mind as something that does not exist, then you could also say precisely how it does not exist. But in fact the mind cannot be identified even in that simple way nor can the mind be identified as something that takes a certain aspect or expression and then changes to something else. One cannot identify the changing expressions or moods of the mind. In this way, the mind is found to be free from all elaboration or complexity. In the text, mind is compared to space. For instance, it is compared to space in the *Sutra of Great Compassion*, which was requested by Maitreya and in the *Manifest Purification of Vairocana* tantra. In these texts, and in many others, mind is said to be like space. Now, when something is compared to space, you might say that it is vast like space or, it is blue like space. But neither of these are the qualities these texts are seeking to attribute to the mind when they say that the mind is like space. Rather, what they are saying is that the mind is nothing whatsoever just like space. It does not exist as something. It has no nature of its own. It does not exist in terms of its own inherent essence.

The same thing was said in the sutras, in the tantras of the vajrayana and was discovered by the great siddhas of the mahamudra tradition. The same thing was discovered through the process of careful and reasoned analysis of the scholars of the Buddhist tradition as they studied the teachings of the sutras and tantras. This can be expressed in a variety of ways. You can say it is the lack of inherent existence; it is the lack of any nature that truly characterizes phenomena. You can say it is emptiness. You can talk about the mind's way of being. In any case, it comes down to the fact that when you look for the mind itself, you don't find anything. This lack of anything is the emptiness spoken about in the sutras. It is the way of being as dharmata of reality. It is the mind's true nature that is described in the spiritual songs of the great adepts of the mahamudra tradition. The text cites many different songs from great teachers such as Saraha, Tilopa, and Shavari. It comes down to this one same thing. When you look for the mind, because it is empty, it is not found.

THE MIND'S NATURE

When we look for the nature of the mind, the distinction between the object (the mind) that is looked at and the thing (the mind) that is looking is a false distinction. Nevertheless, when we sit down to practice meditation, it does seem that there is something that is looked at and something that is looking. Since we are working with our experience, we investigate the way they seem to be. So, settled in the meditative stabilization called shamatha, we look. And when we look for the mind, we discover nothing whatsoever. The mind is not established in any way. So when we look, who, or what, is looking? And who doesn't find something and knows that to be the mind's nature? That looker is called *so so rang dge sherab sherab* in Tibetan, which means "intelligence of discriminating awareness." That intelligence looks for the mind's nature. However, one cannot stop there; one has to look for the looker. Where is it and what is it and so forth. And when that looker is found not to exist as this or that shape or nature, one has arrived at what is called *nam par tog me yeshe*, which means "thoroughly non-conceptual wisdom." At that point, one finds the mind to be like space.

When we say that the mind is like space, we do not mean that it is in every respect identical to space. What is the difference between space and mind? Space has no awareness of itself. The emptiness of space is characterized as a lifeless emptiness, a corpse, as lacking the quality of luminosity. The mind's emptiness, however, is not like that. The mind is empty but that emptiness knows. Although the mind does not exist, nevertheless, it sees, it knows, it understands. In particular, it knows and understands and illuminates itself, and from that point of view, it is called the wisdom that is aware of itself. It does not exist, yet it knows and understands that non-existence.

Tashi Namgyal cites a passage from the great siddha Tilopa. It begins with the exclamation, "Je ho!" which expresses the pleasure that Tilopa has discovered as he has expressed the mind's nature. For the mind's nature is a luminosity that is free from all pain, free from suffering, so Tilopa exclaims, "Je ho!" and then says, "This is the wisdom that is aware of itself. It is beyond speech. It is not to be found within the sphere of the mind." When Tilopa says that it is beyond speech, he means you cannot say that the mind exists; you cannot say that the mind does not exist. This exclamation by Tilopa echoes the well known passage in praise of the *Prajnaparamita*, which says that it is *ma-sam-jenei*, which means it cannot be expressed by speech or thought. Tilopa echoes that sentiment here, saying the mind's nature is beyond the paths on which speech travels. It is not really an object that falls within the sphere of mind, not an object within the sphere of an ordinary intellect. For that reason, Tilopa says, "I have nothing whatsoever to teach," meaning since the mind cannot be said to exist or not to exist, I can't say that it's this and I can't say that it's that." But he does go on. For what can one do if one cannot say anything about it really? He says, "The mind is nearby. It is within you. You can look yourself. You can discover it yourself, identify it yourself, point to it yourself and you can know it and that's what you should do."

MISTAKES IN PERCEIVING MIND'S NATURE

That much expresses the experience of real meditation. It's possible to make three different kinds of mistakes at this point. One of these mistakes is to think that shamatha, the simple peaceful state of the mind at rest, is the mind's way of being. This is to say, when the mind looks at the mind, and the samadhi of shamatha arises. One might make the mistake of thinking that one has then seen the mind thinking, "Ah, this is the mind's way of being." That would not be true because at that point, you have not really seen the luminosity that is the mind's nature, and you have not really gained genuine knowledge and conviction of the mind's lack of any inherent existence. A second mistake is to consider the various appearances that sometimes arise within meditation to be the discovery of the mind's actual way of being. Sometimes, due to the force of latent predispositions and habitual tendencies, when one sits down to meditate, various things appear. One might then think, "Oh, now I have seen the mind's nature." That's not so, for the same reasons that were outlined above. A third kind of possibility would be to mistake different temporary experiences that arise in meditation to be the mind's way of being. There are three kinds of *temporary experiences* (Tib. *nyam*) that arise during the practice of meditation. They might be a temporary experience of luminosity or a temporary experience of emptiness. But these are merely superficial and are not actually the mind's way of being. These temporary experiences are not really the mind's way of being because one has not recognized the mind's lack of inherent existence. One has not ascertained that with certainty and come to have great conviction about that. Ascertaining it with certainty and arriving at it with real conviction is extremely important. In each of these cases, one has made the mistake of stumbling upon something and thinking, "This is the mind when it is not."

MIND'S EXPRESSIVE POWER

The mind's expressive power is its ability to move and change extremely rapidly. When the mind moves quickly, it appears in two different ways: externally as appearances and internally as thought. The mind is empty, nevertheless, things appear. When something appears externally, it appears as visible forms, sounds, smells, tastes, and tangible phenomena. When it appears internally, it appears as thoughts such as liking not liking something. The mind is empty, yet it prefers this to that. If we understand that external appearances and internal thoughts are the mind's expressive power, then we have understood the essential point of meditation. If we do not understand this, then sometimes our meditation will go well and other times it will seem we've lost it. So it's important to understand that appearance and thought are the mind's expressive power.

External appearances in the mind appear as visible forms having color and shape, and as sounds, as smells, and so forth. These things are really the expressive power of the mind and they are not something other than the mind. But one might ask, "How are these really just the internal mind because they seem to be external phenomena, appearing to be something apart from mind. External things are also hard and solid things; how can you say that this is mind?" The answer is what are called *latent predispositions* or habitual tendencies (Tib. *bag chag*). Due to the energy of latent predispositions, various kinds of appearances appear. Sometimes they manifest as things that are quite hard, but are not actually so. An analogy of this is a dream. You fall asleep, you move into the luminosity of the mind, and gradually from that luminosity various things begin to appear to you. As they appear and develop, they begin to look like real, solid things. However, it's just a dream, created by your mind and not separate from your mind, even though they are created by mind, they appear external to the mind. It's the same with the appearances of waking life. They are not truly other than the mind. They are not truly some solid thing, but they certainly do appear that way.

5. REALIZING THE NATURE OF APPEARANCES

[196] We are not able to realize the nature of external appearances right off, but we can look at our own mind and directly experience their emptiness. When we see this, we will also understand the nature of apparently external appearances. For the nature of the mind and the nature of appearances is identical. The nature of the mind is the same as reality, dharmata, that is, the nature of all phenomena. The text cites two lines from Saraha that says: "Since the mind alone is the seed of all, It is this that unfolds samsara and nirvana." This is to say, all the phenomena of samsara and all the phenomena of nirvana arise from the mind. For that reason, when we realize the mind's nature, we will naturally understand the nature of all the things that appear.

Thoughts arise and appearances arise and they are both merely expressions of the mind. Their nature is the same as the mind's nature. One might think that it would not be necessary to set out any further techniques for understanding their nature. However, there are the quintessential instructions that enable one to recognize the nature of thought and the nature of appearances. There are stages of meditation that one follows in order to arrive at the realization. The text says that the way in which one understands the nature of appearances and thoughts is quite similar to the way that one understands the egolessness of phenomena as it is taught in the sutras. One begins with investigating the nature of thoughts because it has been found that it is easier than appearances. First of all, there are the essential points of the body, which means how you hold your body. The way in which you take the posture of meditation and the gaze you use has been described. You begin the session by resting briefly, for just a moment, in the luminosity and emptiness that cannot be identified as anything at all, and that is the nature of the mind. You rest in meditative stabilization in that way for a moment, and within that, you cause a thought to arise. You quite deliberately cause a strong thought to arise, for example, hatred or some very strong emotion or thought to arise. When it arises, know that it has arisen. Then ask, "Where is it? Is it inside? Is it outside? What is its nature?" Don't follow after it. Don't think about something that's already happened, and don't follow that thought to be seduced by it, But look at it nakedly and directly and analyze: "Where is it? Where does it dwell? Upon what does it depend? What is its shape? What is its color?" And so on. When you look in these ways, you see that this thought of hatred or pride does not really exist. When that thought has been recognized as not truly real it is pacified, which is to say it dissolves into non-conceptuality. That's the way you have to meditate.

Do this again and again and again. For instance, let your mind wander a little bit from the state of merely resting in peace and think, for instance, of someone who has harmed you. Think of the harm that he or she has done to you in the past and arouse anger. Then look at that anger. "Where is it? What is it? Where did it come from? Where is it going to? What is it actually?" When you do that, its lack of establishment will dawn for you. When that appears and you understand it, you can say you have realized the nature of hatred or the nature of thought or the nature of mind, because those three are the same. You can do the same with attachment or desire. Think about something that you desire, something for which you feel attachment, and when that desire arises, look at its nature. Look at what it is, where it rests, and where it goes. Look at that desire itself. When you look in this way, that thought becomes non-thought. It becomes union of luminosity and emptiness. When you understand this luminosity-emptiness, you have understood the mind's nature and you have understood the nature of thought. You have cut through superimpositions[29] and you have resolved all questions about what the mind's nature is. You have found it to be the absence of inherent existence, of any nature or characteristic or quality that truly defines or belongs to the mind. Do this again and again and again and again, until you have real understanding. When you have gained some experience with this, then, as thought arises in meditation— though at first it may seem to be some sort of obstruction—when you discover its lack of inherent nature, that thought itself becomes part of the quality of meditation.

When you realize that the nature of individual thought, the nature of the mind and the nature of dharmata are all the same, then you turn to the appearances of visible forms, sounds, smells, tastes, and so forth, to determine what their nature is. From the point of view of mahamudra, we say that these appearances arise through the force of latent predispositions, that the mind begins to appear as different kinds of objects: mountains, houses, rivers, whatever. It seems to have some particular shape and some particular color; it seems to be a thing. In the sutra tradition there is a process of reasoned analysis. One begins with large external phenomena, such as a building or a mountain, and through analysis, begins to understand that it is composed of particles, that the particles are composed of still smaller particles, coming down to something that is irreducible, and realizing that, in the end, that irreducible particle itself does not exist. So, through analyzing very minutely, one discovers that the apparent object is not really there. That is the way one goes about this kind of analysis in the tradition of the sutras. However, in this tradition of practicing quintessential instructions, rather than looking at and analyzing external objects, we look at the mind that apprehends these appearances. We analyze and settle decisively the nature of the mind that apprehends these appearances. Then we recognize the emptiness that is the nature of the mind. We will also understand that emptiness is the nature of the object apprehended by that mind. For instance, when a visual form with color and shape appears to an eye consciousness, rather than analyzing that form, we look at the mind seeing that form. We ask: "What is it really? What is the mind to which that form appears? Does it have a color or a shape? What sort of thing is it? Where is it?" As we look in that way, we discover that the seeing mind is not to be found. When the seeing mind cannot be found, then we also realize that the external object does not exist either. Once the seeing mind does not exist, then the object seen by that mind does not exist. The same applies with sounds and smells and so forth. Something hears a sound. Look for the mind that hears: where is it, what is it? And so on.

We have described how we work with the appearances of the five sensory consciousnesses. What about the sense of things as being pleasant or painful? Sometimes things seem to be very delightful, and other times they are misery. What about the mind that is experiencing that pleasure or that pain? That is investigated too, in just the same way that we've been discussing. One looks for the mind that feels that pleasure or suffers that pain. When one looks, one finds nothing whatsoever. Rather, that experience is resolved into union of luminosity and emptiness. If we do this again and again and again, we come to find the nature of thought and the nature of appearance, is the dharmata, or reality, that is the nature of mind itself.

(f). ELIMINATING DOUBTS ABOUT THE ROOT OF SAMSARA AND NIRVANA

[200] The reason why it's important to meditate upon the nature of thought and appearance, and to discover the luminosity-emptiness that is the nature of thought and appearance, is as follows. If you know how to meditate upon the nature of the mind itself, that is helpful; but if you have not learned to recognize the luminosity-emptiness that is their nature, then thought and appearance will seem to be obstructions and obstacles to your practice of meditation. Without realizing luminosity-emptiness we will be able to meditate smoothly as long as you can just focus upon mind itself. But then when you have to work with appearances that dawn for any of the consciousnesses or for thoughts and emotions that arise, if you haven't learned how to meditate with them, then the process becomes very rough and bumpy, difficult, and harsh. There's a sense

of internal conflict and that's why it's extremely beneficial to take up these further practices of meditating upon the nature of appearance and thought.

Chapter 10

Eliminating Doubts about Vipashyana

D. THE MAIN MEDITATION OF VIPASHYANA
1. Thoughts and Appearances are of Mental Origin
2. ELIMINATING DOUBTS ABOUT VIPASHYANA

[200] It is very important to know mistakes that might be made in meditation so we can recognize them in our experience and steer clear of them. For example, we might think we have arrived at this stage when we really haven't. We might experience the mind in meditation as very relaxed and at ease, and interpret this as being Vipashyana. Well, that's not Vipashyana. Or having relaxed we might experience unusual appearances and forms such as flowers, different colors, or bright lights and mistake them for the nature of mind and think our meditation is going well. These are really just appearances of mind and in fact this is not Vipashyana. Sometimes one might experience a sense of a vivid emptiness, just huge, open, clear, empty space and think that is Vipashyana. But it is not.

What is Vipashyana, then? The Vipashyana of which we are speaking at this point is not the creation of something new and sensational. It's a matter of understanding what our mind has always been all the time, naturally, from the very beginning. The only problem is that we have not simply recognized it. But it has been this all along. It's not a matter of it having been hidden and we've missed it. It is just that we haven't looked directly at our mind and therefore we haven't experienced our mind as it is.

So what is important is to look directly and to experience our mind as it is.

This chapter is literally called "severing superimpositions with regard to the basis and the expressive power." Superimpositions are doubts and mistakes that one generates, and severing them means abandoning them. In the previous chapter we talked about three phases of looking at the mind: Looking at the mind itself, looking at thought, and looking at appearances. These three apply also to the process of cutting through doubts that one generates in regard to the ground and the *expressive power* (Tib. *tsal*). Thus, within this discussion of eliminating doubts, the first of three sections talks about settling doubt in a decisive way that cuts through all hesitation and mistaken ideas about thought and appearance as mind itself. When we say that they are mind itself, it means that they are not to be found somewhere other than mind.

(a) DOUBTS THAT APPEARANCES ARE CREATED BY MIND

[200] In the previous section we looked at the nature of mind itself. This section talks about clearly and decisively cutting through doubts, that movement of thought and the appearance of phenomena are nothing other than mind. What is the difference between these two? When we talk about settling decisively the nature of thought, the nature of appearance, the nature of mind itself, we investigate the shape and the color of mind, thought, appearance and so forth, and we see that thought and appearances do not exist by way of their own nature. When we cut through doubts and discover that thought and appearances are mind itself, we look to see the source of these thoughts and appearances. Where do they arise? Where do they come from? Where do they rest? Where do they go? When we investigate in this way, we discover that thought and mind cannot be separated and that appearance and mind are inseparable.

THE TECHNIQUE OF STRONG THOUGHT

Ratna Lingpa suggested another method which we might call "the method of strong thought." We begin by resting in meditation upon emptiness and then give rise to a strong thought such as anger, causing it to arise. When it arises, we then look. The first step is to ask from where does it arise? Where did it come from? Generally when we think about these things, we would say, "Well, I started thinking about someone I hate and the terrible things that person did to me, and from this a thought of hatred arose." Well, roughly speaking, that seems to be so, but when we look very closely, that's not a very satisfactory answer because it doesn't answer the question of what is really the origin of this thought, of hatred. We are looking for the point from where it emerges, where it arises, where it then stays. We look and look but do not find such a place. We may then think that it arises from the mind. If it arises from the mind, then what is the manner of its arising from the mind? Does a thought arise from the mind in the way that a child is born from its mother, so that they become distinct and individual entities that can exist each in their own? If not that way, does a thought arise from the mind in the way that light radiates from the sun or the moon, so that each has its own power and dawning? If it's not that way, is it that the mind itself becomes the thought? First it's mind, then it transforms and becomes thought. Is that how it is? If we look carefully, we see that none of these three processes describe it; in fact, thought is unborn.

When a strong thought arises, then we look to see where it abides. How does it abide? We tend to regard hatred as some very strong and forceful thing, it seems to be quite real, and we cling to it considering it to be a real thing. However, when we begin to look into it carefully, we find that even this powerful thought that has so much energy to i, cannot be identified as anything whatsoever. There is no way to grab hold of it and say, "This is it," and to say exactly what it is.

When a strong thought arises we also look to see where this thought goes when it departs. We look and look for its point of disappearance, and one does not find it. So that leaves two possibilities: Has this thought having ceased become a non-thing, or is it that this thought has been naturally cleansed, pacified, and purified?

Obvious thoughts, subtle thoughts, both are investigated and looked into. From where do they arise? Where do they abide? Where do they go?

Sometimes we are looking at thoughts in the way we have just described, and sometimes you might take to mind thoughts that are contradictory with one another, such as the sense of something as pleasant, delightful, and comfortable, and a sense of something as painful. And one looks at those two, one after the other. What actually is the difference between them? They certainly seem to be quite different, but we can't find a place where a sense of pleasantness arises, or where that sense of pain arises. The same is trũe for where they abide and where they go. So if it turns out that you're doing all this looking and you're not finding anything, what was the point of doing the looking in the first place? There is a point to it, which is that we tend to have very fixed ideas about these things, in particular about what we think of as pleasant and what we think of as painful. We think of them as very distinct from one another. We may also think of mind as inside and thoughts that appear as being on the outside. We have some notion about these things. And when we carefully investigate our experience as it actually is, then those conceptions that we have about our experience fall to pieces. When one look, one realizes that the mind and thoughts are of the same nature; they are inseparable. One can recognize them as such and experience them as such, and that's the point of this looking: to experience mind and thought as inseparable.

Taking that a little further, if we do not meditate in this way and do not find that thought is inseparable from mind itself, then thought will serve as a hindrance to meditation. We will be content to meditate upon mind itself; but when thoughts arise, they will present a problem for us and tend to destroy our meditation. On the other hand, if we have investigated the nature of thought and find that it arises out of nowhere, rests nowhere, and disappears to nowhere, at that point we understand that the mind experienced in meditation and thought are actually identical. When we realize that thought no longer poses an obstacle to our practice of meditation, we experience thought as simply another expression of the mind's true nature.

(b) DOUBTS ABOUT RESTING AND MOVING MIND

[203] The next section tells us how to cut through our doubts with regard to appearances and to resolve decisively that appearances are mind. As before, we rest in meditation, and this causes appearances, such as visual images, to arise. Then we look as before for the place of abiding, and the eventual point of dissolution of that form. When a visual form appears, there is a mind that apprehends it. From where does that mind arise? Where does that mind dwell? Where does that mind go? That's what we are investigating when we are investigating the mind that apprehends appearance. What is the relationship between the visual image perceived and the mind that sees it? Are they the same or are they different? With investigation we find that we cannot separate them. They are in fact not different. When we

investigate this way, it's very helpful to look in particular at the mind that perceives beautiful and ugly forms, or pleasant and displeasing sounds. What is the difference between the mind that sees the beautiful image and the mind that sees the ugly image? We look at it in terms of where it begins, where it rests, and where it goes.

When speaking about the mind itself, it is helpful to identify two different phases. Sometimes the mind is at rest, and when it rests, there is not much thought; the mind is peaceful, smooth, even. Other times the mind is moving. When it is moving, it goes here and there, and many different thoughts naturally arise. We investigate the difference between mind at rest and mind that moves. Where does the mind at rest come from, where does it abide, and where does it go? When the mind is moving, where does that mind come from, where does it abide, where does it go in the end? What is really the difference between the mind that is still and the mind that is moving? It may seem at first that the still mind has a certain nature and the moving mind has a different nature. When we look, however, we cannot find a difference between them. The nature of both still and moving mind is empty. We cannot find a difference is.

At first it seems that there's a big difference between the mind that is still and the mind that is moving. It seems that the mind that is still is peaceful, free from thought, smooth, even, and that the mind that is moving has a very different character. Rest within deep meditative state (Skt. *samadhi*) and look at the mind that is still. It is empty of any nature of its own. It is nothing other than luminosity and emptiness. Look at the mind that is moving. Look at thoughts and say that they are *rang ramsel* or that they know themselves and that they are *rang cha rang cho* or that they are self-liberating. They arise on their own and they are released on their own. That's the kind of language that we use to describe the experience that we have when we look at thoughts. If we look at the still and moving mind with this kind of technique, we discover that they do not have different natures. They are empty of any nature that is truly their own. From that point of view, the still mind and the moving mind can not be differentiated.

It's quite easy to think that resting and moving mind have completely different natures and when the mind is moving, that stillness has been lost. Some think that one must clear away the motion, and when it is cleared away, the mind can be at rest. This is believing there is a contradiction between the mind at rest and the mind when it is moving. In fact, both are union of luminosiy and emptiness. The differences that one tends to see between these two states of mind are really one's own confusion. Because they are of the same nature, these two states do not obstruct one another. Stillness does not obstruct motion and motion does not obstruct stillness, for in fact they are simply one inseparable entity.

(c) DOUBTS ABOUT APPEARANCES AS UNBORN

[205] The third section is called "cutting through and resolving decisively that everything that appears is unborn." Here, as before, one rests within the unity of luminosity and emptiness and within that state the mind looks at itself. When you look and finally settle that everything which appears is unborn, you realize that mind is just a name. It's just a name that has been given. That is the mind's actual way of being; that is its real character. You're looking to see where does the mind arise? From what cause does it arise? Once it has arisen, where does it abide? In the end, where does it go? And when you look in this way, you cannot find any point of origin of the mind, any place where the mind dwells, and any point at which the mind ceases. When you have realized that none of these three apply, you have also understood that the mind is not established by way of its own nature. And in that sense, you have been able to identify this mind without identity.

E. CHARACTERISTICS OF EMERGING INSIGHT

[208] This section is concerned with the measure of whether or not one has given rise to Vipashyana. You ask, what is the difference between Vipashyana and shamatha. Because of the strength of mind at rest, you are not able to realize mind's nature. You cannot give rise to that certainty, conviction, and realization. Within the experience of the mind dwelling in peace, other experiences arise, such as temporary experiences that seem quite dramatic and persuasive. You think you have now experienced something truly and profoundly. But in fact, you have not. You have not understood the mind's nature. You may have had some sort of temporary sensation that you think is an experience of the mind's emptiness.

But in fact you have not realized the mind's way of being. Actually it is the shamatha itself that is obstructing your realization. It's necessary to relax further, to separate from this temporary experience and then meditate upon insight to achieve the actual purpose of this practice and realize the mind's true nature.

There are other kinds of problems that students experience. Some have inferior minds and are obstructed by karma, that is to say, obstructed by the imprint of actions done in the past. For those, there is some difficulty in realizing the mind's nature. No matter how much they analyze, they are not able to see mind itself. For them it is necessary to work at other practices for a while, particularly at accumulating the collections of wisdom and merit and at purifying obstructions that they have accumulated in the past. When they have done so, they are able to give rise to shamatha with a real crisp and keen edge to it, and through sustaining that, eventually are able to realize the mind's nature; that is to say, give rise to the insight of Vipashyana. For others, the problem is that they are too intellectual. Their reasoned way has become so strong that it's getting in their way and they haven't actually given rise to real experience. They need to apply themselves more to the actual practice of meditation, set aside intellectualization, and just look very simply at the mind's point of origin, place of rest, and point of disappearance, until their meditation actually bears some fruit.

F. THIS VIPASHYANA AND OTHER KINDS OF VIPASHYANA

[209] The text makes a comparison of the practice of Vipashyana of mahamudra that we have been discussing with the Vipashyana that is presented in other texts in this section. Tashi Namgyal names many kinds of Vipashyana mentioned in other Buddhist texts and analyzes them to see if they are a different kind of Vipashyana. The general point he's making is that this practice of Vipashyana which investigates the mind's way of being, is essentially the same as all the other kinds of Vipashyana.

Questions

Question: We spoke about shamatha as being resting in a state of peace, and that when that was looked at from the point of view of

Vipashyana, we would say that in shamatha delusion has been suppressed.

Rinpoche: Yes, it's true that delusion is like dream and like illusion. But that has not been realized when one is resting in the state of peace known as shamatha. In the state of shamatha, there's less delusion. But the nature of the mind and the nature of that delusion have not been realized. And for that reason shamatha does not serve as an antidote to delusion. It's merely a temporary solution, though it's also a stepping stone on the way to a permanent understanding. The mind becomes very relaxed in shamatha, and as the mind becomes relaxed, so the delusion relaxes too. But the nature of that delusion has not been realized. Then, in Vipashyana, the mind and delusion, all of it is realized to be empty, like a dream and like an illusion. In that sense, we say that shamatha suppresses delusion and that Vipashyana cuts it from the root.

Question: I thought that the increase of auspicious coincidence and virtue were related. I'm just trying to find out if there is a relationship between the increase of virtue and auspicious coincidence.

Rinpoche: The relationship between the increase of virtue and the gathering together of auspicious coincidences and the practice and realization of mahamudra is principally through the practice of virtue. The conditions that are harmonious with the practice of mahamudra can come about if one practices virtue, for it can come to pass that you meet with a guru who holds the lineage of mahamudra and who can teach it, that you actually hear these teachings, that you will feel faith and devotion when you hear these teachings, that you have the necessary resources and suitable conditions to allow you to practice mahamudra meditation. So it's mostly to be understood that the increase of virtue brings about the auspicious coincidences that allow one to arrive at realization. If you have not accumulated virtue in that way, then those auspicious coincidences don't come about.

Question: My understanding is that mahamudra can be applied not just on the cushion but when we're at work and other situations. My own experience with work is that it's really a time for awareness to go to sleep. When I go to work, I feel like I've been slammed into a mental dungeon. But then I sort of get used to it, and it kind of becomes numb, but I cannot think of how to combine awareness with that. I think it's partially because I'm not grinding sesame seeds, which doesn't require that much concentration. But at work I write code for computers, and it takes one hundred per cent of my mind staring at this code.

Rinpoche: When we're talking about these investigations such as looking to where the mind arises, where does it rest, and where does it go, that's the work that you do within the formal session of meditation, the period of sitting on the cushion. When you do that, particularly if you have the opportunity to do it in a retreat session, then some experience does arise. You do get some sense of what that's about. The point, then, is that when you get up off the cushion or leave the retreat, do not forget about that experience completely, but sustain it by just maintaining mindfulness and recollection and awareness of that. When you sit down and do these investigations, you get some feeling of what it means to say that the mind is not a real thing in the way that it seemed to be. And the point is to maintain some awareness of that when you go back to the rest of your life, not to forget that.

Now, of course, that's not the easiest thing to do, and particularly for a beginner, it's difficult. But it's crucial that you not become discouraged by that difficulty and just cast the whole thing away when it becomes difficult. That's really the critical point, not to just give up on it.

It might be a little bit easier if we were just pounding sesame seeds, like Tilopa did. But, if you think about it, there are certainly examples of people like Nagarjuna who had extremely complex intellectual work to do, and managed to conjoin that with the practice of mahamudra. He did so well and achieved supreme enlightenment. That should give us some hope and inspiration that, indeed, it is possible to do truly serious intellectual work and at the same time mix it with our experience of mahamudra, with the practice we've done, and with our sustaining that awareness into the rest of our life. So when Nagarjuna was sitting composing the books on Madhyamaka, he really had to tighten his awareness and focus and concentrate. That's somewhat similar to the situation in which many of us find ourselves now and certainly the situation you're describing. But, just as he was able to find a way to conjoin that kind of study and intellectual complexit, with the practice of mahamudra, so that's possible for us, too. It's not easy in the beginning, but it's important not to become discouraged by that difficulty and to continue. Stage by stage, it will get better and better.

Question: You were speaking about looking at the looker. When I look into the face of the looker, it ceases, and then the experience of cognizance of looking arises. Is that cognizance another looker, or also what was translated as the "prajna" or "discriminating intelligence" What exactly is this?

Rinpoche: What does it mean to talk about prajna or the intelligence of discriminating awareness? Calling it prajna or intelligence is to say that it is not stupid. It's not obscure, it's not dull, it is not deluded. It understands things as they are. When it sees something, it sees it accurately. It knows that certain things are of good or poor quality or whatever. Think about it this way: you take two sticks and rub them together, eventually that creates fire and the fire then burns up the two sticks. In a similar way, if you look at mind, you see that mind is an emptiness that is unidentifiable as anything at all. In that way, you experience the union of luminosity and emptiness. That prajna of discriminating awareness, that intelligence of discriminating awareness or individual realization, experiences and knows that union of luminosity and emptiness which pervades all of the mind and all of one's experience. Because that's what it knows, then the prajna itself does not become solidified. You don't hang onto that. You don't experience that as some kind of real thing that you can fixate on.

Question: If you're looking at the mind, you're looking at the looker, and when you look at the looker, that brings a second looker, and then if you look at that one, there's a third looker, and this could go on endlessly.

Rinpoche: Well, logically speaking, that's so. But it doesn't actually happen that way. If you're just thinking about what might happen, then it could happen that way. But if you do the practice, it doesn't happen that way. This is because it's not like an eye consciousness looking at a visual image. It's mind looking at itself. And, in particular, since you have a mind that is of the nature of emptiness looking at its own nature, the object and the apprehending subject are not two things to begin with. Being of the nature of emptiness, they dissolve into that emptiness. So there's a slight fluttering, but this is not really going to go on that way. It will quickly resolve itself if you actually get in touch with the emptiness.

Question: Would it be correct to say that the insight known as Vipashyana has to be induced? In my own experience if you just kept doing shamatha practice, there is not much room for intelligence to work there. So does the insight associated with Vipashyana have to be induced? Does the practitioner then have to ask the questions and look at the mind in the way that you just spoke about?

Rinpoche: No matter how long you persist exclusively in practicing shamatha, it will not become Vipashyana. No matter how much you develop the principal shamatha qualities of stability and clarity, it will not bring about Vipashyana. Shamatha is very good, important, and necessary to do and is extremely helpful and very beneficial. But techniques of shamatha will not bring about Vipashyana.

Vipashyana means "the prajna that realizes in a very precise way." In shamatha we look at mind, but not at what mind is. Looking at our mind, we assess the mind's stability, clarity, wildness, and so forth. But we aren't examining what is mind? What it its shape? What is its color? Does it have any of those qualities? That isn't part of the practice of shamatha.

The Buddha says in the *Prajnaparamita*, "Form does not exist, feelings do not exist, discriminations do not exist," and so forth. In this list of things, starting with the second one, feelings, we are talking about mind. When we look for the mind, we find that we aren't a long way off. These things are nearby, and we can just look at them. But we find nothing there at all. Well, if there is nothing there at all, does that mean mind is nothing more that a corpse? No, because the mind's emptiness is infiltrated by luminosity. Sometimes we talk about this as the "union of space and wisdom" (Skt. *dhatu* and *jnana*), where space refers to emptiness and wisdom refers to luminous clarity. If we experience that, that is Vipashyana.

Question: Is the term translated as "*superimposition*" the term that we sometimes understand as projection?

Translator: I don't know. The Tibetan is *dron dok* with *dron* meaning "feathers" and *dok* meaning "attaching." It literally means "attaching feathers to things." It means only adding things that are not there. That is only half the story. The other half would be taking away things that are there. Another term is used to describe the other half of the story, saying something doesn't exist when it does. For instance, saying there is no such thing as a result of one's actions, or karma. That is not superimposition, that is *gur dep* or deprecation, such as saying the Buddha is not enlightened or literally "hurling insults at something.

Chapter 11

The True Nature of Mind

X. THE STAGES OF VIRTUOUS PRACTICE

[213] We will now examine Tashi Nagyal's section called "The Stages of Virtuous Practice" which has several parts to it. The first part of the chapter here discusses the mind as it is and the second part discusses coemergence. The first part has three sections: what the mind is or the essence of mind; the nature of mind, and the definitive characteristics of mind. This discussion is not from the point of view of meditative experience. It is an explanation that is to be studied and examined with one's prajna.

A. THE SYSTEM OF MAHAMUDRA MEDITATION

1. THE TRUE NATURE OF MIND

[213] The essence (Tib. *ngo wo*) of mind is luminosity (Tib. *salwa*). When we say the essence of mind is "luminous and clear," we suggest it is like light. But that is not so because the Tibetan word *salwa* has the meaning of "knowing" rather than light. Furthermore, this essence of mind is peacefulness, which is to say it is mind without discursive thought and conception.

[216] The nature (Skt. *svabhava*, Tib. *rang bzhin)*[30] of mind is that it is not produced, it does not abide, and it does not cease. If the mind were an actual thing, then it could be produced, it would eventually cease, and in between these two it would abide. However, when one examines carefully, one sees that the mind is not produced, it does not cease, and it does not rest between these two. Therefore one can say that the mind is not truly existent, that mind is empty (Skt. *shunyata*). One can also say that it is the sphere of reality (Skt. *dharmadhatu*). In the word dharmadhatu is the syllable *dhatu* that basically means "that which offers no obstruction." If one were

talking about space, one would say space is everywhere and there is no place one wouldn't find space. Therefore, anything can come into the space and pass through the space, but nothing will ever be limited by the space.[31] Here, the notion of non-obstruction indicates principally, that there is an opportunity for anything to appear without anything obstructing it. It is not like a mountain which stands in the way of something. So, that is the notion of *dhatu*. When this is connected with the syllable *dharma*, the dharmadhatu means that place where it is completely suitable to abandon faults and a place for all the good qualities to increase. So, if one were to say that mind is empty and is dharmadhatu, one would be saying it is not inherently established and it is free from creation, abiding, and cessation.

[218] The characteristic of the mind is that it appears as samsara and nirvana. Because the mind is not a solid entity, it can appear as samsara and as nirvana. It might seem to us, to ordinary persons, that the appearing of samsara is contradictory to appearing as nirvana, but it isn't a contradiction.

A discussion of the view of the Madhyamaka or Middle-way School will help us to understand this point. There are two aspects to the Middle-way school: the *Svatantrika* and the *Prasangika* School. The Svatantrika School is a lower view than the Prasangika School. In the Svatantrika School, relative or conventional reality refers to appearance and absolute or ultimate reality refers to emptiness. So appearances appear on the relative level, but they are empty on the absolute level. However, there is some sense of contradiction between them. Still, the way things are explained in the Svatantrika School is very helpful when we are beginning to understand emptiness.

The explanation presented by the Prasangika School is somewhat higher. In this school emptiness and appearance are not contradictory to one another. Appearances are themselves empty. And emptiness itself goes right with the dependent arising of appearances. Just as things appear, so they are empty. Just as they are empty, so they appear. Thus the *Heart Sutra* says, "Form is emptiness, emptiness is form. Form is no other than emptiness, emptiness is no other than form." When it says that form is emptiness, it is saying that the very nature of form is emptiness. When it says that emptiness is form, it says the very nature of emptiness is this form. Form is not something other than emptiness, emptiness is not something other than form. They exist together. It is like the appearance of an elephant in a dream. The elephant appears in one's dream, the elephant is seen, but in fact there is no elephant actually there. Even though one sees an elephant, it doesn't exist. The non-existence of this elephant and the appearance of this elephant might seem contradictory, but in fact they occur together.

When we are on the path of inference, then we consider form and emptiness as being like the elephant that appears in a dream. We come to understand the non-inherent existence of various phenomena in this way. However, when we are on the path of direct perception, we look straight into our mind and see mind as emptiness, as lacking inherent existence. However, the mind's emptiness does not come about from looking or not looking into the mind. Mind lacks inherent existence when we look at mind and when we are not looking at it. The mind is there from the beginning of time without any inherent existence. It is primordially free of production, cessation, and abiding. This then is the nature of mind and the characteristic of mind.

2. THE MEANING OF THE COEMERGENCE OF MIND

[220] The second part of the chapter on the stages of virtuous practice discusses *coemergence* (Tib. *sangye chepa*) which could also be translated as "innate," because it quite literally means "born together." Coemergence refers to the fact that the wisdom (Skt. *jnana*) that realizes the true nature of phenomena,[32] is already present within us. It is not something that is newly generated at some point, but it exists within us already. Although we have this wisdom, we have not realized it. Because we have not realized things as they are, or mahamudra, we suffer the distorted states of mind called disturbing emotions within samsara. We speak of *coemergent wisdom* as a way of connecting with the reality of things that are already present within us.

(a) THE TERMINOLOGY OF COEMERGENCE

[221] First of all, we need to understand what the term coemergent means. When we are speaking about coemergence, we are not talking

about something other than the mind's true nature. Coemergence is the mind's way of being or we could say the mind's true nature. Thus, we would say that by coemergence we mean the clear light that is like space and that is the sovereign of all of samsara and nirvana. When we are speaking about coemergence, we are talking also about the inseparability of emptiness and luminosity. These two are not contradictory. Ordinary people such as ourselves, when we understand something about the emptiness of the mind, we do not understand its luminosity; and when we understand something about the luminosity of the mind, we misunderstand its emptiness. But in fact these two are perfectly integrated and they are not separate things. The emptiness of the mind is not an emptiness that negates luminosity; it is the utter groundlessness of the mind. And the luminosity of the mind does not solidify its ability to know. From that point of view, emptiness and luminosity are not contradictory in any way. They are coemergent.

What about the term coemergence itself? What emerges together is phenomena (Skt. *dharma*) and their essence or suchness (Skt. *dharmata*). To begin, there are phenomena which are stable and phenomena which move (animate and inanimate). That's one way of talking about what we experience. At the same time, there is the reality (Skt. *dharmata)*. There are the appearances of phenomena and there is the real nature or essence of those things.[33] This can be described in slightly different terms: the union of appearance (phenomena) and emptiness (their true nature). We tend to treat appearances or phenomena as being external to us and having inherent nature and as being real things. The appearance of things and their suchness—their reality, their emptiness—do not follow one another with one of them happening first and the other happening later. It is not, the case, for instance, that first things exist and later they become empty. Rather, the appearance of things and their emptiness are simultaneous. Nor is it the case that when we meditate upon reality, we somehow bring that coemergence and that emptiness into being, and that when we do not meditate, coemergence is not the nature of things. It is just that we do not understand and do not realize the coemergence that is the nature of the mind and the nature of phenomena. Through meditating, we begin to understand it.

(b) TYPES OF COEMERGENCE

[222] There are a variety of types of coemergent wisdom. In the teachings of the Buddha in the sutras and the siddhas coemergent wisdom is divided into ground, path, and fruition coemergent wisdom.

Ground coemergent wisdom is the reality of luminosity and emptiness, the mind in its basic nature which has always existed within us. However, because we have not realized this, we have to listen to a guru's teaching, think upon what we have heard, and meditate upon what we have understood. When coemergent wisdom is born within us, this is referred to as path coemergent wisdom. When we become accustomed to coemergent wisdom and our familiarity with it increases further and further, eventually all of the adventitious stains upon the mind are eliminated and cleared away, and all good qualities blossom fully. At that point we achieve what is called the supreme siddhi or enlightenment which is the fruition of coemergent wisdom.

In addition to these three types of coemergent wisdom, two more are described. The tantras of the vajrayana include contemplative practices involving the manipulation of the subtle winds (Skt. *prana*) and working with the subtle channels (Skt. *nadi*) and the subtle drops (Skt. *bindu*). Through these practices there arise the fourth type of coemergence. And finally, there is the unity of bliss and emptiness, referred to as the coemergent wisdom of bliss and emptiness, the fifth type of coemergent wisdom.

The categories of coemergence just covered are those that are discussed in the sutras and tantras. Other ways of speaking about coemergence have also been given by great teachers in the Kagyu lineage based upon their own experience.

THE INSTRUCTIONS OF GAMPOPA

[222] Though the presentation of coemergent wisdom in the tantras and the treatises composed by the siddhas (Skt. *shastras*) are very clear, they are not joined with the quintessential instructions.

Therefore it is very helpful to look at the quintessential instructions that were given by Gampopa which describe coemergence and the practice of meditation. Gampopa describes two types of coemergence: coemergence of mind and coemergence of appearances.

The coemergence of mind refers to the point of realization when shamatha and Vipashyana have been integrated so that we realize mind as it is: empty, luminous, and free from any complexity. At that time we rest in this true essence of mind. Mind has a resourcefulness that does not cease. That resourcefulness is a power of the mind and this power dawns as various appearances. Because those appearances have not passed beyond the nature of mind, they are called "coemergent appearances." This is how we join the instructions on coemergence with the practice of meditation.

GOMCHUNG'S THREE TYPES OF COEMERGENCE

[223] One of Gampopa's students, known as Gomchung (which in Tibetan means "small meditator"), developed Gampopa's terminology somewhat further to help students understand their experience. He pointed out that we have many different types of thoughts and emotions, for example, joy and passion. We might think of them as good or bad, but whatever thoughts are churned up, they are nothing other than mind itself. They never go beyond being mind and they are nothing other than luminosity with no independent nature of their own. It is not as if the mind were one thing and the thoughts were something else.

Gomchung described three types of coemergence. First, there is "coemergent mind itself," which could be regarded as the dharmakaya. Second there is "coemergent appearance," which could be regarded metaphorically as the light of the dharmakaya. And third there is "coemergent thought," which could be considered as the waves of the dharmakaya. Just as the ocean's waves are not separate from the ocean itself, so thoughts are not separate from mind itself. So there are three types of coemergence: coemergent mind itself, dharmakaya; coemergent appearance, which is like the light of dharmakaya; and coemergent thought which is like the waves of dharmakaya.

There is a term that we need to understand: "application of coemergence" or "connection to coemergence." In the tantras and the shastras of the great siddhas, coemergence is spoken of as ground, path, and fruition. In the quintessential instructions, coemergence is spoken about as mind, appearance, and thought. Then the instruction on mahamudra is called "unification of coemergence." Well then, what does that mean?

There are three elements: mind, thought, and dharmakaya. First of all, mind just means one's mind. Thought means one's mind having become confused and agitated and coarse. Dharmakaya refers to the wisdom that realizes things as they are ultimately. Originally these three were together; later they appeared to us to be separate; then with the oral instructions on mahamudra, it is explained that these are just mind and are unified again. So these three seem to separate and then by the practitioner relying upon the instructions given by a teacher, they are united again. This is why the instruction of mahamudra is referred to as "the instruction that unites these coemergent elements." Mahamudra is the method that enables one to realize them as coemergent, as existing together.

Gomchung further states that the coemergence of mind itself is the actual dharmakaya. What this means it that the mind's way of being, a union of luminosity and emptiness, from the very first is not established. The mind's integration of luminosity-emptiness, when realized such that it becomes manifest for the yogin's or yogini's experience, is the actual dharmakaya. Once this dharmakaya has been recognized, then something further can be understood. Gomchung states: "The coemergence of appearance is the light of dharmakaya." This is to say, various things do appear; this dawns, that dawns, the other dawns. All kinds of things appear. But because one has understood them to be an integration or union of luminosity and emptiness, one does not conceive them to be true or real. Rather, you understand that they have no nature of their own. And because you understand that they have no nature of their own, you develop the wisdom of dharmakaya. Many different thoughts arise, but these thoughts have no nature of their own. When they are not misconceived to have a nature of their own, they are found to be the waves of the dharmakaya. The inseparability of mind, appearance, and thoughts is the actual dharmakaya, and it is the same as the meaning of dharmakaya. In other words, there is the dharmakaya which is the undifferentiability of coemergent mind, coemergent appearance, and coemergent thought. At the same time, dharmakaya has a meaning. What is its meaning? The undifferentiable coemergence of those three. When we speak about them as undifferentiable, what we mean is it's not the case, for instance, that mind is good and thoughts are bad or that appearance is good and mind is bad. Rather, these are inseparable and undifferentiable; and from that point of view, they are coemergent.

HAMOTRUBA'S COEMERGENCE

There is another term that is famous in the tradition of mahamudra in regard to coemergence, and it's called "the joining of coemergence." When Gampopa spoke about the joining of coemergence, what he meant was looking at thought from different points of view and seeing in thought the four embodiments of enlightenment (the four kayas). That's one way of thinking about it. This was then taken further by one of Gampopa's students, Hamotruba. Hamotruba applies this notion of the joining of coemergence to the three elements: mind, thought, and dharmakaya. These three exist together. Mind, thought, and dharmakaya are naturally from the very first joined. However, we don't realize that is the case. Through the instructions given in the tradition of the practice of mahamudra, it becomes possible for the practitioner to see and discover the undifferentiability of these three. And when the student does this, that is called "the joining of coemergence."

B. THREE ASPECTS OF COEMERGENCE

[225] In this section we will begin looking at what is called (1) pointing out coemergent mind, (2) pointing out coemergent thought, and (3) pointing out coemergent appearance. Basically what's being discussed is the nature of coemergence. The focus is changed slightly from the last chapter. Here we are talking about discriminating among the different experiences we might have when we are meditating. So now we need to identify which is actually the experience of coemergence. The meaning being discussed concerns

pretty much the same thing. But the value of looking at it again and again from many different points of view is that, gradually, the meaning becomes more and more clear.

1. COEMERGENT MIND

[225] The appearances to mind, the mind itself, and mind's lack of inherent existence: these three go together as what we call coemergence. One might think that the existence of something conventionally, and the nonexistence of that thing ultimately are different things. In fact, it is not so. They go together and their being together is coemergence. Gampopa said that mind is coemergent, thoughts are coemergent, and appearances are coemergent.

Saying the mind is free from production, from cessation, and from resting does not mean that it is dead like a corpse. Rather, it indicates freedom from these three. In the context of the sutras, we say it is the union of luminosity and emptiness. Because that luminosity has an aspect of bliss to it, we say in the context of the tantra that there is a union of bliss and emptiness. In the sutra context, we speak about a union of the two truths, relative and absolute truth which are not separate from one another. All this is concerned with the way in which mind itself is coemergent.

We approach coemergence of mind by examining coemergent mind itself. The initial step is to settle into shamatha and then the mind looks at itself. In looking at itself, the mind does not stop thought, but rather the mind simply purifies itself and becomes at peace with itself. At that point, it cannot be identified as anything at all. The mind rests vividly and clearly in its own state. This is a state of awareness that does not become dull or unclear. Mind doesn't wander anywhere, but remains clear and luminous. The text says that "the mind itself remains luminous and does not stop understanding." The mind doesn't lose its intelligence. It is said that at that point it is aware of itself and is illuminating itself. But if we were to ask how it does this, it cannot actually be explained, but has to be experienced. Even though we cannot actually express this state, we can say that it is an experience of knowing things as they are. We can further say that it gives rise to real certainty, so we know exactly what it is. That's the experience of Vipashyana.

We begin this meditation when our mind is free from sinking and wildness and we rest in a very relaxed way. Then simply by looking at itself, thought is pacified. This brings forth the experience of shamatha in the context of mahamudra. This shamatha or resting in peace is not mere equanimity.

We then investigate the qualities of luminosity and emptiness. If our mind appears to be luminous and vivid, we then look into that asking just what is that vividness? If our mind seems to be empty, we investigate that emptiness. What is that emptiness? How is it empty? These are not questions that we need to put to someone else because we answer them from our own experience. When we understand that, it is given the name Vipashyana. Within that experience, the quality of stability is regarded as shamatha and the prajna or intelligence that realizes the nature of things is given the name Vipashyana. However, they are not two separate things. That's simply a way of talking about different aspects of one thing because at that point shamatha and Vipashyana are united and integrated. When one's experience of this settles, that is called coemergent mind.

2. COEMERGENT THOUGHT

[229] Now thoughts are also coemergent. Sometimes the mind and its thoughts seem to be different things and at other times they seem to be similar. For instance, in Milarepa's song to Palpapung he says that mind is like an ocean and thoughts are like waves on this ocean. Waves do appear and arise in the ocean and one sees them. However, they are not different from the ocean itself. Similarly, thoughts appear and are perceived but are no different from the mind. However, in certain circumstances they seem to be something other than mind. When we say mind, we mean chiefly the factor of luminosity, and when we say thoughts we mean the various things; that come from the mind—joy, suffering, desire, devotion. However, when particular sensations appear these things are called discursive thoughts. For instance, when we described the five aggregates, we discussed the aggregates as mind (Tib. *sem*) or as mental factors (Tib. *sem jung*). The mind and the mental factors are the eight consciousnesses. Mental factors refer to various states and transformations that come about within this factor of luminous

clarity such as feeling, discrimination, and the other fifty-one mental factors.

As for these thoughts, mind is their nature. However, they are experienced and seem to be something coarse. Jampal Dzangpo, in the Kagyu Lineage Supplication, begins one stanza with, "The nature of thought is dharmakaya." Some scholars may say that doesn't make any sense because how could these confused thoughts and the pure dharmakaya be the same thing? They have a point, for if you consider all the different aspects you will have to say there are some ways that thoughts are not dharmakaya. However, in the context of meditative experience, the nature of thoughts is dharmadhatu, and dharmadhatu is dharmakaya. From that point of view the nature of thoughts is dharmakaya. In that way thoughts are coemergent. The mind and thoughts seem to be different on the conventional level. But in the experience of meditation, the nature of mind (Tib. *ngeluk*) is dharmadhatu and the nature of thoughts is dharmadhatu; thus their nature is the same and in that way they are not different.

Other people misunderstand the teaching "thought is dharmakaya" to mean that when a thought arises, it has been pacified, which is to say when it has dissolved we are then left with dharmakaya. Still others misunderstand "thought is dharmakaya" to mean if we don't realize that thought is dharmakaya, then it's not dharmakaya. However the word dharmakaya is made up of *dharma* meaning "the truth," and *kaya* meaning "embodiment." Thus, dharmakaya refers to the ultimate mind of the Buddha. So there are these two ways of misunderstanding what it means to say that "thoughts are dharmakaya." Both of these are a misunderstanding of the fact that from the very beginning, thought is nothing other than the reality of the Buddha's omniscient mind. It is, from the very beginning, the ultimate reality. It doesn't become dharmakaya at some later time, and it doesn't depend upon whether you are aware that thought is dharmakaya or not. Thought is identical with reality.

In the *Four Dharmas of Gampopa*,[34] the first dharma is, "May the mind go into the dharma." The second dharma is "May the dharma go on the path." The third is, "May the path destroy confusion." And the fourth is "May confusion dawn as wisdom." The fourth dharma refers to thoughts. When one looks into the nature of the thoughts, one sees the union of luminosity and emptiness. In that way thoughts are seen to be of the very nature of wisdom. That is what is indicated by the fourth dharma of Gampopa.

Now we will discuss how we experience coemergent thought. We begin with meditative equipoise of coemergent mind and within that state, we deliberately cause a particular thought to arise. This is the procedure discussed earlier when we were identifying coemergent thought of deliberately creating a strong thought. It might be a pleasant or an unpleasant thought. We give rise to it so that it is very vivid and sharp. When it arises, we look right at it nakedly. It's important that the way this thought appears be vivid and clear, not just an ordinary thought. In this context, the thought is regarded as not truly existent, so when it arises, we don't latch onto it as if it were some real thing.

What is the nature of that thought that arises from within coemergent mind itself? It is an emptiness that cannot be identified as this or that. Its nature cannot be fixed as this or that. Still, the thought is vivid and clear, and the clarity of that thought is inseparable from its emptiness. These two—the luminous aspect of thought and the emptiness that is its nature—are inseparable. When this thought arises without any obstruction and the meditator does not become attached to it, then that's shamatha. When the meditator sees that this thought has no nature of its own, that's Vipashyana. To accomplish the meditation fully, shamatha and Vipashyana must be completely integrated.

Why do we need to point out coemergence of thought? We tend to think that we must meditate with a relaxed, peaceful state of mind that is isolated from conceptual activity; and indeed it is very helpful to do so. However, that is not the only way to meditate. In fact, just the opposite is true. It is also helpful to meditate with lots of thoughts to recognize the nature of mind. If one can meditate in that way it is extremely helpful. Therefore there is the instruction of pointing out coemergence of thought.

One begins by meditating within the samadhi or stabilized mind in which the recognition of the mind's nature and the mind resting in peace in shamatha are united. Within that, we cause rough sorts of thoughts such as pleasure and joy, or passion and aggression to arise. Because they seem to be very strong, very vivid, they are described as quite coarse. Whatever thoughts they are, whether pleasure or revulsion, we look directly at what they are. We look right at the thought itself. We look to see where this thought arises from? Where does it dwell? And when it leaves, where does it go? We look directly at it. What is it? Where is it? We look clearly and precisely and when we do so, the meaning of coemergent mind itself and the meaning of coemergent thought are the same.

We tend to see the coarse mind and peaceful mind as different, but in fact the nature of coarse mind and the nature of peaceful mind are the same. The mind's nature does not change when its state changes. These rough states of mind might appear to be something, but in fact they have never been born. This thought isn't what it seems to be. At this point this realization is not just a theory to be deduced, rather it's something that is seen directly. This is why we say in the Kagyu Lineage chant, "Whatever thoughts arise, their nature is dharmakaya," which means that the nature of thought is itself mind itself, dharmakaya.

3. COEMERGENT APPEARANCE

[233] Later Gampopa's student Gomchung separated coemergence to make it easier to understand. What we have been discussing is the pointing out of coemergence of appearances as it pertains to feelings of pleasure and pain, and so on. Here, we are talking about pointing out coemergent appearance as it applies to external things such as colors, shapes, sounds, and so on. We are talking about investigating the appearance of colors, shapes, sounds, and smells that appear in common perception and that arise because of the actions that all of the people who inhabit the environment have performed in a similar way. We experience an environment as having common features, features that we apprehend in common.

We begin the meditation by resting in the meditative equipoise of coemergent mind itself, as that has been previously explained, and look at mind itself. Then we pay attention to what is appearing as external phenomena, such as a vase, buildings, or houses. At this point, we might experience some difficulty. The reason is that in the past, we have established very strong habitual tendencies to see things as external to ourselves. So we think that the mountain is outside and that the mind is inside and that the mind is looking out at the thing that's outside. Practicing this meditation is a little uncomfortable at first because we are introduced to that appearance as simply being regarded as an aspect of our mind. That is, it's not that the eye is looking at a mountain; rather, there is an appearance of the luminosity of our own mind as a mountain. The appearance is part of the perceptive fabric of the mind itself and is nothing other than the mind's innate luminosity. It is not something outside the mind.

When this array of color and shape appears, the meditator does not stop or allow this to become vague. Furthermore, the practice at this point is not a matter of just looking at the mind itself and experiencing luminosity and emptiness, but rather the meditator is looking nakedly at whatever aspect appears. However, the luminosity of that appearance is of a nature that is impossible to identify. It is an emptiness that cannot be grasped and fixed upon. And that's the sort of coemergent luminosity and emptiness and coemergent appearance that the meditator is working with in this phase.

Lingjerepa said: "The mind itself, which is groundless and rootless, is well understood by thinking about last night's dreams. Last night's dreams are an excellent teacher for pointing out appearance as just mind." He concludes by saying, "Do you understand that?" So, the point is that when we dream, all kinds of things appear but when we awaken, we realize that these appearances were nothing other than the mind itself. Dreams, then, are a wonderful teacher for they help us to understand that the appearances in waking life are also nothing other than mind.

A further way to look at appearances is when thoughts appear they have no nature of their own. That is what is called "the union of appearance and emptiness." Whether we realize this union of appearance with emptiness or not doesn't make any difference in what their nature is. With regard to the way things appear to a particular person, there is a difference between realizing the union of appearance and emptiness and not realizing it. But the fact remains that emptiness is the nature of things whether we realize it or not. When we understand this in meditation, we realize coemergent thought.

There is a very practical use for this realization of coemergent thought. When we experience great joy and pleasure and become strongly attracted to this pleasure or when we experience strong pain and are quite miserable, we give birth to disturbing emotions or kleshas. These are painful and cause hardship and our minds become very disturbed. It is at times like this when this teaching on coemergent thought is particularly valuable. If we look directly at the pain that we are experiencing, such as the kleshas, they will be pacified. And if we look directly at the strong attachment, it will diminish. This is the real purpose for understanding and being able to practice this coemergence of thought.

The proponents of the Chittamatra school hold that all appearances are just mind. But this is not what is being talked about here in relation to coemergence of thought. The Cittamatrins say that all appearances are mind only, which includes solid external things such as mountains and buildings. They say apparently solid external phenomena are, in fact, nothing other than the appearances of internal mind, and are not truly external things. While what they say is true, that is not what is being pointed out here. Here the term "appearances" refers not to external appearances such as mountains and so forth, but it refers primarily to the experiential sense of perceiving something, such as seeing a visible form or hearing a sound. There is some feeling that goes with that perceptual experience. We aren't trying to make a point about whether or not apparently external phenomena is external and real. We are simply looking at the experience we have of seeing and hearing, and so forth. We are looking directly at that and as we do, we see the truth of the matter. Then that experience becomes inseparable from dharmata and this experience doesn't go beyond mind itself.

We must realize that "coemergent thought" and "coemergent appearance" are different ways of speaking about one nature, not different natures.

Questions

Question: Appearances are not established as what they appear to be. Why is that? Is it because things do not exist in the way that they appear?

Rinpoche: This is to be understood in terms of coemergent appearance, which means that whatever appears one inquires into the way in which it appears. The seeing of it and the hearing of it is not done from the point of view of inference; it is direct experience, it is direct perception. When one talks about illusion-like appearance in the context of inferential reasoning, one says things such as, "Because things are empty of inherent existence, therefore they are like illusions." That is not what we are talking about here. Here what is being discussed is coemergent appearance. It is looking directly at the experience, or in fact we could say the "experiencing," if you understand what we mean.

Question: Rinpoche, I wonder if you could say more about the Tibetan word *salwa* which is being translated as luminosity?

Rinpoche: When we describe the mind as luminous and empty the word "luminous" might suggest light, but that is not what it means. Rather, to say mind is luminous is to say that the mind knows, that the mind understands. That is what it means to say that the mind is luminous. At the same time it is empty because it isn't anything and it cannot be located.

For instance, we speak about an eye consciousness, something that sees physical forms, colors and shapes. But if we look for it, where is it? It isn't anywhere, we can never find it. That is emptiness. Even though we cannot find it, nevertheless, the eye consciousness does see colors and shapes, and that seeing is called its luminosity.

Similarly, although the ear consciousness hears sounds, it can never be found. But it does hear sounds, and that hearing is called its luminosity. This is true for the five sensory consciousnesses (eye, ear, nose, tongue, and body sensation) and also the sixth, mental consciousness. Where is the mental consciousness? Is it in the upper part or the lower portion of the body or in the body at all? Is it outside the body? No matter where we look for it, we will never find it. Nevertheless, it remembers; it is attentive. Sometimes the mental consciousness is very rough, and at other times it is very subtle. The mental consciousness can realize its own nature. It is the mental consciousness that perceives all appearances of *samsara*. It understands and this understanding is described as its luminosity. So we say the union of luminosity and emptiness.

Question: I heard that the mind has no inherent nature, but it has qualities like luminosity, so that means that things can have qualities without existing. Can we have my personality, my nature, my inherent way of being, which can exist without my mind?

Rinpoche: The mind itself is empty and at the same time it has the aspect of luminosity. People have their own individual characteristics or personality. We're talking now about the relationship between the ultimate and the relative. In the context of the conventional truth, there is a sense of something that is covering up and hiding something else. From this point of view everyone has their own particular qualities: some are proud, others angry, still others kind and compassionate. No question about it.

But in reality none of this exists, it is empty; there is nothing there. Because it is empty, good qualities and wisdom can develop. Because things have no real existence, faults can be purified. These qualities are not in the true nature of things, they are just superficial additions and don't need to be there. So we say that because defilements are only add-ons or adventitious, therefore they can be purified. How can they be purified? By realizing this lack of any real existence, the ultimate truth.

Question: I don't understand the difference between coemergent thought and coemergent appearance because I think of thought as no different from your description of appearance or mind, that is, there is a mental phenomenon going on.

Rinpoche: First of all, "coemergent thought" and "coemergent appearance" are ways of speaking about one nature, not different natures. That is why Gampopa classified the different types of coemergence into two: coemergent mind itself and coemergent appearance. Later another teacher, Tsultrim Nyingpo, who is known by the name Gomchung, subdivided one of those two groups, "coemergent appearance" into two, "coemergent thought" and "coemergent appearance." When that division is made, coemergent appearance refers to the different appearances of visible images, sounds, etc. or the appearances of the five sense consciousnesses. The phrase coemergent thought refers to the various appearances for the sixth mental consciousness.

Question: Are samsara and nirvana inseparable because thoughts are confusion and thoughts are empty?

Rinpoche: Yes, basically that is right. We can talk about samsara and nirvana that way. Thoughts are mistaken yet we speak about confusion dawning as wisdom. We are not saying confusion is wisdom. But what we are saying is that confusion is not established primordially and therefore it can dawn as wisdom.

Question: I have two questions. The first question is regarding the Tibetan word *sem* being referred to as mind. Does this include the eight consciousnesses or just the sixth one.

Rinpoche: The mind, or in Tibetan *sem,* generally speaking refers to all eight consciousnesses. However, in this context, the one that is doing the principal work is the sixth consciousness, which is called "mental consciousness." This is because the seventh and eighth consciousnesses are somewhat covered over and they do not identify very much. Then there are the five sensory consciousnesses which are non-conceptual. So, at this point what we are principally talking about is the sixth or mental consciousness. Then in terms of the five aggregates, the first aggregate of form refers to body and the fifth refers to the six consciousness. And the second aggregate feeling, third aggregate discrimination, and the fourth aggregate formation are the mental factors.

Question: When you're doing sitting practice, after a period of time, the mind settles and luminosity begins to come and there always seems to be an observer. Can you expand a little bit on the observer and what it is and how to work with it?

Rinpoche: Yes, one does have the sense of a watcher. That watcher is *namtok* or discursive thought. And if one looks very closely into it, then where is it? It isn't really there. But, I don't think that beginners ought to worry about this very much. There is a story in a sutra in which the Buddha explained that one has a sense of a looker and something looked at, but that it is like rubbing two sticks together to make fire. When fire starts, it burns both of the sticks up. It is like that in your meditation. If you go along in stages, then the two of them will just become nonexistent like the sticks burning up.

Question: Rinpoche, I have a small problem trying to connect the sort of understanding of emptiness that one arrives at through inference and reasoning with the direct perception of emptiness when one looks straight into one's mind. It seems that both are path. It seems that in the first, the emptiness by inference, there should be some nonconceptual aspect of it that would assist or help us with the discovery of emptiness when we look directly at our minds. Could you discuss that?

Rinpoche: The Buddha spoke of the sutra path and the tantric or mantra path. The sutra path is principally just the path of inference. On this path one receives the teachings just of inference, which is a long and protracted path. The sutras say, to reach Buddhahood in this way requires three *kalpas* with each kalpa lasting millions of years. So one needs to accumulate merit and wisdom for centuries to develop certainty about the nature of things. In accumulation of merit, the certainty about the nature of things becomes clearer and clearer until one arrives at direct perception, meaning a nonconceptual state. In this sutra path one has not been introduced to something by a guru. Rather, this realization comes about through one's own ascertainment. In this way one achieves first the path of accumulation, then the path of unification, and then the path of seeing. On the path of seeing one has direct perception of emptiness as being the path in the sutra system. Then comes the path of meditation, and fifth the path of no more learning which is Buddhahood. So that is the way one goes about it in the sutra path.

In the vajrayana one takes direct perception as the path. In this path, millions of years are not required for achieving enlightenment. Rather, having renounced the world, enlightenment can be achieved in this lifetime. Even if one does not succeed at that, then in two or three human lifetimes one will achieve complete enlightenment. In this vajrayana path the guru introduces you to direct perception and you meditate not by analyzing external things, but by meditating simply on the mind to which you have been introduced. Even though you have been introduced to such direct perception, sometimes it is not stable. When this happens, it is very good to study the presentations that are made in the path of reasoning and inference. This will help you to develop stability in what you have ascertained and will help to bring about good experience and realization.

Some people, having been introduced to this nature of mind, think that "I can just forget the sutras and shastras because I have the transmission and I don't need any of that." That is not really so because studying the sutras and shastras will help bring about a very stable, clear meditation in terms of the nature of mind, which the guru has introduced.

Question: Rinpoche, it seems possible to imagine seeing mind and even thoughts as empty and luminous, but I can't imagine as seeing the body as empty and luminous.

Rinpoche: At this point in the presentation of mahamudra we are pointing at the nature of mind. By knowing the nature of mind, we begin to understand the nature of all phenomena. When we proceed by the inferential path, then the analysis of external phenomena is extremely important. However, when we proceed by the direct perception path, because the mind is already right with us and we can look directly into it, it is an easier path. The examination of the nature of mind in the path of direct perception goes like this: Appearances are mind, mind is empty, and this emptiness is spontaneous. When we proceed in this way, first we must resolve that external appearances are mind. We do this by using the two logical arguments of clear and knowing, and the argument of the definite observation to the together. We look into all these external appearances and how they appear clearly and vividly to consciousness. But they are not existent except from the perspective of consciousness. We next determine external phenomena are just appearances for mind. We do this using our body which is merely an appearance for mind like the elephant in the dream. Also by examining mental factors, we would say that the body is an appearance for mind, not a mental factor. It is an appearance of mind and it is an appearance to mind, in short, it is an appearance for mind, it is mind appearing. How this comes about is through predispositions that have been established formerly with the alaya or the eighth consciousness. The mahasiddha Lingje Respa spoke about this in a spiritual song. The song says that when we go to sleep and we dream, these appearances in dreams are the teacher in the way in which all appearances are mind.

Chapter 12

Eliminating Flaws that may arise in Mahamudra Meditation

C. ELIMINATING FLAWS THAT MAY ARISE IN MAHAMUDRA

[237] We have discussed coemergence of the mind itself, of thought, and of appearance. In particular we spoke of the methods for pointing out coemergence with regard to these three aspects of experience. After these are pointed out, we meditate on mind. And when we meditate, sometimes our meditation is mistaken. Sometimes it is simply that our meditation doesn't go well, and at other times even though it goes well, it is not complete. So it is important to know the ways in which our meditation can go astray and the ways in which it might be incomplete.

The two benefits to understanding how meditation might be flawed is that we can avoid those faults in our own practice; and second, that in teaching others, our understanding of the ways in which meditation might go badly or be incomplete can help others eliminate faults in their meditation. For that reason the text goes into these matters in some detail.

1. FLAWS OF INCORRECT MEDITATION

(a) QUALITIES OF GOOD SHAMATHA MEDITATION

[237] Before discussing the faults of having a lack of Vipashyana meditation, we begin by discussing the three positive qualities of shamatha meditation before discussing the faults of having a lack of Vipashyana meditation. The excellent qualities of shamatha meditation include the experience of the three qualities of pleasant

body and mental sensations, extreme lucidity, and non-conceptuality. These three qualities indicate excellent shamatha meditation, but to develop complete mahamudra it is necessary to go further to completion the definitive characteristics of excellent meditation.

The second quality of excellent meditation that must be brought to completion is that our meditation must be joined with bodhichitta. Bodhichitta is a Sanskrit word that means "mind of enlightenment" or "heart of enlightenment." It requires what is called "arousing the mind of bodhichitta," meaning that our meditation needs to be joined with an extremely pure motivation. We could think of it in this way: the practice of meditation is very pleasant, it is delightful, and we might practice just for that nice sensation. But this is only a very temporary happiness. Meditation by itself will not eliminate the disturbing emotions, which are to be abandoned, nor will it bring about all the good qualities of a fully enlightened person. We must practice in such a way as to eliminate all disturbing emotions and to achieve all the good qualities. More importantly, achieving enlightenment for ourselves alone would not do much for anyone else at all, and that is unacceptable.

In this world alone there are billions and billions of human beings and animals who live scattered all over the earth, on mountains, in forests, on plains, in the ocean. For these beings happiness is extremely rare. They experience nothing but suffering and they have no protector whatsoever. If I myself were to achieve the complete enlightenment of a buddha, I would then have the ability and the courage to free others and to show others the path that leads to freedom from the pain of samsara. This is the attitude that we need when we practice meditation. If we practice with this attitude, it will be a very pure practice and will lead to vast results. If we don't think in this way, the result will not be very extensive.

It is very good to have two qualities of good stable meditation and the mind of enlightenment, however, we need a third quality: the realization of emptiness and selflessness. The Buddha spoke about emptiness in everything he taught. If we realize emptiness then we are able to abandon all the disturbing emotions and bring forth the wisdom that realizes the nature of everything perfectly and clearly (Skt. *jnana*). Unless we understand emptiness, our meditation will only temporarily weaken the habitual patterns of the kleshas. So we need to go further and understand the true nature of things as empty of self.

In order to realize the quintessential instructions of mahamudra and the coemergence of thought and appearance, we need to recognize not only the resting mind, but the nature of that mind. We need to see what that resting mind is. Furthermore, we need to understand it not only from an inferential understanding but from direct observation. When we realize emptiness directly we have understood the nature of phenomena and that is called Vipashyana. Therefore, in addition to the mind merely resting in shamatha and having great bodhichitta, we also need the Vipashyana that realizes the nature of phenomena.

When we have some experience of these three qualities of samadhi, bodhichitta, and Vipashyana we have a fully qualified meditation. Yet we might have different sorts of problems and make different sorts of mistakes when we try to develop our meditation experience further. This may be because we don't understand the dharma very well or because we have only been with our guru for a brief period. Perhaps our certainty about what we're doing declines or perhaps our meditation becomes sloppy and the force of meditation and awareness decreases. Perhaps we lose the essential points of meditation to the degree that we are doing something that doesn't really deserve the name "meditation." Various kinds of appearances might arise and we might think, "Oh, this is fantastic, these are the signs of really superb meditation!"

These kinds of mistakes do come about, and it is important to understand them because if we understand them, then we can dispel them. In fact, even if they don't occur in our experience, merely knowing about them can be tremendously helpful.

(b) MISTAKES DUE TO LACK OF VIPASHYANA

[237] Our shamatha meditation may be going extremely well—even to the point of achieving some clairvoyance. In spite of this if we have not fully realized Vipashyana, that is, the true nature of emptiness of self and of phenomena, we have not achieved

mahamudra. In this section we will discuss mistakes or flaws that arise from not having achieved genuine Vipashyana.

[238] Some students' meditation may grow lax, and because they have not listened to the lama's instructions sufficiently, they will not be able to recognize the faults in their meditation. Even though they have had some glimpse of mahamudra, they haven't really ascertained it well, and will lose whatever insight they had glimpsed previously. When they go in that direction, gradually their mindfulness and awareness become lax, and they think that whatever meditation experience they have is real meditation. In fact, they have wandered off into a blind alley and become lost.

Another mistake is that some students will allow dullness and a darkness of mind to arise and increase in their session of meditation. When that happens, gradually the objects that ordinarily appear to the senses of consciousness become vague and unclear. The eyes don't see forms properly, the ears don't hear sounds properly; and as students fall into this state further and further, eventually they don't see forms or hear sounds at all. The consciousnesses have become unclear and actually have ceased to operate. Even if a person doesn't go to that extreme, if through a lack of mindfulness, she or he allows the mind to become unclear, losing its luminosity and its sharpness, that person is not actually meditating properly. These kinds of experiences have to be cast away.

A third kind of mistake is a meditation in which there is a genuine clarity and brightness to the mind, but the qualities of mindfulness and awareness have not been maintained properly. So even though there is a sense of vividness, the mind's awareness of itself is lacking. When mind's awareness of itself is lacking, then the meditation is neither particularly virtuous nor particularly unvirtuous; it falls into a middle range that is described as neutral in character, not terribly beneficial, not particularly harmful. But in the end it doesn't help very much.

The mistakes that students make become subtler and subtler; that's what we're investigating. Another sort of mistake would be to think that the meditation of mahamudra is simply a state in which thought is absent. Which is to say, the meditator might discover the intermediate space between the dissolution of a previous thought and just before the arising of a new thought. In that space, in which you're really just not aware of anything, there's no real quality of mindfulness or knowledge. One simply rests there thinking that this is the meditation of mahamudra. But that won't do at all. The reason is that clear, definite, certain knowledge of the mind's way of being is the essential characteristic of Vipashyana. And if that definite knowledge is lacking, then so is Vipashyana. The actual meditation of Vipashyana is one in which the mind's nature is clearly and knowledgeably understood. One knows that the mind is empty and this emptiness is not a lifeless emptiness. It is, rather, an emptiness in which it is suitable to know, to see, to perceive, to feel. If one has not discovered that emptiness, one has not found mahamudra Vipashyana. And, resting in that state between one thought and another, not really aware of anything, simply will not be genuine meditation.

(c) MISTAKES DUE TO LACK OF SHAMATHA

The mistakes that we have been considering so far basically come down to the absence of Vipashyana. On the other hand the meditation may have arrived at some degree of insight but the aspect of shamatha is lacking. The problem here is that Vipashyana will not be very strong. In shamatha, thoughts tend to be pacified right on the spot, and the mind can rest evenly and peacefully. Then thought arises, but one is not particularly bothered by it, and the thought is pacified, simply and quickly. If a person does not have that kind of meditative skill, then when a thought arises, it will seem to be some kind of obstacle. It will seem to be a threat and an opponent that the meditator will not really be able to deal with easily. Even a very subtle thought will seem to be an interruption and a threat to one's meditation. When you have that problem in meditation, then it's very difficult to meditate even for a short period of time, much less sustain your meditation for any length of time.

It's not as if this meditation were a bad thing. It's just that you haven't actually been able to realize the mind's way of being. Beginners will experience these kinds of problems of the mind and not be able to rest easily. So it's important to train in shamatha to enhance the mind's ability to rest and to develop the mind's quality of stability.

[240] We've talked before about the three types of temporary experiences that arise in meditation whereby the meditator thinks,

"Well, I have discovered something truly remarkable and profound and this is genuine meditation." The text speaks about them at this point and explains why they are not the actual Vipashyana that is mahamudra. One of these is the experience in which the mind has a very strong sense bliss; and the mind rests in that blissful state. Or the meditator may be free from thoughts of the past, present, and the future; and the meditator has the temporary experience of emptiness and can merely rest in that absence of thought. Still, in that absence of conceptuality, there is no genuine ascertainment of the mind's way of being. A third possibility is the temporary experience of luminous appearance, in which the mind seems so fully in possession of its extraordinary abilities that the meditator thinks, "I can see everything now. I can see things that are far away, I can see inside completely and clearly; everything is now vividly clear for my mind." Even though you're inside the house, you have the sense that you could see every last detail of the mountain in the distance. You may have these experiences individually or in some combination. It's very seductive but something vital is missing. What's missing is the definite knowledge of the mind's way of being that is the fundamental characteristic of Vipashyana. In Tibetan that definitive knowledge that is Vipashyana is said to be "the mind that has seen its own face," or "the mind that has cut its own root."

(d) CRITICISMS OF THE SAKYA PANDITA

[241] In the *Moonlight of Mahamudra* there are many refutations of various opinions that other people have held. Since this is not pertinent to our practicing meditation, I haven't discussed these refutations in detail. However, there is an important purpose for these refutations. The Sakya Pandita who was a very learned and distinguished person and who had extraordinary good qualities, wrote two special treatises. One of them was concerned with valid cognition, *Pramana*, in which he refuted the views set forth by many Tibetan scholars who lived before him. In the second book he wrote about the three vows; the Hinayana vow of individual liberation, the mahayana vow of bodhichitta, and the vajrayana vows. In this book on the three vows he wrote many refutations of the Kagyu mahamudra, but not of mahamudra itself. He pointed out problems

and mistakes of those who had mistakenly thought that they had realized mahamudra; those who had confused the various levels we were just discussing; those believing they had discovered the deep nature of things, but in fact had not; and those who had received practices that were not the genuine method. The Sakya Pandita's book has proven extremely helpful. *The Moonlight of Mahamudra* is replying to many of those points, illuminating clearly the various faults and good points of the teaching of mahamudra.

There is a verse in Sakya Pandita's treatise on the three vows that says, "If a fool meditates on mahamudra, that person will probably take birth as an animal or end up in the formless realm." This is not faulting the mahamudra teachings, but faulting the person. In fact this is true of any sort of meditation, not just mahamudra. If you practice ignorantly and you don't understand how to practice properly, or if you make mistakes and don't know that they are mistakes, then indeed such things come about. So, it is important then to recognize mistakes as such and not to make these mistakes oneself.

2. FLAWS OF PARTIAL MEDITATION

What is the distinction between the incomplete meditation that is being described at this point and the faulty meditation that we are considering just a moment ago? The answer is that the states we have talked about up to now are actual faulty states of meditation. The student has made some mistake, doesn't realize it, and is headed off in the wrong direction. Here what we're talking about is meditation in which only some of the important factors are experienced, but not all are present.

The first example is meditation in which the samadhi is clear, lucid, luminous, and we have some sense of things being empty. Although we may have a subjective sense of emptiness, however, we may not have real certainty of emptiness. This passing experience of emptiness, which is quite captivating, and the true understanding of things as they are, are clearly not the same. There is a real difference between this sensation of emptiness and the naked realization that is an utterly certain, penetrating, definitive knowledge that things do not exist as they appear. If this defect occurs, we need to examine our mind and see clearly, directly that things are empty of any inherent existence. We begin to understand with complete certainty that our mind lacks existence in its own right.

Another flaw may occur wherein we have developed a certainty of emptiness, but believe incorrectly that it is necessary to stop thought and appearance. It is at this point that we must understand that thoughts and appearances are also coemergent wisdom. Here the importance of the instruction on coemergent thought and coemergent appearance becomes apparent. Stillness of mind with no thought or appearance is not coemergent wisdom. We must overcome this view. Otherwise, we will begin to feel that thoughts and appearances are our enemies; and because we cannot stop them, our practice of meditation will become extremely irritating. To avoid falling into that misunderstanding, we need to understand coemergent thought and appearance so that whether thoughts arise or not, we are able to recognize them as coemergent wisdom.

A problem may also arise in postmeditation if we believe that thought is contrary to realization, and we feel it is necessary to stop thought and appearance. While it may be possible to cancel out all thoughts and appearances in mediation, we cannot stop them when we leave our meditation and return to the appearances of our daily life. This may become an issue if we think that appearance and wisdom are incompatible.

3. REALIZING FLAWLESS (OR GENUINE) MEDITATION

[243] Our topic is "things as they are." Things as they are refers to emptiness (Skt. *shunyata*), and reality (Skt. *dharmata*). But in mahamudra we are not referring to the emptiness of external phenomena, rather we are speaking about the mind's emptiness and the mind's reality. Understanding the mind's emptiness and reality is a little different from understanding the emptiness of external phenomena which is understood through inferential cognition because we can't realize the emptiness of things directly. Understanding emptiness with reasoning takes a while, and the journey is rather long.

Within the tradition of the quintessential instructions of mahamudra, we are introduced first to the mind's reality which is emptiness. This is in fact considerably easier to realize than the emptiness of external phenomena. The mind's emptiness is pointed out in what the gurus of the Karma Kagyu lineage call *ordinary mind* (Tib. *thamel gyi shepa*).

The best way to understand ordinary mind would be to think of it as "the mind as it is." However, there are other ways in which people might understand this term. The Sanskrit word that corresponds to *thamel gye shepa* is *prakshita*. Prakshita means "natural," and at the same time, it also has the sense of "ordinary" or "common place." The meaning of "common place" is not a correct one because we might think of "ordinary mind" as being thoroughly affected by disturbing emotions. That might be one way of understanding the term, but that is not what we mean here.

What we mean by "ordinary mind" is that the mind is, just by itself, empty and luminous, and that is what the mind is. It is only when we begin to manipulate mind that we become confused and mistaken and the disturbing emotions arise. So when we speak about this ordinary mind, we are talking about a mind that is uncontrived, unfabricated, left just as it is in its way of being.

(a) WHY IT IS CALLED ORDINARY MIND

[244] The name "ordinary mind" was applied to the mind's true nature by teachers such as Gampopa and other great accomplished meditators of the lineage. Their thought in doing so was that when one is practicing the meditation of mahamudra, one is not seeking to recover something that is far away or concealed, nor is one trying to remove the obstacles that prevent one from acquiring something. Rather one is simply looking for the nature of one's very own mind, which is right in one's own mind. What could possibly be closer than that? Furthermore, one could easily tend to think that the nature of one's mind is extraordinarily fine, extremely pure, and utterly unusual, such that one would discard everything that is old and familiar and arrive at something that has never been experienced before. Well, that's just manipulation, contriving something. And no matter how much one attempts to do so, one will never succeed in discovering the nature of one's mind in that way. So to dispel any misconceptions, this was called "ordinary mind" so one would

realize that it has always been, and is just the mind's nature without any manipulation or any contrivance.

(b) THE CHARACTERISTICS OF ORDINARY MIND

[245] A passage from Gampopa says, "Ordinary mind is unstained by any perceptive forms, unmuddled by any levels of existential consciousness, and unclouded by dullness, depression or thought." The commentary then gives the three characteristics of ordinary mind: not polluted by dharma, not stained by worldly consciousness, and not wrapped up in a heavy mind.

Not polluted even by any aspect of the Buddha-dharma means that one's mind is not polluted by the philosophical systems of reasoned analysis and conclusions, that is, inferential conclusions of thinking that something exists or that something does not exist. The mind is not manipulated or fabricated in that way, nor is it effected by various sorts of temporary experiences that come about when one practices. One's mind is not polluted by such temporary experiences. So the first characteristic is that the mind is not some new thing that has to be made up.

The second characteristic of ordinary mind is that it is not of the turbulence filled with disturbing emotions or the busyness of mind. Ordinary mind is free from such preoccupations and is uncontrived.

Thirdly, to say that ordinary mind is not wrapped up in a dull, obscure state of mind, or within conceptuality is to say that ordinary mind is brilliant. It's not dull, it is not unclear, it is luminous.

In brief then, ordinary mind has those essential characteristics. And in some sense to sum it all up, it isn't altered by something else, it is just itself. In particular, there is no need to make it into something better by trying to get rid of something that one regards as bad, or trying to turn it into something that is good. If one realizes ordinary mind, it is said to be the wisdom that knows itself; and if one does not realize it, even though it has always been there, then it is called coemergence ignorance.

(c) WHAT ONE MEDITATES ON WITH ORDINARY MIND

[247] One meditates upon ordinary mind by recognizing it as ordinary mind. One knows it for what it is: if it is empty, it is empty;

if it is luminous, it is luminous. Sometimes through the force of habitual tendencies one loses track of ordinary mind and so what one must do is sustain recognition of it. Recognition of ordinary mind is sustained by way of mindfulness and awareness. Thus Gampopa emphasized that the practice of ordinary mind is simply not to wander from it, not to become distracted, and the way to do this is by mindfulness and awareness.

If ordinary mind is such a crucial point, then what is the difference between a yogin and someone who has no connection with ordinary mind? If there were no difference, then wouldn't a worldly person also be naturally liberated and freed? There is indeed a difference. Gampopa explains this point by saying that although ordinary mind is the nature of the yogin and the worldly person, the worldly person does not have instructions on how to recognize ordinary mind and work with it, and the practitioner of yoga does have such instructions. The person lacking such instructions does not recognize ordinary mind, whereas the person who has such instructions does recognize it. By not recognizing it, all sorts of dualistic conceptions arise; and by recognizing ordinary mind one is liberated from dualistic conceptions and all experience becomes an experience of great bliss (Skt. *mahasukha*).

Gampopa also discusses the dharma practitioner who does not have the instructions on ordinary mind; that is to say, someone who is pursuing a more conventional path and is developing knowledge and good qualities. When this path of ordinary mind is taken into perspective, one would have to say that the ordinary practitioner of dharma is not very different from the ordinary person in the world in comparison to the yogin or yogini who has the instructions and the practice on ordinary mind.

We should not spend a lot of time noticing what the mind is not. Rather we should see what it actually is, that is, what it is with nothing being added or subtracted. When we talk about it beings not polluted, it is not a matter of contriving something that is regarded by the dharma as good, such as wisdom or luminosity. Ordinary mind is not polluted, it is mind as it is without the interference of passion or aggression, which is extra, superfluous. From the point of view of saying that the mind's nature is not wrapped up in thought or in heaviness or depression, all of these are fabrications, contrivances, and the ordinary mind is unfabricated and uncontrived. So it is just one's mind noticing itself. It is not a matter of looking at something else, but it is mind noticing itself, seeing itself, and not trying to fix itself or do anything. It's mind seeing what it naturally is and just resting in that; seeing itself for what it is and resting in that. And the way in which that is sustained and extended is through mindfulness. Mindfulness notices that some thought has boiled up and is about to take one for a ride, and mindfulness just doesn't go with it.

If I were to give an example, I would say this glass of water sitting on the desk in front of me is a glass. I see that it is a glass. If I looked with the quality of analytical intellect, I could stop and think about it and say that this is a glass and it's filled with water, and I could go around and around like that. On the other hand, I could see just glass and water. And if I wanted to get involved in some sort of hyperbole, I could say this is not just a glass, it is diamond, and this is the most magnificent glass; and this isn't just plain water it is the healing nectar (Skt. *amrita*) of the deities itself. On the other hand, I could think this doesn't deserve the name glass and the worst possible things were used to make this glass; and this isn't just water, this is poison. I could become excited about it. But that is not what we are talking about. We are talking about just looking at it and seeing that it is a glass and it has water in it.

So it is the same with one's mind; you don't have to look at it and exaggerate it by saying how wonderful it is or say it is completely rotten and filthy. It is just one's mind, and there is no need to think about it as good or bad. It is just what it is, that's all, without fabricating anything at all. That is what it means to just see what it is; and from the point of view of the quintessential instructions, it is empty.

Chapter 13

Sustaining Mahamudra in Meditation and Postmeditation

XI. MAINTAINING MAHAMUDRA IN MEDITATION AND POSTMEDITATION

A. MAINTAINING MAHAMUDRA IN FORMAL MEDITATION

[251] Devotion and faith are necessary for one's experience in meditation to increase. As said in the *Kagyu Lineage Prayer,* "Devotion is the head of meditation." If one has a head, then one can see, hear, eat, speak, and so forth. If one does not have a head, one can't do much of anything. Similarly, in meditation if one has devotion, one's meditation will improve, become more clear and stable.

THE DOG'S TOOTH

One story in this regard is the story of the dog's tooth. There was an old woman who had much faith in the dharma and the sangha. She had a son who was a merchant, who went back and forth to India buying and selling. Prior to the merchant son going to India the woman said to him, "You are going to India which is the birthplace of the Lord Buddha and the place where many scholars and siddhas lived, taught, and became realized. This time I want you to bring me back a relic that can serve as a basis for faith."

Her son went to India and returned bringing nothing because he had forgoten all about it. So as he was about to go to India again, his mother said to him, "This time you just have to bring something for me. Don't forget it. I really need this." The son went to India and conducted his business and he returned and had forgotten it again. So, the third time she begged him, "This time please, please bring something for me. If you don't, I am going to be very sad and I will die right in front of your eyes." Well, her son almost forgot again. On the very day he was to meet his mother he thought, "Oh no, now what am I going to do? If I don't bring her something she is going to die!" He looked around and saw a dead dog by the side of the road. It had been there for a while so most of the flesh was gone and there was just this dried skull. He went over and yanked out one of the teeth, cleaned it off, and wrapped it up very nicely. He brought it to his mother and told her, "You are extremely fortunate because I have brought you a tooth of the Buddha himself."

The woman believing this was the tooth of the Buddha supplicated it, made offerings to it, and generated extraordinary faith and devotion to it. The tooth had no potency or blessing itself. Nevertheless, there appeared in it what is known as *ringsels* (tiny circular rocks the size of a grain of rice) that spontaneously appear either in the body of a powerful guru or a particularly sacred *stupa,* or in association with a great lama. These ringsels appeared in this dog's tooth and came about because of this woman's faith and confidence, not because of any blessings that were contained in the tooth itself. Just based on her confidence and faith alone, it received the blessings of the Buddha.

This story indicates the potency of faith. In a similar manner when one practices meditation in the tradition of mahamudra, if one has faith and devotion for one's root guru, the gurus of the lineage, and the great practitioners, then with such faith and devotion, one's meditation will increase more and more.

1. THE REASON FOR MAINTAINING MAHAMUDRA

[251] If we have developed meditation through exertion, mindfulness, and awareness, how do we sustain our meditation? The earlier discussions were concerned with shamatha and Vipashyana meditation. In our present topic of coemergence, the text doesn't speak of teaching coemergence but rather it talks about pointing it out, which is to say, what is being pointed out is something that already exists within oneself and there is no need to teach anyone how to become coemergent. Rather one simply needs to recognize coemergent mind itself, coemergent thought, and coemergent appearance.

But having recognized coemergent appearance, coemergent thought, and coemergent mind itself, the question that then arises is how to meditate upon it. It's not enough simply to point it out. One must sustain one's meditation upon it, so that what has not yet become clear does become clear, and what is shaky becomes stable, and whatever good qualities are present develop further.

It is said that having arrived at this remarkable opportunity, having mind as it is pointed out, one's good fortune is inconceivable. One's practice has led to the birth of a profound opportunity within the stream of one's being, and if one doesn't exert oneself in sustaining the recognition and realization, then whatever good qualities might have fallen to oneself will decrease further and further, and whatever faults one has will increase. One should take the attitude that one has found a precious jewel and should take care not to throw it away into the mud, which requires exertion.

Looking into the mind's true nature and finding only emptiness and luminosity is not enough. Even though we have been introduced to the nature of mind, it is necessary to increase that realization. This nature of mind has existed within us all along. But from the beginning of time until the point of our recognizing it, it has stayed there unknown and unrecognized. We have been confused about it for a long time and the latencies and predispositions established by such confusion are extremely strong. Therefore, these latencies will reassert themselves and confusion will return. So, we must meditate again and again. Since the basic meaning for the Tibetan word for meditation *gom* is habituate we must become familiar with it. For our meditation to improve, it is important to hold our mind there. Shantideva said that those who wish to protect their minds and practice the dharma must have three things: mindfulness, attentiveness, and vigilance.

For the most part these are not different things, they are one nature. However, if we analyze them in great detail, we can distinguish slightly different natures and characteristics.

WHY IT IS NECESSARY TO SUSTAIN MEDITATION

[251] The first point has to do with why it is necessary to sustain meditative experience once it has arisen. To say that it has arisen means that one has come to know the mind's way of being. Then one

must extend that meditative experience further. One reason why it is necessary to maintain the meditative experience is that, if one does not do so, one will return to the state of an ordinary person, and then realization will have been meaningless. In particular, if one does not sustain one's meditative experience, good qualities will decrease and meditation will gradually become less and less clear.

Sustaining meditative realization and taking good care of it is spoken to by the great master Tsongbejari: "Not to care for the meditation that has arisen in the continuum of your own mind is like a rich person being carried away by a wind illness." In the Tibetan medical system there are different types of illnesses. One of these is said to be an illness of the *subtle wind* (Tib. *lung*). Wind illness arises when you don't have enough to eat making the wind in the body completely unorganized and sickness ensues. For a rich person who can buy good food and take care of himself, to suffer from an illness that comes about through emaciation is ridiculous. Tsongbejari also says that if you had a very precious jewel, you ought to take care of it properly; wrapping it in good quality cloth and setting it properly. Not to take care of your meditative realization, your insight into the mind's way of being, is like taking a precious jewel and letting it fall into the mud.

2. MINDFULNESS, ATTENTIVENESS, AND VIGILANCE

[253] We could say mindfulness (Tib. *trenpa*) means not forgetting, not forgetting mahamudra, not forgetting mind as it is. The attentiveness that we are speaking about is the right-up-to-the-moment attentiveness,[35] the present, active knowledge that becomes possible by way of mindfulness. So if one has mindfulness, then attentiveness can develop, and if one's mindfulness declines, then one's attentiveness is not possible. Also, when we talk about vigilance (Tib. *sheshin*) we are looking at our mind from the point of view of asking or inquiring: Are faults of this sort or that sort arising? Is samadhi or the stability of meditation declining? One watches to see that disadvantageous aspects don't creep into one's meditation.

Mindfulness and attentiveness are important at all times, and the reason for that is very simple. If they are present, then faults will not arise; and if they are absent, then faults will arise. This is explained by Shantideva who compared disturbing emotions to bandits. If you are protected by people who are strong, then thieves and murderers cannot possibly do you any harm; they see that you are well protected and they will not injure or steal from you. However, if your guardians become lazy or stupid or weak, then burglars can sneak in and harm you and steal whatever they want. So, Shantideva said, it is like that with regard to thoughts and disturbing emotions in that so long as you are well protected by mindfulness and attentiveness, then thoughts and kleshas cannot take control. But as soon as mindfulness and attentiveness slacken or are abandoned, immediately disturbing emotions arise, many thoughts arise, and they bring much trouble by blocking and covering over whatever good qualities there are. For that reason it is important to adhere to mindfulness and attentiveness at all times.

Vigilance tames the mind, which is to say it subdues the disturbing emotions and keeps one from doing things that cause others to give rise to aggression, envy, pride, and so forth. At the same time, vigilance dispels the joy one takes in what are actually harmful things, which is to say it prevents one from seeing attachment and aggression as good characteristics. Vigilance enables one to see such things as faulty and therefore not to enjoy them. It is vigilance that understands the reasons why dharma is beneficial. And it enables one to take delight in the dharma, preventing one from disliking the dharma. In sum, mindfulness, attentiveness, and vigilance are extremely important to the practice of meditation and they enable one's meditation practice to develop further and further.

MINDFULNESS

Generally speaking, mindfulness means not forgetting about the object upon which one is meditating. The text says, "As for mindfulness, it enables one not to forget the meaning that one is seeking to accomplish." It keeps your mind on the point that you are contemplating in your meditation, and it maintains clarity within your meditation. In particular, the sutra called the *Sutra Requested by the Student Who Had a Jewel upon the Crown of his Head,* called the Tsugna Rinpoche sutra in Tibetan, points out the different functions of mindfulness. One of these is: "Through mindfulness, delusions do not arise." Because we have become so well accustomed to disturbing emotions and have established such strong predispositions and habitual tendencies in that direction, through the force of those habitual tendencies, disturbing emotions will arise. But if we sustain mindfulness, then those disturbing emotions of desire, hatred, pride, and so forth do not arise. Secondly, through mindfulness, we do not become involved in demonic activity. These two are related as root and branch. First of all, through mindfulness, we protect our mind so that disturbing emotions do not arise. Once disturbing emotions do not arise in the mind, then the activities of body and speech do not go in the direction of *demonic action* (Skt. *mara*) Thirdly, through mindfulness, we do not stray from the correct path. That is to say mindfulness keeps us on the path that leads to genuine benefit. In this way, mindfulness can be understood as a doorway.

In the Buddhist tradition, when we talk about mind, we often talk about mind and mental factors, mental factor being "that which arises from mind." Through the force of mindfulness, the mind does not go in an unvirtuous direction. For that reason, the text says, "We should exert ourselves at genuine mindfulness." To speak a bit more about mind and mental factors, what we're talking about is very subtle kinds of thought. In fact, mindfulness is itself one of these mental factors, and it has the particular aspect of causing one not to forget whatever one is trying to pay attention to. Mindfulness has the role of keeping the mind on the point that one is meditating. If we guard our mind well with mindfulness, then we will not wander from it. We will not sink into dull states of mind or wild states of mind. When we have understood the dharmata that is the mind's way of being, then through the power of mindfulness we will not stray from that to something else. Thus, mindfulness is critical in guarding the realization that comes about as the insight of Vipashyana.

VIGILANCE

Vigilance (Tib. *sheshin*) has a sense of presently knowing what's going on in your mind and looking very closely at it. The text says that first you have to establish mindfulness. When you have established mindfulness, then this quality of vigilance, knowing at the present moment what's going on in your mind, can arise. Vigilance arises in dependence upon mindfulness. It inspects or examines the activities of the three doorways of body, of speech, and of mind. And this vigilance knows what to accept and what to reject. So this vigilance is critical for nourishing a healthy state of mind. There is a passage from Shantideva's *A Guide to a Bodhisattva's Way of Life* which says very simply, "Once you have established mindfulness, and mindfulness is serving the function of guarding your mind, then vigilance (or knowing what's going on in your mind at that moment), will naturally come about."

It is important to rely upon mindfulness and vigilance because their particular activities in the context of mahamudra meditation sustain one's realization of the mind's way of being and brings forth the enhancement of that realization. Mindfulness and vigilance very precisely enables one to know what to accept and what to reject. Without mindfulness and vigilance, different faults arise. In *A Guide to the Bodhisattva's Way of Life* it says that if you do not have vigilance, then your practice of listening to the dharma, reflecting upon its meaning, and meditating upon what you have understood will really not go anywhere. It will turn out to be a waste of time. And your good qualities will not increase and you will not be able to retain what you have accomplished.

When you have proper mindfulness and vigilance, then the self-restraint or carefulness of which we spoke earlier can arise in the continuum of your mind. What exactly is this self-restraint or carefulness? It knows when delusion is arising. It sounds the alarm. It says, "Oh, I think there's some delusion coming around here." And then you can respond to that appropriately.

3. MINDFULNESS AS THE ROOT OF THE OTHER CHARACTERISTICS

Mindfulness is the root of attentiveness and mindfulness is the root of vigilance. If one sustains mindfulness, then meditation, samadhi, and all good qualities will increase straight away. If mindfulness declines, then so will one's meditation and one's good qualities. Therefore, the siddhas of the Kagyu lineage talk about "holding mindfulness." This notion of holding mindfulness is explained with the metaphor of the shepherd. Mindfulness allows one to remain within the state of meditation. Just as when sheep wander into a place where there are fierce animals that would devour them, then the shepherd will bring the sheep back. Or if a sheep wanders to a precipitous place, the shepherd will bring it back to a place that has water and grass, where it will be happy and want to stay. In the same way when the mind strays from meditation, it is mindfulness that brings it back to meditation and places it in the relaxation of meditation so that one can enjoy its benefits.

Mindfulness is vital to the practices of listening, contemplating, and meditating upon the meaning of the dharma. Furthermore, it is important for sustaining meditation because it focuses the mind into one-pointedness. This means that it prevents the mind from becoming distracted into some other activity. If you do not have mindfulness, then you will also lose the purpose that you are attempting to accomplish. You will become confused and get lost. So mindfulness is important if you're going to practice meditation. If you don't have it, then you lose the meditation. It's mindfulness that tells you whether or not your meditative stabilization is coming along well or not. If you have mindfulness, then you can maintain your meditative stabilization; if you do not, then it gets lost. For that reason, it's important.

The text cites a number of texts which have spoken about the necessity of mindfulness: Nagarjuna's *Friendly Letter of Advice*; a passage from Gampopa; a passage from Pamotruba; and, one from Je Drikhungpa, who said, "The main highway for the Buddhas of the three times is mindfulness that is never interrupted." How did the Buddhas of the past, the Buddhas of the present, and the Buddhas of the future progress to enlightenment? The great highway on which they travel is the highway of mindfulness, in all cases. They have a mindfulness that is without gaps; it never lapses. That's how one proceeds to enlightenment. The passage from Je Drikungpa continues, "If you do not know undistracted mindfulness, then you will fall prey to resistive tendencies of body and mind" If you don't have that kind of mindfulness, you simply won't attain the fruition that is Buddhahood.

4. NATURE OF MEDITATION AND POSTMEDITATION

[261] First of all, what do we mean by meditation and postmeditation? When faults such as heaviness and wildness of mind have been cleared away and the mind rests within meditation, resting within recognition of mind as it is, that is what is meant by

meditation. And when one has "risen from that," which does not mean getting up from one's cushion but rather that one's mind has shifted, and then one's mindfulness of fundamental nature is restored, that is what is referred to as postmeditation or subsequent attainment, indicating one has recovered what one had before.

It is particularly important to consider how one sustains the meditation, and how one comes to have postmeditation, because once one has risen from the period of meditation, one is particularly prone to becoming completely wild in thought. So that is the time one needs to sustain meditation. If one learns how to do this, then the meditation can be joined with whatever activity one is doing through the power of mindfulness and awareness.

In the tradition of the quintessential instructions it is often said that meditative equipoise or meditation is like space, which is to say that in the main practice, as one recognizes just what the mind is, it is said to be like space. Then the period of postmeditation is said to be like an illusion; whatever work one is doing between the sessions of meditation appears to be like an illusion. If that activity can be joined with the definite knowledge, certainty, and mindfulness of mind as it is that one experienced at the time of meditation, if one can do that, then worldly activity is said to be like an illusion. Saying mediation is like space emphasizes the factor of emptiness. Saying that postmeditation is like an illusion emphasizes the factor of appearance.

In this chapter we will discuss meditation and the insight that is achieved in postmeditation. First, we need to identify meditation and postmeditation. When discussing the practice of mahamudra, we classify the stages of a practitioner's journey somewhat differently than the general way that we usually speak about things. Ordinarily we talk about the student's journey from confusion to liberation in terms of the ten bodhisattva levels. In mahamudra, we speak about the *four yogas*. Those four yogas are one-pointedness, freedom from complexity, one-taste, and non-meditation. The first yoga, the yoga of one-pointedness, is really the stage of a beginner. Here the student has an experience that is temporary in nature, which may be quite dramatic, but it doesn't last. So at the time of one-pointedness, the student's practice of meditation is really that of a temporary experience of insight rather than genuine realization. For that reason, the student at this point does not have genuine meditation or postmeditation.

The latter three yogas—freedom from complexity, one-taste, and non-meditation—have actual meditative equipoise and actual postmeditation. The meditation and postmeditation that the student or practitioner experiences in these stages is genuine and complete.

The first yoga of one-pointedness is free from the fault of a heavy and wild mind. It is also a mind that rests upon the true nature of mind, which is to say the coemergent mind itself that has been pointed out to the student previously. Thus, you come to rest within luminosity and emptiness. Moreover, the meditative equipoise of one-pointedness is free from other thoughts and mental activity. It does not wander or become involved in thinking about this or that. It does not lose this mindfulness. Rather, the meditation of one-pointedness is a mind that has come down into its own nature and that rests there, without being distracted to anything else.

In the *Quintessential Instructions on the Middle Way*, Atisha says, "One abandons all mindfulness and mental engagements." Of course, we've been speaking about the importance of mindfulness and the instructions on meditation. You may wonder, "What in the world does he mean when he says to abandon all mindfulness and taking to mind of various phenomena?" The answer is that this is not to be understood as casting aside mindfulness and one's intelligence. It is mindfulness that causes you to remain with the understanding of reality and causes you not to wander from that. Rather it means that you should not take other things to mind when you are resting within meditative equipoise upon the nature of mind. You should give up mindfulness and consideration of anything other than the meditative stabilization within which you are resting. So long as you remain mindful and do not wander, then thoughts of other things will not arise. But when you do lose your mindfulness, then you wander from that and other things come to mind. If you were to give up mindfulness altogether, then it simply would not be possible for meditative experience and realization to come about.

So long as mindfulness remains steadfast, then mind remains upon the meaning of reality and thoughts do not arise. When mindfulness wanders just a little bit, a very subtle thought will arise; and then when mindfulness wanders greatly, obvious thoughts will begin to arise, thoughts that involve the apprehension of and assent to the appearance of things as if they were inherently established. The arising of those thoughts and appearances means you are no longer within meditative equipoise; rather, you have passed to ordinary subsequent knowledge and appearance. Subsequent here means you've gone back to being an ordinary person with a very ordinary sort of mind, as if you've never experienced meditation. Later, when you rediscover the mindfulness of the former state, you can again rest within that without having to stop thought and appearance. Your awareness will then be, as is said, affected by the mindfulness that is aware of and rests right on the mind's way of being. When you have rediscovered mindfulness in that way, you have found what is called the union or integration of appearance and emptiness. Although thought or appearance is not obstructed in any way, it is understood as merely inseparable appearance and emptiness, the nature of which cannot be identified as anything at all.

Thus, we begin with the meditative stabilization of meditation right upon the mind's way of being. Then that is lost. And after it's lost, your mindfulness returns, and, as the text says, you achieve that again. For that reason, it's called subsequent attainment. Meditation is spoken of as being like space, meaning it is free from dullness, heaviness, sinking mind. Postmeditation is said to be like an illusion, meaning that appearance is illusory in the sense that although it appears, you know that it is really nothing.

5. FURTHER SKILLS FOR SUSTAINING MEDITATION

[263] Gampopa talked about sustaining meditation and postmeditation in terms of three skills: meditation in the beginning; skill in adhering to experience; and skill in cutting through elaboration.

The first skill in the beginning is mainly a matter of understanding that meditation is valuable and brings with it good qualities so that we delight in meditating. We have a strong aspiration toward it because we understand that if we have meditation, then good qualities come about; and that if we do not have meditation, then whatever good qualities we have will disintegrate. So we have great confidence in it and feel strongly inspired. At the same time we do not feel averse toward it nor do we take great delight in the opposite of meditation, that is, we do not particularly enjoy a flurry of thoughts and disturbing emotions.

The second skill is that we become skilled in recognizing heaviness and wildness, the two basic faults in meditation, and we know how to repair the situation. Furthermore, experiences that are temporary in nature, that are rather seductive and deceitful tend to arise in meditation. There are three types of temporary experiences, or *nyams* in Tibetan: experiences of great clarity or luminosity, experiences of emptiness, and experiences of bliss. We must learn not to become attached to these temporary experiences of pleasure, clarity, and non-thought. They seem to be real, real luminosity and so forth. But in fact they are like the husk around something, they are false, and one has to strip these nyams away to get down to the mind as it is, nakedly, unfabricated, and uncontrived. So the second skill is called the skill in how to avoid becoming attached to such experiences.

The third skill of cutting through elaboration occurs when we have developed our meditation to the point that we are not easily seduced by these fake experiences. Yet we are not able to sustain our meditation for any length of time, so we begin to resent it, and find it to be irritating. When we begin to feel this way about meditation, it is very difficult to continue meditating. We don't view the inability to sustain our meditation as a good thing, and become displeased. So we must become skilled in not resenting our meditation, but rather see this totally unelaborated meditation as a good thing and something delightful. When we see our meditation as good and delightful, then we want to practice. The name of this stage has the sense of getting rid of what is left over after the main part of the meal. So it is eliminating our resentment and irritation with regard to the practice of meditation.

6. METHODS FOR MAINTAINING MAHAMUDRA WITHIN MEDITATION

[264] We will look more closely at the way in which mahamudra is sustained within periods of meditation. The text is divided into two principle sections, the first of which is concerned with methods for sustaining meditation itself.

(a) THE SIX POINTS OF MEDITATION OF TILOPA

We will first consider Tilopa's famous six points for sustaining meditation, also known as Tilopa's six ways of resting. The verse from Tilopa says:

Do not recall,
Do not think,
Do not anticipate,
Do not meditate,
Do not analyze,
Do rest naturally.

In terms of the words they all mean more or less the same thing, but we can consider the meaning and observe some distinctions between them.

"Do not recall" means do not follow after thoughts that are concerned with the past. "Do not think" means don't fabricate or ponder in the present moment. "Do not anticipate" means do not invite thoughts that are concerned with the future, that is, making all sorts of arrangements and plans for what one will do later. These first three points are concerned with how to sustain meditation within a formal session of meditation by working with thoughts of the past, the present, and the future.

The fourth thought "Do not meditate" means that one simply sustains the awareness of mind without trying to manufacture something else. For example we would not meditate upon emptiness because then we would manufacture emptiness, or intend to meditate upon luminosity and thereby fabricating some luminosity upon which to meditate.

"Do not analyze" indicates that the meditator is not to become involved in speculation and analysis of the quality of his or her meditation, thinking that the meditation is good or bad. One does not investigate using theoretical speculation or inferential realization; rather one's mind is placed directly, unimpeded, without any intermediary, upon one's own mind.

Finally, "Do rest naturally" means that the mind rests with mind as it is in an unfabricated way. Mind is placed in ordinary mind, the mind's own nature. These then are six methods taught by Tilopa for sustaining a session of meditation.

(b) THE FOUR POINTS OF GAMPOPA

[267] Another set of instructions includes the four ways that are renowned in the Kagyu tradition, and which were first explained by Gampopa. The first instruction is for the meditator not to tighten or constrict or concentrate, but to relax.

The second is to experience freshness, newness, mind just as it is originally, just as it is without theories and classifications, and free from fabricating it as either empty or luminous.

The third instruction by Gampopa for sustaining meditation is to let the mind be. As we look at these different instructions, they all really say the same thing in terms of their meaning, but the words and the viewpoint are slightly different. "Let the mind be" means not dressing it up, not fabricating, not manipulating the mind at all; not looking for something special or unusual, but just sustaining the awareness of that which was pointed out previously.

The fourth instruction principally has to do with not fabricating, not manipulating, not worrying about whether one's mind is good or bad, not feeling that there is something that needs to be stopped and something that needs to be established; not getting involved with thoughts about that, but realizing that the nature of the mind already exists within one's mind. So there is no need to dress it up as something else or think, "I'm not sure I'm doing this right." There is no need to get involved in pride thinking, "I have figured it out." Understand that the recognition of the mind comes simply through the blessing of one's guru, and for that reason simply relax.

(C) OTHER METHODS OF MAINTAINING MAHAMUDRA

[270] There are three more main points discussed for maintaining meditation. The main point of Tilopa's six points is the one which says, "Don't meditate." This is to simply rest in ordinary mind without fabricating anything. So from that point of view, meditation is not a mental activity. This is well-illustrated by the advice given by the great master Saraha in which he likens the practitioner's mind to the red thread worn on a Brahmin: it must be neither too tight nor too loose. If your mind is too tight, you will have problems in your meditation. Here, the antidote is, "Don't meditate." This advice allows you to relax. However, if you relax too much, pretty soon you

will not be meditating on the mind's true nature. And the antidote to excessive relaxation is, "Don't be distracted." These two contain within them the advice you need for training and extending your meditation on the mind's true nature.

The second point has to do with when the mind begins to scatter, all sorts of thoughts begin to arise, and the mind cannot rest. It wanders here and there and one begins to fall under the sway of different patterns that arise. At this point what is helpful is mindfulness and awareness, and of these two, in particular mindfulness. The essential point is not to wander. Thus all the instructions on how to sustain meditation could be summed up in these two points: "don't meditate" and "don't wander."

The third point considers how "don't meditate" and "don't wander" include within them the essential points of meditation. The instruction not to meditate is principally connected with shamatha in that the mind is to relax; and the instruction don't wander is principally concerned with Vipashyana and instructs the meditator to tighten or to focus appropriately. For a beginner some care is required in that it is easy to fall into a state in which the mind sinks, becomes dark and heavy. As the antidote to sinking and heaviness of mind, the instruction is not to wander. As the antidote to wildness of mind the meditator is instructed not to meditate.

B. MAINTAINING MAHAMUDRA IN POSTMEDITATION

[279] In the previous chapter we spoke about the ways in which meditation is sustained in order that one's meditation can develop further and increase to a higher level. And in particular we spoke of how meditation is sustained within the meditative session. In this section we discuss specifically sustaining mahamudra in post-meditation, that is, when we return to worldly activity.

Between meditation and postmeditation, sustaining our mahamudra within postmeditation is the more important of the two. The reason for this is that in any twenty-four hour day, we can spend only a small amount of time in the meditation session and we spend most of the rest of our time doing something else. If we can sustain our meditation experience of mahamudra in the times of post-meditation, then it will be extremely beneficial to us, enabling our experience to develop further and further. It will also reduce the amount of stress that we have in our work and make our living less of a hardship. So the methods for sustaining meditation in the periods of postmeditation should be regarded as extremely important. This is why I spoke the other day about the particular usefulness of the teaching of mahamudra for the western world and for the twentieth century.

It does require some exertion to maintain mindfulness in the states of postmeditation. Principally what is required is that our mindfulness be unbroken. It is a mindfulness that is a definite understanding and awareness of the experience of coemergent mind. And the aspect of mindfulness that is required is that we not forget that coemergent mind itself.

(1) MINDFULNESS IN MEDITATION

If we maintained mindfulness completely and never wandered from our experience of coemergent mind itself, then that would still be the period of meditation. So what then is the difference between actual meditation upon the nature of the mind and the periods that follow? In the periods of postmeditation, the force of that application of our mind to the mind's way of being is maintained slightly. The text suggests, "It's just not lost." We just don't stray from it. In other words, there's still a bit of mindfulness of the mind's true nature.

So long as we maintain that little bit of mindfulness of the mind's way of being, then when different kinds of thoughts or appearances arise, we don't fixate upon them as some real and true thing that must either be rejected or affirmed. Rather, we remain right with that thought or that appearance, experiencing it and experiencing the luminosity of it. In particular, because we have that kind of mindfulness and since we are able to refrain from clamping down on things as real and true, we don't get involved in attachment and aggression. We don't have to form opinions—thoughts or appearances evaluating them as good, bad, and so forth. The example for this is that of a young child in a vajrayana shrine room. When a young child sees the depiction of the peaceful and wrathful deities, then the child will just look, without having to decide that they are good or bad. In the same way, the meditator's mindfulness allows him or her to experience whatever thoughts or appearances present themselves in all their vividness and all their brilliance without fixating upon them, without giving rise to various views and conceptions of them. And so the meditator is able to remain in a state that is not only spacious but also pure and unadulterated because it is not harmed by thinking of things as being either good or bad, attractive or unattractive.

2. MINDFULNESS IN POSTMEDITATION

The method for sustaining the meditative experience in postmeditation is mindfulness. We spoke of the three types of coemergence: coemergent mind itself, coemergent thought, and coemergent appearance. In the meditative session we are concerned with coemergent mind itself in which we are recognizing and studying the coemergence of mind and its own nature.

When we rise from a meditation session, we must make some effort at mindfulness while we go about our business, engage in conversation with others and in other activities. This mindfulness doesn't come about naturally but requires exertion, and sometimes we have mindfulness and other times we do not. But as we exert ourselves, mindfulness becomes more steady; and as we become more familiar with it, it becomes more continuous.

In the meditation session we are mindful of the mind's nature. The mindfulness of postmeditation is not to separate from that. We have the mindfulness of reflecting, thinking, remembering the nature of the mind, and our mind is affected by the force of that mindfulness. Thoughts arise, various appearances arise, we don't attempt to stop them. At the same time we don't become attached to them. As different thoughts and appearances arise, we do not become afraid of them or uncomfortable in the face of them nor do we give rise to the disturbing emotions. Rather we feel peaceful, free from attachment, and free from fear. To use the example again of a very young child who has wandered into a shrine room and is looking at various things in the shrine room. The child sees everything, but doesn't stop to think this is white, this is red, this is a deity, this is the Buddha, and so forth. If we have that attitude and mindfulness in postmeditation, then our mind becomes very relaxed, very spacious, and vast.

Now that we have some idea of how a practitioner will work with postmeditation. We will talk about exactly what we do with thoughts and appearances as they arise? The text comes at this by setting out two kinds of mistakes that we could make, and then explaining what the proper way to go about it is.

The first sort of mistake would be to dam up thought and appearance, to obstruct it, so that it is either halted or it doesn't appear clearly. It's like, pressing on and confining it. The other mistake is to follow after or be led along by thoughts and appearances, so that we become completely distracted. When we become thoroughly distracted in that way, then we have lost the mindfulness. Because we've lost that mindfulness, then we get involved in the very ordinary thoughts that we have, as if we'd never practiced meditation at all. We just become like ordinary people harshly rejecting some things and affirming others. Rather, we work with whatever appearances arise for the six consciousnesses: eye, ear, nose, tongue, body, and mental consciousness. Whatever their objects are, however they appear, we maintain the understanding of them as being of a nature that defies any of our efforts to categorize, grasp, define, or say precisely what they are.

The fruition of that meditative experience of coemergent mind is that all thoughts will be the appearance of emptiness. They appear but we do not grasp; and with that mindfulness, we don't contrive, fabricate, or manufacture anything. Rather, we maintain a meditative awareness in which the mind has settled into its own way of being, and we are able to sustain that. That's the kind of mindful understanding that we need to maintain our meditation as post-meditation.

We need to keep this kind of mindfulness active in whatever we do, sustaining it in a way that we're just not losing touch with the mindfulness. The text points out that, for beginners, most of the time we're distracted. What can we do about that distraction? Well, there's two things, one in meditation and one for postmeditation. The most helpful thing for meditation is to give rise to a very strong mindfulness that is right with the mind's coemergent nature. For postmeditation we must rely upon some exertion in applying our mindfulness. It doesn't arise naturally at this point, but takes some work and exertion. When we have done that, then it won't be necessary later to continue in that way because whatever thoughts and appearances arise will arise quite naturally without our having to apply much exertion. We will be able to stay in luminosity and emptiness.

If it's difficult for this mindfulness and this experience of thoughts and appearances as luminosity-emptiness to arise, then it's a sign that we've not related sufficiently with meditation, we've not understood sufficiently coemergent thought and coemergent appearance. It is an indication that when we practice formal meditation, we need to make an effort to experience coemergent thought, coemergent appearance, examining them in terms of where they arise, where they abide, and where they go.

3. BRINGING EVERYTHING TO THE PATH

The third section regarding postmeditation is concerned with how one brings thought to the path. Gampopa suggested that you do this in three ways. First, do this with what he literally calls, "destroying whatever is met with." In the context of having some familiarity with the experience of postmeditation, it's like suddenly meeting an old friend. When thoughts arise, then you at the same time give rise to mindfulness and awareness that understands their nature. Very soon after the thought arises and without having to get involved in one's analysis, you're able to recognize its nature. When you can do that, then when thoughts and appearances dawn for you, without having to analyze, you are able to go into the state that is the unborn mind. You can recognize the non-arising of mind, its birthlessness.

The second term for describing the meditator's practice in postmeditation is "reviving awareness." This is like where a friend has been visiting you and has already left. Suddenly you notice your friend has left something behind. You have to run after the friend and try to catch up with her or him to return what they've left. That's the sort of the way you're practicing at this point. Here you've really fallen under the spell of thoughts and appearances, you've been somewhat overwhelmed by them, and you have to put your whole meditative process back together, sort of start from scratch, looking at things carefully, and revive your mindfulness of what's going on.

The third phrase literally says, "emanation of non-existence." This is speaking about a situation in which you are thoroughly familiar with the practice of mindfulness in postmeditation and it's like a great fire blazing in a forest at this point, so that, whatever you throw at it, it is consumed right on the spot. If the fire is in its early stages, then damp wood or a gust of wind tends to threaten the fire. But once the fire is blazing in the forest, then whatever it comes upon just becomes more fuel for it. So here, for the meditator, whatever thoughts or appearances arise, you have become so familiar with the practice of mindfulness in postmeditation that any kind of thought or appearance, even one that would ordinarily be quite difficult, is for you just the spontaneous expression of reality, dharmata.

These three ways of working with thought and appearance in postmeditation really come down to a matter of how familiar you are with this practice. If you are very familiar with it, then you can practice in the third way described; if you're somewhat less familiar, then it's the first way described; and if you're still less familiar than that, then it's like the second.

4. SEEING EVERYTHING AS A MAGICAL DISPLAY

The fourth topic in this section is a discussion of what it means to say that appearances are like illusions. We said earlier that meditative equipoise is like space and postmeditation is like an illusion. So what are we talking about here when we say like an illusion? Here what we're concerned with is that the things of the world—colors and shapes, sounds, smells, tastes, tangible objects—are like illusions meaning that they are not established as what they seem to be. They appear in a certain way for a consciousness that does not see suchness, that does not see things as they are. That's what it means to talk about appearance that is like an illusion.

Two things need to be present if we are going to truly realize reality as an illusion. First, we must realize that phenomena are empty and that appearances are an illusion. When the mind understands this definitely and clearly, you have what is called illusion-like appearance. An example for this is a magician who is able to create the appearance of different kinds of things, such as horses and elephants that others would actually see with their eye consciousnesses; but because the magician created this appearance, the magician is not fooled by it. The magician knows that these appearances, whatever they may be, are not what they seem to be; they are not established as what they appear to be from the perspective of, in this case, the eye consciousness. They certainly do appear that way, but the mental consciousness knows without a doubt, without hesitation, that these appearances are not what they seem to be. So when those two, the appearance and the definite understanding that the appearance is false, are both there, then you have illusion-like appearance.

The *King of Meditation* sutra says:

Meditation on perceptive marks
Is empty of the unborn essence,
Like mirages and the phantom city of the gandharvas,
Like illusions and dreams.
Understand all things as such.

The text suggests illusion could mean (a) that reality (Skt. *dharmata*) and complete realization (Skt. *sarvajnana*) are illusion and (b) that phenomena such as the five aggregates are an illusion. What does "illusion" mean in the term "whatever appears is like an illusion?" In regard to the latter, phenomena as illusion, the text identifies the meditator's knowledge that things are not established, or do not exist in the ways that they appear, as "illusion-like appearance." That is what "illusion-like appearance" means.

Having identified the mind that understands illusion-like appearance, the text then explains the way in which illusion-like appearance arises. Various things will appear, for instance, to the eye consciousness or to the ear consciousness, but the mental consciousness knows that these things are without essence and that they do not truly exist. All sorts of things appear to the sense consciousnesses, and the mental consciousness understands that those phenomena do not intrinsically exist and are merely appearances to the sense consciousnesses. That then is the dawning of illusion-like appearance in postmeditation.

The text gives an account of ways in which one could deceive oneself about illusion-like appearance. In the quintessential instructions of mahamudra it is said frequently that one should not manipulate one's mind, that one's mind is to be recognized as it is without fabricating anything, and that one allows one's mind to settle into the space that is natural to it. There are ways to misunderstand these instructions. One might, for instance, give rise to many different thoughts and distrubing emotions based on experiencing external objects and be quite confused about them. One would then think, "I will just relax within this without trying to alter it or fix it." That would be a big mistake. Or one might experience the mistaken appearances that are dependent upon and polluted by ignorance and think that it would be the practice of illusion-like appearance to just relax within that. There is a big difference between relaxing within mind as it is and relaxing within ignorance. To relax within ignorance and conceptuality that does not understand things as they are, is not correct.

5. UNION OF MEDITATION AND POSTMEDITATION

[289] The text goes on to talk about the way in which the period of meditation and postmeditation can be brought together. However, that is not something over which we have much control or much power at this time; we have not achieved independence with regard to mixing meditation and postmeditation. This comes about through tremendous exertion.

This occurs only at a very, very high level of experience and realization, but it is set forth here for the purpose of clarifying this point. The answers come from the answers that were given by Gampopa to questions that his students asked of him. When Gampopa was asked what it means to talk about the mixing of meditation and postmeditation, he replied that it refers to never being separated from clear light and the realization of clear light occurs in anything you do: sleeping, eating, anything. When you are never separated from clear light, then that is the blending of meditation and postmeditation.

Questions

Question: When one does not recognize ordinary mind (Tib. *thamel gyi shepa)* and is in a mess, then how does one go about practicing the dharma and trying to be of use to sentient beings?

Rinpoche: It's wonderful if one can give birth to the realization of mahamudra in the stream of one's being. If one is unable to do so, all of one's actions are not worthless and futile, so that there is nothing one can do to develop the dharma. You can revivify your faith and devotion to your root guru, generate love and compassion for sentient beings, practice shamatha which helps to pacify one's own mind when it is in a worried state, and do virtuous activity. When one does such things, then that causes one's understanding to increase and one will be of more help to others.

Question: The three definitive characteristics of ordinary mind are that it is not polluted by mental postures appropriate to the dharma, it is not sullied by passion and aggression, and it is not encased within conceptuality of any sort. Do we recognize this from noticing the absence of something that's usually present? For a brief period of time, we sort of notice either on the spot or later, that something wasn't there.

Rinpoche: Well, it's not necessarily a matter of talking about a short period of time. In any case, the thrust of this is not so much noticing what the mind is not, but noticing what it actually is. When we talk about it being unpolluted, it's not a matter of contriving something that is regarded as good, such as wisdom or luminosity, but rather it is the mind without the interference of attachment and aggression, which are superfluous. By saying that, the mind's nature is not wrapped up in thought or in heaviness because all of these are just fabrications and ordinary mind is unfabricated and uncontrived. It's not a matter of looking at something else, but it's the mind noticing itself and not trying to fix itself or do anything. It's just mind seeing what it actually is, and resting within that. The way in which that is sustained and extended is through mindfulness. Mindfulness notices that some thought has boiled up and is about to take one for a ride, and mind just doesn't go with it.

Question: Of mindfulness, awareness, and vigilance which is the most important?

Rinpoche: From among these three, mindfulness, awareness and attentiveness, mindfulness is the main thing. Mindfulness is keeps you in, or brings you back to, meditation. It may involve some intention and effort, "I am going to meditate," and if one slips and loses the meditation, mindfulness thinks, "Whoa, what happened here," and then restores the meditation. If mindfulness is present, then awareness will come about. If mindfulness is not present, then there is no possibility of awareness.

Awareness looks to see how well the meditation is going, and takes a closer look: "Now that I am meditating I can look and see how well my meditation is going." It is on the lookout for different faults that might creep in, different faults that might arise. It is looking to see what the state of the meditation is, you know, have thoughts arisen, are they taking over, whatever. But the relationship of awareness and mindfulness is that awareness depends on mindfulness.

Attentiveness is a bit different in that it runs through everything. It is a care, a very definite concern, or a heedfulness that one not allow certain problems to arise. So it is not so much an inquiry into whether something is happening as it is a very definite taking care of one's state of mind.

Question: If we are practicing this particular meditation without object, and a thought arises, do we just not feed it and just let the thought die down? How does this relate to not regarding thought as an enemy?

Rinpoche: Meditating upon the nature of mind, upon mind as it is, is somewhat easier than meditating upon other sorts of things. One is simply recognizing mind's luminous emptiness which is already there. It is not like meditating upon external phenomena in which one cannot apprehend their emptiness except by meditative and analytical strategies, and that inevitably involves some difficulty and distance and technique and contrivance, fabrication. Whereas looking at one's own mind involves only looking at one's own mind, with one's own mind. You don't have to look somewhere else, you don't have to concoct an elaborate strategy for how to do it. So it is a good bit easier. And as for how one regards thoughts that arise at that time, one is not looking to negate them; one is simply investigating their nature, recognizing them for what they are. Suppose some very coarse thought arises in one's mind. One simply looks at the thought to see what it is: from where did it arise, where is it, where does it cease, where does it go? And just as bubbles that arise in water appear to arise from somewhere, abide somewhere, and disappear somewhere, in fact they don't, they just seem to, and it is the same with thoughts. They seem to arise, abide, and cease, but in fact they don't. One is looking in this way not in order to stop thought, but because one is simply investigating the nature of one's mind so when thoughts arise, one investigates them in this way. One is looking at them in this way not because one wants to do anything to them, to get rid of them. One simply wants to know what they are. So that is how one investigates them.

Question: I was wondering if you could explain how we actually would remedy dullness by using non-distraction and remedying wildness by using non-meditation. A passage in the book says, "Beginners should know that non-meditation connotes tranquillity and relaxation, but that an excess of relaxation will produce dullness; and that non-distraction includes insight and exertion, but an excess of exertion will produce wildness." So how do we work with these in our practice?

Rinpoche: Those instructions are indeed given. Mainly the point is displayed in this way. The essentials are non-meditation and non-distraction. Through non-meditation the mind rests in peace or shamatha, but if that becomes too strong the mind becomes dull. Through non-distraction sharp insight develops, one experiences Vipashyana, but if that becomes too strong wildness arises. The essential point is that the two have to be balanced, they both need to be present and they need to be in balance. And what has been described as developing something as an antidote and then falling into the other situation is a matter of the two not being in balance. That is to say, either the factor of non-meditation becomes too strong or the factor of non-distraction becomes too strong. So what is required then is a union of shamatha and Vipashyana in which the principle of non-meditation and the principle of non-distraction are completely balanced.

Question: Then is it spinning one's wheels to exert in mindfulness with the intent of mixing meditation with postmeditation, since we don't have much experience in this?

Rinpoche: No, it's not a waste of time to exert oneself at mindfulness during postmeditation. Within that postmeditation we tend to forget samadhi and because we forget it, then the force of it doesn't come into our experience. But if we were to develop some mindfulness of it, to remember the keenness and the feeling of samadhi, then later when we return to samadhi it's strength will increase. Therefore the mindfulness of samadhi within postmeditation is very helpful for meditative equipoise.

It also is very helpful for the postmeditation period because it will tend to weaken kleshas. And it is very helpful given all the difficult experiences we have during postmeditation, for the times in which our body is in pain or our mind is ill at ease, frightened, or undisciplined. If we can bring the sense of samadhi, the memory of it, the mindfulness of samadhi to bear on the life we live in postmeditation, that will help to pacify our fears, to tame our disturbing emotions, to ease all the physical and mental suffering that we have such that it doesn't do us much harm. So it is a very helpful thing to do, it helps our body, our mind, and it helps everyone else.

Question: In that case is it useful to use reminders, an object of focus in postmeditation, to encourage meditation. For instance I have this ringing in my ears, reminder type, or protection cords, anything.

Rinpoche: Within samadhi we experience our mind as lacking any nature of its own. And when that experience is remembered, when we are mindful of that experience, that helps a great deal with the suffering that we encounter within postmeditation, suffering such as strong passion and attachment, strong aggression and hatred. If we can remember that feeling and the sense of samadhi, in which we have experienced the mind's lack of any nature of its own, that is very helpful for increasing the stability of our mind. It helps at the time in terms of pacifying the pain we are feeling and it also helps when we practice meditation again.

For instance, if we were to practice meditation and then get up, with no effort to sustain the meditation during postmeditation, and then a month later sit down to meditate again, we would feel, "What happened, I meditated last month, there doesn't seem to be anything happening now?" However, if we have maintained some awareness during postmeditation, that will help a lot during meditation practice the next time we sit down to meditate.

Chapter 14

Eliminating Obstacles to Mahamudra

XII. ELIMINATING OBSTACLES TO MAHAMUDRA

A. ELIMINATING OBSTACLES TO MEDITATION

[293] In mahamudra, first the nature of mind is pointed out; then one trains in that, learning to sustain one's recognition of it in meditation and in postmeditation. When one trains in meditation on mind itself, different kinds of obstructions and adverse circumstances may arise. Tthese are regarded as errors into which we can fall and mistaken paths we can take. All of these need to be abandoned, cleared away, overcome, and from that point of view, we must understand the dangers and the faults of meditation. These are known as the four ways to go astray and the three mistaken paths.

1. ELIMINATING THE FOUR WAYS OF GOING ASTRAY

In talking about the *four types of strayings*, each of these four has two different ways in which you could go astray. In the first you may make a mistake in meditation in the way of practicing or the manner of meditating itself. This is a "temporary straying." The second has to do with how you develop your understanding and mental image of the nature of things. If your understanding of the nature of reality has gone astray, this is called "an original straying." An original straying occurs when you have not give rise to meditation properly in the continuum of your body and mind.

The first way one might go astray is through misunderstanding emptiness. This is not understanding the fact that emptiness is a characteristic nature of all phenomena and that it is everything that might appear in one's mind. Learned persons have identified the emptiness that one needs to understand as "the emptiness that possesses the supreme of all aspects." What this means is that while phenomena are empty of any inherent nature, nevertheless, that emptiness allows everything to appear in it despite having no nature of its own. This emptiness is in no way opposed to the idea of dependent arising or the interdependent relationship of phenomena.

The *Heart Sutra* which is part of the Prajnaparamita sutras says, "form is emptiness," which means that forms of any kind have no nature of their own, they are not inherently existent. The next line is "emptiness is form," which means that even though forms do not exist, it is entirely appropriate for them to appear. The next two lines are "emptiness is not other than form" and "form is not other than emptiness." These lines mean the two do not exist in separate places. It is not as if the form is here and emptiness is somewhere else. Related to our mind, these lines mean that the emptiness that is the nature of our mind is not a voidness. Someone may infer from this that this is a dead emptiness or nothing at all and therefore it is not worth meditating upon because meditating on nothing is a waste of time. Or someone might think that this emptiness means there is no relationship between our actions and their effects (i.e., karma) and therefore, there is no such thing as a virtuous action that brings a result of eventual happiness or a wrongful action that brings about eventual suffering. Thus, the first way one might go astray is to misunderstand the real meaning when it is said the nature of phenomena is emptiness.

The second way we might go astray is to misunderstand the way in which we take emptiness as the path. In the practice of mahamudra one is meditating on mind's very own nature, in its unfabricated state; the mind that is naturally empty. If we do not understand that mind in its natural state is already the ground, the path, and the fruition, we might think that "I want to achieve enlightenment and therefore I will meditate on this emptiness; and later as a result of this meditation I will achieve some fruition." That is not the correct path. Rather we are meditating on dharmata that already exists within ourselves and we bring it from an unmanifested state to a manifest state. If we don't understand this, then we have misunderstood the way emptiness is taken as the path.

The third way we could go astray is to regard emptiness as the antidote. If we do not understand that the disturbing emotions themselves lack inherent existence and we don't understand that the disturbing emotions are coemergent thought and their nature is coemergent wisdom, we might believe the disturbing emotions are things and that emptiness is the proper remedy for them. In this mistaken way we would think of the disturbing emotions as one thing and emptiness as something else. We would not realize that emptiness is the very nature of the disturbing emotions. We would therefore meditate with the wrong point of view, not understanding that the kleshas already lack any true reality.

The fourth way we could go astray would be to think that we must realize phenomena with emptiness, which is to say, that we might not understand things already lack inherent existence. We might not recognize the actual way our mind already is. Not understanding the mind is empty, we feel we must fix things up, manipulate them, and transform things that aren't empty to things that are empty. That is, however, unnecessary because emptiness is their nature already.

Tashi Namgyal actually discusses eight ways to go astray, but these are two levels of each of the four just discussed. One level is fully misunderstanding the concept, and the second level is occasionally misunderstanding the concept. Of these four strayings, the first one is the most important to abandon. What is most dangerous is the first mistake in which one misunderstands the emptiness that is the essential characteristic or nature of all things. That above all needs to be understood properly.

This bears repeating. The most problematical of these four ways of going astray is the first one: misunderstanding emptiness is the nature of everything that appears to one's mind. Why is this such a problem? It is a problem because such a nihilistic view causes one to think that there is no interdependent relationship between phenomena. We mistakenly think that emptiness is mere voidness or nothingness. Because the word "emptiness" causes us to naturally think of nonexistence, the instruction of the Kagyu tradition uses other terms for emptiness. In the Kagyu tradition we speak of "mind as it is" and "mahamudra" and "ordinary mind." When we hear such terms we are not so liable to think of mere nothingness. If we misconstrue emptiness, we will not travel the genuine path. How can such a misconception be cleared up? It is cleared up by the mind resting in the unfabricated state of equipoise. When we do that, it clears away any misconceptions.

Of these eight points of losing the meaning in meditation, the worst mistake is with regard to wisdom in the context of virtuous deeds and unvirtuous deeds. The worst thing is to think things are utterly nonexistent, therefore it doesn't matter whether one engages in virtue or nonvirtue, because virtue being empty doesn't help and nonvirtue doesn't harm. The great mahasiddha Saraha said, "To conceive of things as being real is foolish. But to hold on to emptiness is even more foolish."

So, there are two mistakes which we have just discussed that are extremely dangerous. The others are not so dangerous, but they do prevent our meditation from going well. In this way they serve as instructions for our meditation to proceed properly. And for that reason it is important not to stray into them.

So, how do we eliminate these aberrations? We must realize that true nature exists in us primordially and that it is not newly constructed. The third Karmapa, Rangjung Dorje, spoke to this point by saying, "When one looks into one's mind, one will not find anything." When one says one sees one's own mind, it is not that one sees anything. However, by looking directly into one's mind, one sees that the true nature of one's mind is beyond any thing such as being true or false, existent or nonexistent. One passes beyond doubts of thinking the mind is like this or like that.

TWO ADDITIONAL STRAYINGS

[298] In addition to these four ways of straying that involve a misunderstanding of emptiness, there are two other strayings which were pointed out by Gampopa. The first is confusing experience with realization. Mistaking experience for being real is related to the extraordinary method (Skt. *upaya*) of mahamudra meditation in which the winds begin to move through the channels in the body. One then experiences bliss or luminosity and if one regards these experiences as genuine realization, one becomes very attached to them. This is confusing experience as realization.

The sixth straying is confusing realization for experience. With the blessings of the guru one realizes the nature of one's mind which is not established in any way and cannot be identified as anything in particular. When we try to continue meditation, we are not able to stay with that and our meditation begins to degenerate into various temporary experiences such as bliss and luminosity. But we don't realize the meditation has degenerated and we think this is realization. We don't understand it to be just a passing thing and not realization. The remedy for this problem is that we must meditate with certainty and a definite knowledge of the true nature of mind.

2. ELIMINATING THE THREE MISTAKEN PATHS

(a) THE TEMPORARY EXPERIENCES (NYAMS)

[299] There are three kinds of mistakes a student can make that are concerned with the practice of meditative stabilization itself. When a student has been introduced to the mind's true nature and meditates within that, gradually there comes to be some sort of separation of the purified, brilliant quality of consciousness from literally, "the dregs" of consciousness. Some sort of separation of those takes place as the student continues to meditate, and, as the purified aspect of consciousness begins to be experienced through sustaining meditation, different kinds of things appear to a student's mind. You see different forms, hear various kinds of sounds, smell things strongly, different kinds of thoughts appear. All kinds of meditation experiences occur. But if we were to summarize we could talk about three types of temporary experiences: bliss, luminosity, and non-thought.

The first is an experience of bliss or pleasure and can be experienced both in the body and the mind. Physically there can be a sense of bliss pervading the body. Mentally you might feel extremely happy and joyful. With the experience of luminosity or clarity (Tib. *salwa*), there's a sense of extraordinary brilliance. You might have the experience that there's really no difference between night and day. You might have the experience of the appearance of a very brilliant light. With the experience of non-thought, it's the sense of all things as being empty. The mind then feels very steady, free of projection, straightforward, free from thought.

If a person has one of these temporary experiences and does not become attached to them, there is no problem. But if one regards one of these experiences as wonderful and wants to replicate it again and again, then one has imprisoned oneself creating an obstacle for further development.

How might these temporary experiences affect your meditation? What is the problem with them? You may have the experience of bliss, clarity, and non-thought all together or you may have them individually. You may experience just a sense of bliss or pleasure, a sense of clarity and luminosity, or you may just experience non-thought. In any case, you take them to be extremely important. When they arise you feel very glad, and when they don't happen, you feel that there's something wrong and you become depressed. This is because you have become attached to them. You have become so absorbed with them, thinking they are the true nature of phenomena and you are having genuine meditation, that you don't understand you've not realized the nature of things. In fact, you've just become distracted by something and have mistaken these three temporary experiences for the nature of reality.

These kinds of experiences will naturally arise when you practice meditation so the important thing is to understand that there's no need to feel particularly happy if they come about or feel sad if they don't. Whether they come along or not, so what? These things will happen. Sometimes you will have a good experience in meditation; sometimes your meditation experience will be painful. There's no need or purpose in fearing difficult or painful experiences in meditation and there's no purpose in becoming attached to good experiences. The important thing is to sustain your meditation within the mind's way of being. Whatever comes along, let it come and go. If you get involved in hope and fear with regard to meditation, then your meditation will not progress properly.

The best way to work with these temporary experiences is to realize the cause of your going astray, and to turn that around in the other direction. The basis for becoming attached to these experiences and entering into hope and fear with regard to them is not understanding that they are empty; that is to say, not recognizing the mind's way of being. So whether it is the experience of bliss or luminosity or non-thought, it is the emptiness that cannot be identified as one thing or another. All these experiences are free from arising, free from abiding, and free from cessation. If you don't realize this, then you will regard them as being truly existent. Thus, the antidote for attachment to nyams is not to think of them as real, but to recognize them as the union of luminosity and emptiness. When you recognize them as the integration of luminosity and emptiness, you will avoid becoming attached to these temporary experiences.

[305] Gampopa described these three kinds of temporary meditation experiences and how one has to work with them, saying, "You must understand bliss, luminosity, and non-thought as unborn. If you do not understand them to be unborn, then you have not ascertained appearances. If you do not know them to be unborn, then you do not understand the nature of appearances." He's talking particularly about meditation subsequent to the mind's nature being pointed out to you. First you have recognized the mind's nature, but then later these kinds of experiences conceal or obscure the mind's nature. Because they conceal the mind's nature, you are unable to ascertain them as the luminosity and emptiness that is the mind's way of being. Gampopa says, "It's necessary to enter into the knowledge of all these as unborn."

Gampopa spoke about two more types of mistaken paths. The first is the temporary experiences of pleasure, clarity, and nonconceptuality just discussed. The second type of deviation of Gampopa involves developing realization through the blessings of one's guru and recognizing the nature of mind. Then later one experiences these temporary experiences of bliss, clarity, and nonconceptuality and thinks, "these are wonderful, I want them, I need them" and develops attachment to them. So the first type involves beginning with these temporary experiences and becoming attached to them which prevents genuine realization. The second involves beginning with genuine realization, but then when such experiences come along one becomes stuck on them.

B. METHODS FOR REMOVING OBSTACLES ON THE PATH

1. REMOVING OBSTACLES TO GENERAL MEDITATION

[308] How do we clear away obstacles? Obstacles, or hindrances, are divided into two classes: (a) the general hindrances and (b) the inner and outer hindrances.

Previously, we have discussed the methods of tightening or concentrating as an antidote to heaviness and loosening or relaxing the mind as an antidote to wildness. But at this point in meditation such methods are not employed. Rather we simply look directly into their nature. They are, after all, just sensations and feelings having no inherent existence of their own. We do not need to regard them as false. We do not need to make an effort to clear them away. Rather, we see them as we look directly into them, seeing their true nature as emptiness. There is a verse from Gampopa which says, "At this point if one were to engage in the methods for clearing away this heaviness and wildness of mind, it would be like lighting a lamp in the day time to clear away darkness." Of course, if you light a lamp at night to clear away darkness, that is fine; but to do so in the daytime is silly. In other words, once you recognize the nature of mind there is no need to apply the traditional antidotes to heavy and wild mind.

Another way to put this is that, there are two basic kinds of hindrances that may interrupt or interfere with the practice of meditative stabilization. There is the kind of impediment that interferes with the factor of luminosity and there is the impediment that interferes with the aspect of steadiness. Whenever you practice meditation, you need both the luminous clarity and the steadiness that are intrinsic characteristics of the mind. When the factor of luminosity is not fully present, then the mind feels heavy and dull. When the mind is not stable enough, then it becomes wild. It's very helpful at that point to rely upon the kinds of techniques for working with the mind that were presented earlier in this text by Tashi Namgyal. To put it simply, if the mind has become dull and sunken, then it can be brightened by thinking about, for instance, the Buddha's good qualities. If the mind has become wild and scattered, then it's too tight and it needs to be relaxed somewhat. The way to relax it is to think about what's wrong with samsara and to think about the painful situations that sentient beings must endure in the lower realms. If you think about those, then your mind will become less wild.

The second class of obstacles or hindrances, the outer and inner hindrances, cover many different things. An interesting hindrance which has been described by a particularly accomplished meditator is one having to do with the *mara* or demon of darkness entering into one's head, the mara of speech entering one's tongue, the mara of scattering entering into one's heart, and the mara of motion entering one's feet.

The mara of darkness entering one's head means that no matter how much one tries to meditate, one's mind is dull and unclear and one cannot experience clarity. The mara of speech entering one's tongue is that one just cannot stop talking, one just always has to talk all the time. The mara of scattering entering into one's heart means that one is just beset with thoughts, one's mind just will not settle down, just endless thinking. The mara of motion entering into one's feet is that one just cannot hold still and sit down and meditate, one has to get up and go somewhere immediately. These hindrances happen sometimes and when one is beset with these situations, one supplicates one guru. One imagines one's guru to be at one's head, or one's throat, or one's heart. Meditating in that way has been found to be an effective way to deal with this obstacle.

Other hindrances that can occur include: sickness, harm from human beings, from non-human beings, all kinds of thoughts that arise, and emotional turmoil. Nonhuman beings are the different kinds of spirits, ghosts, hungry ghosts, and also animals such as tigers and poisonous snakes. These are not things that come about because of meditation practice. You don't get sick or harmed by others or fall into emotional turmoil because you're meditating. They happen because that's the nature of samsara. One wanders from lifetime to lifetime through the power of different kinds of actions and different deluded states of mind. Sometimes you get sick, sometimes you're having such a good time with your friends and family that you become thoroughly distracted by that and don't seem to get around to meditation. Sometimes thieves take possessions from you and harm you, and cause all kinds of problems for you. That's just the nature of samsara. So what should you do at that point? You should then supplicate the guru by imagining the guru sitting upon the top of your head. And supplicate that your efforts to understand the view and to practice meditation will go well. Later on in the text, we're going to talk about how you can bring sickness to the path, how you can turn the experience of adversity into the path of mahamudra. Similarly, we will discuss how you can work with painful, deluded states of mind and bring them to the path of meditating in mahamudra. But at this point in the text, the general advice is given that when these kinds of obstacles arise, supplicate the guru upon the crown of your head.

Questions

Question: Rinpoche, you spoke about looking into our dreams to help us see the illusion of our daily life. That night, I had a very bad dream, and woke up upset, and had a moment of impression of my being upset and the illusion of the dream. The next night I had a worse dream and woke up crying out to Guru Rinpoche. Then, last night, I had a very wonderful dream with Kalu Rinpoche, I realized I wasn't looking at the nature of my mind at all. I wasn't realizing the illusion of the dream at all, I was just daydreaming. Can you give us any further indication on how to wake up in the dream, or become aware in the dream.

Rinpoche: In answer to your first question of how to recognize dreams as dreams: if you maintain mindfulness and awareness of what's going on in your mind, in the daytime, then that will carry into the nighttime. If, during the day, you are mindful of what you're doing, with your body, your speech, and your mind, then this will establish predispositions for mindfulness, and, as you become used to that more and more, then these predispositions will help you to recognize your dreams as dreams. The most important thing is the practice of mindfulness. And if you get used to it in the daytime, it will carry into the dream time. If you don't carry out your activity mindfully in the daytime, then you will become confused when you go to sleep.

In reply to your second question, it's just as you say. Usually suffering encourages us to practice the dharma and happiness encourages us to enjoy and not practice. So, suffering has the advantage of encouraging us to practice the dharma but it's not very much fun; and happiness is fun, but it discourages us from practicing the dharma. So, when everything is comfortable and sweet and happy, remember that it's impermanent and is going to change, and you don't know when it's going to change. This realization encourages an attitude of renunciation, of wishing to emerge from this endless cycle of cyclic existence. It actually brings a little discouragement. So that's quite helpful.

When things are bad, remember that this is impermanent so it is not going to last; it will change to happiness. If you do that, then that will tend to cheer you up. You can also remember that the suffering you are experiencing is quite similar to the suffering that limitless numbers of people are experiencing right at that moment, that they are suffering in a way that is quite similar to you and that you have the good fortune to have heard the dharma and to be able to practice it. So that will help.

Question: You said that one of the major obstacles is when you have the experience of luminosity and bliss, and it's an obstacle if you don't recognize that the mind is unborn. Is that because there is still a reference point of someone experiencing that?

Rinpoche: Yes, the temporary experience of bliss and luminosity serves as an obstacle to the practice of meditation and is an obstacle because it involves the fixation upon the conception of self. That's because the conception of a self is what leads to the attachment. And from that point of view, it tends to get in the way of your meditation developing further. So the absence of that attachment is necessary and the way to bring about the absence of that attachment is to rest in the mind's way of being.

Chapter 15

The Practice of Utterly Releasing

XIII. EXCEPTIONAL METHODS FOR ENHANCING ONE'S MEDITATION

We began in the preceding chapters with a discussion of Vipashyana and then went on to how the nature of mind is pointed out. Later we considered the way in which this realization is sustained, and in the last chapter we discussed the presentation of the methods for abandoning various mistakes that arise in meditation.

Abandoning these various mistakes is not enough. We must also enhance our meditation further. In this chapter and subsequent chapters we are concerned with the methods for enhancing our meditation, which is to say enabling it to develop to higher levels, increasing it stage by stage. Some people are extremely fortunate and their meditation develops by itself naturally. But for other people they must exert themselves at exceptional methods to develop further.

There are two exceptional methods to increase one's meditation. The first is known as *lada,* which means a decisive, doubtless understanding of emptiness which is discussed in this chapter.

The second special method discussed in the next chapter involves bringing everything to the path and involves training in the resourcefulness of this realization. This is concerned particularly with working with meditation during pleasant or painful experiences and whether one is meditating in a solitary place or in the midst of turmoil. This involves meditating in the midst of busy and complicated situations, because that is how one really trains in the understanding of emptiness.

[314] In this chapter we will look at a practice that is known as *lada* in Tibetan, which is translated as "utterly releasing," and how this practice brings forth an enhancement of one's practice. By utterly releasing, we intend to convey the notion of having no doubt

whatsoever in one's meditation. We first train in the meditation on the nature of the mind and then identify the different mistakes in meditation and dispel them, such that we arrive at a point at which it is appropriate to our meditation to rise to a higher level. The term *lada* has the meaning of abandoning all doubt and hesitation, of settling decisively what mind is. Generally, we know that mind is empty, but due to the force of habitual tendencies that have been established from beginningless time, we still have some doubt about that. At this point, we cut the doubt completely, called "cutting the rope," meaning cutting through all complexity and all elaborations such as the arising, abiding, and ceasing of our mind. In cutting the rope of these hesitations, we are moving decisively into what is called the "unborn great unimpededness" (Tib. *zangtal*).

1. THE TERM LADA

[314] The term *lada* conveys the sense of doubtlessness and a complete resolving of any qualms that one might have; of practicing with complete freedom from doubt, having complete conviction. It is like going up a mountain in a car, with one long route winding up in a slow careful way, and the other short, difficult route going straight up the mountain and requiring exertion. We're not going to take the easy route, we are going to take the short cut which is very quick but very difficult.

When is the appropriate time to do that? Beginners frequently have temporary experiences, and if they continue to meditate stage by stage then the husk of this nyam is broken and actual realization comes forth. When that has happened, then it is the time to engage in the practice of *lada*, of going straight up the mountain. There are possibilities of doing *lada* too soon and doing it too late, and each has with it its own particular peril. If you don't yet have the proper experience, and you have perhaps some intellectual understanding, that would be too soon. For example, a person may be knowledgeable about the dharma and talk quite eloquently about a high view, but in fact be someone who doesn't really have an attitude of renunciation or the realization and deep experience. For this type of person it is too soon to do this practice of going straight up the mountain. On the other hand, if one waits too long, there is the danger of becoming strongly attached to the meditative experiences that one has, which then serve as obstacles to one's meditation practice developing further.

2. DETERMINING THE NATURE OF MIND

[316] Where are we going in *lada*? This refers to the nature that is the ground of all phenomena, all things as they are, wherein birth, production, arising has never been experienced. One does this within the recognition of the nature of the mind that has been settled and pointed out by the lama, and within that one moves very strongly and directly to the mountain peak. It is the place to which one is going, and this is the emptiness of all phenomena, the true nature.

Lada is a manner of going about it directly. It is leaping rather than going step-by-step. In the mahamudra tradition we speak about lada and it corresponds to what in the Nyingma tradition of Dzogchen is called *thögyal,* which literally means "leaping over." So, it is a matter of going directly rather than gradually.

3. WATCHING MIND TO DEVELOP DETERMINED MIND

[318] How does one go directly up the face of the mountain? The third section of *Moonbeams of Mahamudra* explains the way in which one does this by releasing utterly, or doing lada. There are two parts to it. The first is utter release through looking at thought and appearance; the second is utter release through looking at the object of meditation and the meditator. In both cases, one begins by supplicating one's root and lineage gurus, because further development of one's meditation depends upon faith and devotion.

To begin the practice of looking directly at thoughts and appearance, as already mentioned, one give rise to devotion. This is a point at which it is particularly appropriate to practice guru yoga so as to enable one to recognize and meditate within dharmata. Having aroused devotion for the guru, who is understood as the dharmakaya, one supplicates fervently to bring about the realization that any appearance that occurs is the dharmakaya. Then, as was explained before, one extends meditative equipoise one-pointed by resting in that equipoise. The mind rests in a way so that insight does not waver, with even the slightest flutter of distraction. At the same time, the mind has no target whatsoever; it rests in an unadulterated manner. Whatever dawns at that time, whether it is a subtle thought, an obvious thought, or no thought at all, it is looked at nakedly and directly.

Generally speaking, what we are talking about now is no different in meaning from the introduction to coemergent thought that we discussed previously, but there is a slight difference in the way one meditates.

It's basically a matter of the meditator's capacity, in that, at this point, the meditator has a very powerful ability to look directly and nakedly at whatever thoughts arise, not just at obvious thought, but even at the most subtle thought that might arise. The meditator can look within a state that is undistracted and yet not focused on anything that is unadulteratedly pure and spacious. The meditator can investigate the two kinds of thoughts, for instance, a subtle thought and an obvious thought, and see if any difference between them exists or one can also investigate the difference between the mind when it is resting and when it is moving. What is the nature of the mind that is recognized in lada? Whether thoughts are subtle or strong, the mind's nature does not change. Whether there are many thoughts, few thoughts, or there seem t be no thoughts at all, the mind's nature does not change.

Also, the meditator is able to look at whatever pleasure or pain arises, or at any of the eight worldly dharmas, and can cut through them all, settling decisively just what their nature really is. Sometimes thoughts will cease, sometimes thought will radiate; the meditator can look at them all clearly and see exactly what they are. In looking at external phenomena, whether it is a visual form that is beautiful or ugly, large or small, or a sound that is pleasant or unpleasant, the meditator is able to look nakedly and see them as they are. Moreover, the meditator is able at this point to study very precisely, the difference between appearances and mind, between appearances and thought, and by severing all superimpositions whatsoever, release utterly into the mind's way of being.

4. THE ACTUAL RELEASE

[323] Now that we have some understanding of what it means to release utterly into the mind as it is in terms of thought, appearance,

the object of meditation, and the meditator, we come to the fourth section, which describes the actual utter release into the unborn unimpededness. This word *zangtal* has a sense of "utterly penetrating" and "completely penetrated" at the same time. What's being worked with here, is attachment to meditation itself. When you are a beginner, definite knowledge of the mind's way of being, which is of course the object of your meditation, is absolutely necessary and indispensable. But when you have become accustomed to the mind's way of being, then the instruction that's given is that you allow that certainty to crumble. Which is to say, at this point there is a sense of something extra, which is the certainty; some special thing, some exceptional certainty. And you allow that to dissipate. Furthermore, as important as mindfulness has been, there is the sense that the mindfulness of the meditator is allowed to relax, that the deep desire for that which is to be experienced is set loose. You cast off the exertion of the experiencer. In brief, you relax.

This practice of *lada* is called "the actual *lada* to the transparent unborn." One begins by sitting unconditionally in samadhi, resting the mind upon the emptiness that is the unborn, and one does so without any hope of anything happening. One doesn't have thoughts such as, "Now I have to have a good meditation," because one is trying to recognize one's mind as it is. Whether one's meditation goes well or not, the nature of one's mind doesn't change. Therefore one simply practices very straightforwardly one can do this practice in all different situations, whether one is going somewhere, or eating food, or involved in passion.

This is a period of practice that requires tremendous exertion. The text says if one finds it to be very difficult, one should rest three or four days and then undertake the practice again. And if one does so, then it can bring about a very powerful development of one's meditation.

5. MIXING DAY AND NIGHT

The fifth section is spoken of as mixing day and night continuously, in the manner of surrounding all of your experience with meditation. It could also be thought of as the mixing or blending of meditation and postmeditation. This is applied not only to your experience in the daytime, but, moreover, to your experience at night. The way in which you sustain your meditation through meditative equipoise and postmeditation is in accord with what we just spoke of as the utter release into unborn unimpededness. The particular skill that the meditator must master is to relax the mindfulness, because mindfulness involves a certain intention that. The force of mindfulness at this point tends to give rise to *zin*[36] a kind of holding and at the same time emotional, attachment. This kind of conceptual and emotional attachment is released through relaxing mindfulness. It's important to keep in mind that, at this point, we are talking about the meditation of someone who has traveled a long, long way along the path, and has given rise to, has given birth to excellent experience of the mind's way of being, and has learned to sustain that experience. For that person, the way to progress further is to relax even the most subtle desire to maintain mindfulness and to identify things.

You might think, "If I were to practice in that way, wouldn't that mean that I would be falling into a completely unmindful state and how could that be a beneficial thing?" That's not what's going to happen. What's being pointed out is that the mindfulness that we have had up to this point still involves some kind of emotional and conceptual fixation. In this relentless journey and progress toward discovering the mind's genuine way of being, we have now arrived at the point at which we can allow to dissipate even that slight conceptual and emotional fixation that is a component of mindfulness. One rests within a state that is free from any mental work, any deliberate bringing of anything to mind at all. Within such a state, one is mindful of things as they are, the mind as it is, genuinely, accurately, authentically. And thus this kind of mindfulness is greatly superior to the mindfulness we have been able to develop previously, which is either too tight or too loose.

What then does it mean to envelope or surround your experience with this kind of meditative realization? The very best, of course, would be to be able to extend this even into your sleep. When you began to sleep, in just the way that in the daytime you had learned to meditate within the mind's way of being without any kind of deliberate taking of anything to mind, so you would be able to continue into sleep in just that fashion, and you would be able to bring sleep and dream to the path. That, of course, would be the best; however, even for a yogin or yogini at this level, for the most part that's not possible. It does happen, but not that much. And, thus, what is more realistic, even at this point of the path, is that when you go to sleep, you will lose your mindfulness of the mind's way of being. Dreams will dawn in a confusing way. However, when you wake from sleep, almost immediately, you will recognize and will have insight into the way of being of that sleep and that dream. Then your insight into the mind's way of being will resume in an uninterrupted way, such that your daytime experience is again saturated with this meditative realization.

So as to enhance your practice of meditation, you train in the mind's expressive power through the activity that is known as "bringing to the path." That's our topic at this point. When you have gained a good experience of the coemergence of mind thought or appearance, it is time to bring various experiences to the path. If you do so, this will enhancement your practice. If you do not learn how to do so, then most likely it will be difficult to enhance your practice further.

To summarize, the topic at this point is a matter of indicating some of the essential points of carrying difficult situations onto the path, which will include also where you go to practice. So you may well, at this point, go to a place that you find to be terrifying, and practice meditation there. And we'll talk about that in more detail tomorrow, when we speak about the six types of situations, just to put it as generally as I can, that need to be brought to the path, can be brought to the path, as a way of enhancing your meditation.

What is it that is to be brought to the path? That's the main point that we would like to understand right now. It's the very ordinary kinds of thoughts that involve the sense of something that is apprehended and something that apprehends it, that involves an obscuration by ignorance. Those ordinary kinds of thought are what cause you to fall into samsara, and it is for that reason that they must be brought to the path.

THE HEART OF ENLIGHTENMENT

[330] When you meditate upon mahamudra, the most important thing is to meditate in the mind's nature. Upon realizing the emptiness of

the mind, you progress gradually over the stages of the paths. Sometimes students wonder, what is the relationship between mahamudra and compassion and bodhichitta and compassion for other sentient beings. There is a close connection between them. In his *Aspirational Prayer for Mahamudra*, the Third Karmapa, Rangjung Dorje, said, "The nature of migrators is always the Buddha" "Migrators" means those who travel from lifetime to lifetime without having any fixed home. Which is to say, Buddhahood is not something foreign to sentient beings. It is the very nature of sentient beings, it has always been the nature of sentient beings, it always will be the nature of sentient beings. The second line says, "Due to the power of not realizing, they wander in samsara endlessly." "Not realizing" means not realizing one's own nature. As they wander in samsara, they never come to the end of that wandering. One lifetime follows another one endlessly. And in those various lifetimes, sentient beings experience many hardships, delusions, obstructions and different kinds of pain. The third line says, "For sentient beings who have suffering without end." Which is to say, sentient beings whose suffering is never exhausted. The fourth line says, "Arouse compassion. You should give birth to compassion." The point is that realizing this, compassion arises.

When you meditate upon mahamudra, if it goes well, that's great for you. But what about all those sentient beings who have not had the good fortune to realize mahamudra? You should give rise to compassion for them. If you have understood mahamudra just slightly, that is inconceivable good fortune. And you will find that compassion will naturally arise for those who have not been able to understand, to have the good fortune to encounter the teachings on mahamudra, to practice them, and to achieve any realization. If you have had the good fortune to give birth to profound and extraordinary realization of mahamudra, that's very good; and if you have understood mahamudra just a little bit, that's also very good. And remember that you have achieved a human body, you have been able to enter into the door of the dharma, you have been able to hear these extraordinary instructions and you have had the opportunity to practice these quintessential instructions. That, in and of itself, is inconceivable, incomprehensible, good fortune. It is so rare as to be incalculable. For those who have not had such an opportunity, give rise to compassion, and think about how you could help them. Thus you can see how one cultivates compassion in the practice of mahamudra.

So please bear in mind that you have had the opportunity to receive the instructions on mahamudra, to meditate upon them, and consider that you will do whatever you can to further the welfare of sentient beings and to make it possible for others who have not had this opportunity, to have this opportunity. Thinking in that way, you are arousing the mind of enlightenment, the heart of enlightenment, bodhichitta. Do that all the time, and please listen to the teachings in this way.

[330] This chapter discusses the way various difficult situations can be brought to the path. Sometimes we can experience very strong thoughts, strong disturbing emotions, or difficult physical circumstances. It is important that we not fall under their influence but rather bring them into our meditation or samadhi.

Questions

Question: How do we relate to nyams while they are happening? Are we to enjoy them or to avoid them?

Rinpoche: Nyams tend to come in two flavors. Either one thinks one's meditation is going really well or one thinks one's meditation is going very poorly. These are the two main ones, and so we can say there are good ones and bad ones. But the point is, when we are having a good one, we should not be too happy about it and take too much delight in it; when we are having a bad one, we should not be too discouraged by it. If we exert ourselves in meditation, then the intensities of these experiences will diminish little by little until we separate from them. We do not need to regard nyams as good and become attached to them, or regard them as bad and try to get rid of them. We simply continuously exert ourselves in meditation, and gradually they lessen and meditation and realization become clearer. When we talk about the husk with something inside, it is like the nyam is covering over something, enclosing it, and gradually as the husk falls away, the inside becomes manifest.

Whether or not we are able to realize things as they are, separate from misery of samsara and achieve enlightenment, depends upon the kindness of the guru. Also if one has confidence in one's guru, then one will have confidence in the instructions of the guru. If one has confidence in those instructions, then one will practice them. If one practices them, one will achieve fruition. Without confidence in one's guru, one will not have the confidence in the guru's instructions and one will not practice. If one's confidence is 100%, one's practice will be 100% and one will get 100% of the result. If one's confidence is 50% then one's practice will be 50% and so on. So conviction, faith, and devotion are extremely important. If one understands this properly, then faith and devotion are not attachment.

Question: How does one understand this properly so one's faith and devotion is not attachment?

Rinpoche: The reason faith and devotion to one's guru does not become negative attachment is similar to how a mechanic relates to his tools. The hammer, wrenches, and so on are quite valuable to a mechanic for fixing a car, but the tools are nothing more. Similarly, the realization of mahamudra is born in one's being dependent upon the guru's kindness. Because it is very important to realize mahamudra, the guru is very important. But the guru isn't a relative or husband or wife. It's a different kind of relationship.

Question: In meditation the purpose is to make butter, to mix meditation and postmeditation. Is the mantra by analogy the churn that churns the milk that makes butter?

Rinpoche: In the practice of mantra one is generating the experience of mind as it is by looking directly at one's mind. In the practice of the stage of generation, one uses this stage as a skillful method (Skt. *upaya*). In regard to shamatha, meditation on the body of the deity causes the stability of the mind to become enhanced. In Vipashyana the stage of generation is helpful and effective in inviting the *wisdom deity* (Skt. *jnanasattva*), who dissolves in one's body and mind; and one has the sense that one has now received the compassion and wisdom, of that wisdom being in one's own body and mind. One feels great connection from this and it alters one's experience such that it may give rise to realization. From that point of view it is very beneficial to mahamudra.

As for the particulars of the generation stage, the recitation of mantra serves to keep one's mind from becoming distracted. It also brings with it the blessing and potency of practice which enters into one's own being. So you can think of it as the tools to make butter.

The emanation of rays of light that goes out to all sentient beings in the practice at this point has the sense that one is helping them and giving them pleasure and happiness. It also has the sense that one is purifying the obstructions that they have accumulated by way of body, speech, and mind. Principally the point of that is to embrace one's own kindness and good thoughts. Because as the force of that increases, then one comes to have the capacity to help others. This is the reason for the emanation of rays of light in the practice.

Chapter 16

Bringing Obstacles to the Path

B. BRINGING OBSTACLES TO THE PATH

1. WHEN TO BRING OBSTACLES TO THE PATH

[331] The discussion of bringing obstacles to the path is divided into three sections. The first concerns when it is appropriate to do so and what this activity actually is. We do these practices of bringing obstacles to the path when the appearances in our life have become very strong because we have become attached to them, or when we have a strong passion or aggression that we cannot overcome. We might also encounter extraordinary circumstances that hinder our meditation such as becoming very ill. So that we not fall under the influence of such adversity, through the force of our stable meditation we actually use these adverse circumstances and make them part of our path.

When is it appropriate to engage in such action? It is when our meditation shows signs of development and we have arrived at the point of some confidence. To undertake such action prematurely runs the risk of falling under the power of the *eight worldly dharmas*. What is the purpose of such action? We engage in such action to further stabilize and clarify our practice of samadhi. What kinds of actions are there? There are those of the *father tantras* and those of the *mother tantras*. There is also a particular way actions described by the practice lineage. If we go to a place where it is very nice and isolated, we will not know whether our samadhi has any real strength and endurance, any integrity. However, if we seek out adverse circumstances, we can discover whether our meditation has truly become steady and clear. So the practice lineage seeks out an undesirable place that easily generates disturbing emotions such as a charnel ground, or a very crowded place where the disturbing emotions can easily arise.

Generally speaking there is not that much difference between the people of the East and people of the West in terms of the way of practicing dharma. But in this particular practice one seeks out unusual situations that bring adverse conditions to the path. In the East there is a great deal of fear of evil spirits and powerful deities. In Tibet there have been people living in a certain place for many generations. And everyone believes quite strongly in locations where there are powerful deities and harmful spirits; and everyone is afraid to go there. So in Tibet if a yogi wants to discover whether his or her practice is going well, they go to a place said to have demons. This is particularly specified for those who have taken up the ordained life of monks and nuns. The situation is different in the West, however, where the people have not lived here that long and don't have that conviction about certain spirits and deities living in such and such a place.

When should we do this practice of bringing some strong emotional experience to the path? It is at the time that we experience either great happiness or great pain. For instance in America, if we are married and our spouse runs off with another person, we may feel great pain, or hatred and envy; or if we lose our job or cannot make an adequate living, we will feel hardship and pain. This is truly the time to practice to see whether or not we can bring feelings of pain and hardship, or emotions of envy and jealousy to the path.

2. HOW TO BRING OBSTACLES TO THE PATH

[335] On the other hand, there may be times when we want to test our ability to overcome the emotions that might arise when we encounter difficult situations. For instance, perhaps we have been meditating in an isolated, very pleasant place, where we are not irritated by situations such that disturbing emotions would arise. Generally speaking that can be quite good. But sometimes that is not a very good way at all because it does not allow us to find out whether or not we can overcome the disturbing emotions that arise in adverse situations. So we deliberately go to a place that is fairly crowded and mix our meditation with our experience and realization to see whether our realization is sufficient to overwhelm the disturbing emotions. We go to a place where there are lots of people,

lots of distractions, and all kinds of obstacles, and there develop our experience and realization further.

3. SIX PRACTICES OF BRINGING OBSTACLES TO THE PATH

[337] The text describes six different kinds of situations that are to be brought to the path. From some point of view, these would be regarded as adverse conditions. The instruction here is advice on how not to fall under the influence of these situations. Rather, you use them as companions and friends that enable you to enter into meditative stabilization and to develop your meditative stabilization further.

Before discussing these six practices, the text gives three instructions that apply to all six of these practices. It's thus important to understand them at the outset. The first of these has to do with identifying dualistic thoughts or appearances arising from either good or bad circumstances, and not coming under the influence of these. For instance, if conditions are good or pleasant, one might become attached to these; or if a situation is adverse or painful, one might give rise to dislike or the wish to do harm. The point is to identify whether the circumstance is positive or adverse, and not come under its influence. Simply understand what is going one in order not to succumb.

The second step is to cast away the idea of self, which is to say, both the conceptual hanging and the emotional hanging onto self. Whatever has arisen in your mind, do not become attached to it, do not develop aversion for it, don't think of it as something faulty, or good; just rest in meditation.

Just as the first instruction is to recognize what's going on right at the outset, and the instruction for how to work with it in the intermediate period is to cast away the idea of self, the instruction for how to work with the conclusion is to avoid the narrow straits of hope and fear. Hope and fear mean, very simply, hoping that some good thing will come about or fearing that some terrible thing will happen. These are a types of confinement and the way to work with them is to forget about hope and fear and just relax. So these three ways of working with whatever situations arise are the root for any practice of bringing apparently adverse situations to the path and turning them into friends that help you in your practice of meditation.

The first of the six specific practices discussed in the text hs to do with bringing thoughts to the path. The first step, of course, is to recognize thought as thought. Different things arise in our mind and we sometimes believe these to be obstructions to our meditation. Obviously thoughts may arise and appear powerful and vivid. When they do so, don't become heedless; rather, apply mindfulness. Also, we may have thoughts going on that we're not even faintly aware of; they go on and on and we go along with them, not even realizing what's happening. Don't allow yourself to be carried away by your thoughts; rather, as the text puts it, "Squeeze them with mindfulness." It's not necessary to overdo the matter, just apply mindfulness and hold your seat, as it were, rather than being taken for a ride by your thoughts.

Then when you have identified thoughts as thoughts, cast away the idea of self. How do you do that? The text lays out three possibilities of what you might think you should do with thoughts, and points out that each of them would be a mistaken way to proceed. You might think that the way to work with thought is to avoid it, rather than apply your mind to thought. You would draw your mind in and would consider nonconceptual wisdom to be the antidote to thought; you would try to meditate upon nonconceptual wisdom. That's not the way to work with thought. Secondly, you might think that the way to work with thought is to analyze where it arises, where it dwells, and where it goes, and through doing so, you could settle decisively that it has no nature of its own. That's not how you work with it here either. Thirdly, you might think then, if neither of these is the way to do it, you could just give thought its own head and let it go. You would follow along with it, somehow trying to be mindful while all that's going on. That's not how you do it either. The instruction given here is: having identified that thought, without nibbling away at a little angle of it, actually apply your mind right there. Don't think of it as faulty, don't think of it as good, don't try to stop it, don't go after it, don't pursue it, don't do anything to it with your mind. Thought is colorful, pure, relaxed, spacious, brilliant. Sustain that without fixating in any way, sustain it just as it is, without any ideas or any attitudes about it, without hanging onto it. Just sustain that. If you practice in that way, then it will dawn vividly as meditation. That is called "raising thought to the path."

Sometimes you will be able to raise thought to the path and other times you will not be able to do so. Whether you are successful or not successful, do not tumble into the narrow straits of hoping that you will be able to do so or fearing that you will not be able to do so. Without any worry or hesitation, don't calculate, don't figure, don't fixate; once the whole thing is over, just let it be over, and just forget about it. Don't think about whether you did it well or did it badly, but let the whole thing dissolve without a trace, and then just go about your business. The above explains the basic procedure for these six ways of bringing situations to the path. Now, as we look at the other five, we'll see slight variations, but what has just been said is, in essence, how you work with all of them.

The second practice for bringing various situations to the path focuses upon bringing disturbing emotions to the path. Usually this is said to be "transforming poison into healing nectar; you are turning something that kills into something that gives life. We are talking about transforming the five major disturbing emotions of attachment, aggression, ignorance, pride and envy into the *five wisdoms*: mirror-like, equality, discriminating awareness, all-accomplishing, and dharmadhatu wisdoms. How do we bring them to the path? The first disturbing emotion or klesha is desire or attachment. This may be desire for a person or thing and because the mind is attached and stuck, one must realize that the desire has arisen. The second klesha is anger or aggression, such as regarding someone or something as brings about a uncomfortable feeling inside. The third disturbing emotion is ignorance or bewilderment. This bewilderment is when the mind has sunken into some kind of darkness and dullness. Basically, your mind has just become vague and unclear. It's important to recognize bewilderment when it arises. The fourth is pride. Pride is a matter of becoming attached to yourself, thinking "me, me, me." You think that "me" is superior to others so you become quite arrogant and haughty. First of all, you have to recognize that kind of state of mind has arisen. The fifth is envy or jealousy. It's a kind of discomfort with others' prosperity or others' well-being. Whether it is for their wealth or their good qualities, you cannot be content with their good situation. You have some sort of harsh, obstinate, state of mind. Recognize that when it arises.

Usually we don't recognize when a disturbing emotion has arisen. It's important here to recognize our thoughts when they arise. When they appear, don't follow after them; don't try to stop them; don't analyze them in terms of where they arise, abide, or go. Just look right at them. In terms of coemergent mind we look and rest in the mind's luminosity and emptiness. The mind is clear, knowing, and luminous, but it cannot be identified as this or that. Whether we are successful at bringing delusion to the path, that is transforming the disturbing emotion into healing nectar or not, we let it go. We don't hope for something or fear something else, but rest in a very relaxed way, therefore, we see that the way to practice with the mental afflictions is the same method that we practiced in terms of thought.

The third turning of obstacles into the path is working with gods and demons. In Asia there are many beliefs about gods and spirits, and people believe in them. Here in America, it's not quite the same belief. But what's relevant in this section is to think about it this way. Whether magical activity of gods and demons actually arises or not, nevertheless, you may well have this sense of your mind going in a particular direction that's very hard to explain. You may feel sad for no reason at all. Or you may feel frightened, without there being any reason as to why you're frightened. Or you may just feel anxious when there's no particular reason why you should feel nervous. That kind of thing could be regarded as the magical tricks of gods and demons. I think if you can identify that kind of thing in your experience, then the advice given here is quite helpful.

The first thing to do is to recognize that you have become sad, depressed, frightened, anxious, or whatever. The next is to trust yourself to the practice in the way that has been described all along. Whatever sort of magical trick seems to be going on such as fear without any apparent cause, look into its nature, in other words, the nature of luminous emptiness and, having done so, let go of the whole situation. So these three stages that we've been talking about are, again, the essence of this practice too: first, recognize what's going on; second, work with it properly; and third, let go of it, without a trace, and relax.

[337] This third practice of bringing gods and evil spirits to the path works if one has conviction that such gods and evil spirits exist. Whatever fear arises, fear because of our conviction that those supernatural beings are there and that they have a certain power, one works directly with that fear, pacifying it. And by doing so our meditation practice is enhanced considerably.

In the East we have a behavior that is appropriate to those who have taken vows, which is called *kuntu zangpo* meaning "entirely good." The point here is that one would deliberately go into a situation in which there might be a threat to one's vows, and one would preserve one's vows. Householders don't have such vows so there is nothing to talk about in terms of protecting their vows. However, one who has taken vows, by going to graveyards or other places where there are harmful spirits.

How we dispose of the dead is different in the East and the West. In the East the body is just tossed in the charnel ground, and sometimes the body is chopped up and there are limbs scattered around; blood pouring out, and many pieces of bodies in a cemetery. It can be frightening for people to go into the charnel ground. But in the West you put them away very nicely, so nobody knows what is under there; and then of course nobody is afraid.

Also in the East, people would have the conviction that a certain rock or tree is the abode of a particular malevolent evil spirit, or and everyone says, "Don't go there!" and so no one goes there. So the yogins deliberately go there to test the power of their realization. But if you don't think there is something there, then you won't feel afraid, and if you don't feel afraid; then there is nothing to bring to the path. Or similarly, when you go to the graveyard where there are pieces of bodies scattered about, then you can feel horrified. But if all you see are a bunch of white gravestones standing around, then you won't feel afraid and there is nothing to bring to the path.

The fourth practice is to bring pain to the path. This refers in particular to the mental pain of feeling sad and poverty-stricken. Usually one tends to feel that such pain is doing one considerable damage. The practice is not to fall under the sway of such an impoverished state of mind. Usually one feels that the situation is unbearable; but here one mixes one's mind with this sadness and looks directly at this disheartened state and sees its actual nature, which is emptiness. This enhances one's meditation. One can do this in either of two ways. If one is considering the pain of others, then the meditation is a gateway to developing love and compassion for others. If the pain is one's own, then it enables one to recognize the nature of one's mind.

The fifth practice is bringing illness to the path. When illness arises one looks directly at it. This includes both the affliction of body illness and the affliction of mental suffering that goes with it. Generally illness interrupts our practice. When one feels well, one is able to practice meditation; but when one is sick one is not able to. However, we can bring even sickness to the path and through doing so, increase the strength of our meditation. Generally when we are sick, we become quite concerned about the body, think a lot about it, and experience illness as something very harmful. However, by meditating on the true nature of our mind, we can look directly into the very nature of the illness. "What sort of thing is it? How is it?" We will see that the nature of the illness is just the way we see the nature of our mind. This meditation doesn't make the illness go away, but it renders the illness into something that doesn't harm us in quite the same way. We diminish its capacity to strike us and so it will not be so destructive and harmful.

We may wonder why lamas of extraordinary realization, such as Gyalwa Karmapa and Dudjom Rinpoche get sick. They are so highly accomplished, how can this be? These people have very deep realization, however, they also have bodies of flesh and blood. If one has a body that is a composite of flesh and blood, then occasionally one does gets sick. However, people of profound realization don't experience the illness as painful, as ordinary people such as ourselves experience it. For instance, in the film *The Lion's Roar,* His Holiness Karmapa was quite sick from terminal cancer. But in the film, he is smiling and laughing and talking with people. And when people ask him how he is doing, he replies that he is fine. How can this be? The sickness affected his body, but he brought the illness to the path, and looking directly into it, he saw its true nature and did not experience it as suffering in the way that ordinary people would.

Similarly, we can bring the suffering of an unpleasant mental experience to the path. We can look directly into it and see the true nature of this suffering. And through this, the suffering is naturally pacified because the nature of mental events is not truly established.

They are simply the union of emptiness and dependent arising. When realization of this emptiness dawns, the suffering that is experienced does not seem so problematic.

It is very important for us to bring suffering and illness to the path. However, it is very difficult to bring a serious illness to the path from the start. My own guru, when talking about bringing sickness to the path, had us pinch ourselves hard and ask, "Does it hurt?" Then he said, "Yes, it hurts. Look right into it, look right into that painful feeling. How is it going? Oh well, it is not so bad. It diminishes, you can actually look right into it." The point is to start with something small rather than starting with extreme suffering.

The sixth practice is to bring death to the path. We are usually very afraid of death; our mind is very shaky when it comes to the matter of death and to the fact of death. Here one looks at death itself and discovers that it is nothing other than dharmata, nothing other than reality itself, and that in that reality there is no change. There is nothing that exists in and of its own nature, and therefore there is nothing that could serve as a basis for pain. From this viewpoint one overcomes one's fear.

This last practice includes bringing the intermediate state, or *bardo* in Tibetan, to the path. Bardo (pronounced "pardo") means "an in-between state."[37] There are many intermediate states but here we are talking about the intermediate state of dharmata which is the intermediate state between death and rebirth. In both in sutras and tantras, this intermediate state is said to last seven days or sometimes up to forty-nine days. It is the time between leaving the old body and taking up a new body, and during this time all sorts of confusion and false appearances occur. What we mean by bringing the bardo to the path is that we must recognize various sorts of appearances in the intermediate state as dharmata's own light and dharmata's own sound. The practice is to begin to familiarize ourselves with dharmata's own light so that when we enter into this intermediate state, we will be able to practice. To illustrate this light, close your eyes very tightly and press slightly on the side. At first it is completely black because you have your eyes closed very tightly, but then a bit of light begins to dawn, even though your eyes are still closed. In that light will be various forms and many different colors. Then many different little drops may also appear. This is actually dharmata's own light. Similarly, if you put your teeth together, grind them a little, and then stop, there is a silence; and then there is a sound that is like a purring sound, like "drrrrr." After awhile it becomes very loud, but there is no source from which it is emanating. This is the sound of dharmata. Experiences of light and sound such as these come about in the intermediate state. At this time we must look right at the very nature of them and if we do so, they will decrease. The important point is to familiarize ourself with this light and sound now, so that when we die we will be able to do this practice in the bardo, bringing this intermediate state to the path.

Chapter 17

How Realization Dawns

XIV. THE DAWNING OF REALIZATION

[350] As we understand quite well, it is necessary to sustain our meditation experience, and having learned to sustain the experience, it is important not to wander off into distractions and false paths. Not only must we remain on the genuine path, but our meditation must develop further to ever higher levels. We must engage in the practices that we discussed to bring about an enhancement of our meditation, through deliberately getting involved in adverse situations that provoke obstructing conceptions. A variety of methods are taught for doing so; and when a person has learned to sustain realization through all sorts of situations, then realization dawns in stages. Realization becomes more profound, more clear and one progresses on the path. In this chapter we will be discussing the ways in which realization arises.

THE NEED FOR PURE MOTIVATION[38]

Whether we are practicing meditation, studying the quintessential instructions or listening to instructions, or giving teaching ourselves, pure motivation is required at all times and is extremely important. We can speak of this pure motivation first as a seed, which is to say, we think, "I'm going to practice the dharma and my reason for doing so is not to subdue my enemies or to accumulate wealth, but so that I'll be able to achieve liberation from samsara and achieve the omniscient state of complete enlightenment." From that point of view we listen to instructions, meditate and practice, and in this way accomplish our own welfare. Moreover, we earnestly try to further the welfare of others, and think, "As I listen to these instructions and practice them, I do it not for my sake but for the sake of the many, many sentient beings, so that later I will be able to teach the dharma to them properly and protect them from the suffering of samsara. I will be able to help them find liberation and complete enlightenment by showing them the paths that lead to such a state.

In that sense, the intention to achieve supreme enlightenment for the sake of all sentient beings is vital when we listen to instructions and it is vital when we teach the dharma to others. It is absolutely necessary that whatever activity we are engaged in be directed by this aspiration to complete enlightenment for the sake of all sentient beings.

THE NEED FOR DEVOTION TOWARDS THE GURU

[350] We need also to generate devotion to develop one's practice further. The object of one's devotion may be one's root guru or it may extend to the gurus of the lineage such as Milarepa, Marpa, Naropa, or Tilopa. By reading their spiritual biographies, one may begin to feel great faith and devotion towards them, offer supplication to them, and achieve their blessings. Why is that possible? The very nature of our mind is emptiness, and it is undifferentiated from the vast space that is inseparably united with insight. Our mind is really pervaded by this union of space and insight. Similarly, the great gurus of the lineage have mixed their minds undifferentiably with this union of space and insight. Since our mind is undifferentiated from the union of space and insight and the minds of the gurus of the lineage have mixed and manifest with this realm of space and insight, they are not so distant from us. If we feel and ascertain the mixing and inseparability of the minds of the gurus with our own mind, then we achieve their blessings and the great potency of the minds of the gurus enters into us.

We may also meet face-to-face with accomplished teachers such as Chögyam Trungpa Rinpoche, Kalu Rinpoche, or the Karmapa. If we supplicate to them by visualizing light pouring from the three centers of their bodies and dissolving into the three centers of our own body, the exalted body, speech, and mind of the guru mixes undifferentiably with our own ordinary body, speech, and mind, such that we generate a confidence and an unusual sensation that the blessings enter into us. When our meditation has poor clarity or stability, we can supplicate the gurus with devotion and their blessings enter into our continuum and will benefit our practice and make our meditation more clear and stable.

A. THE THREE LEVELS OF PRACTICE

[350] Depending upon how much and how well one has trained in former lifetimes, there are three families of practitioners. First, in the case of those who have extremely sharp faculties and for whom realization dawns all at once (Tib. *cik charwa*), the levels of realization dawn for them simultaneously. Second, those who "suddenly cross" (Tib. *thogalwa*) have a situation such that, though they may be practicing a lower level, nevertheless the realization of a higher level occurs. But this higher realization is not stable, being sometimes clear, sometimes vague, being present and then absent. The third type (Tib. *rimgyipa*) are those who proceed gradually, bit by bit, step by step, stage by stage.

There are also three different levels of knowing the nature of dharmata: understanding (Tib. *go*), experiencing (Tib. *nyong*), and realization (Tib. *tok*). Understanding uses the mental consciousness by investigating, studying, and thinking about how phenomena are empty and in what way mind has nature of clarity. One investigates in terms of what is known as valid cognition (Skt. *pramana*), whereby the meaning (Tib. *tunji*) of emptiness or the nature of dharmata is known by way of words.

As our understanding of dharmata becomes clearer, we arrive at the second level of experiencing dharmata. At this level we are not just putting words together, but we actually experience the concept in our meditation. Events arise and we have the experience of the deep nature of mind. However, at this point we do not have great familiarity with the nature of mind as sometimes it appears clearly and other times not very clearly.

At the third level, direct realization, we experience the deep nature of mind clearly and directly. We know the meaning of the dharma or phenomena without any intermediary and as a result our knowledge of dharmata is decisive and does not waver.

In terms of these three ways of knowing the dharmata, it is possible when looking into the nature of mind to mistake one type for the other. One might think that mere understanding is realization or that realization is just understanding and so on. However, one must work towards realizing the deep nature by seeing it nakedly and directly. Sometimes when one has only understanding, that understanding actually obstructs realization. One must move further by recognizing that understanding is not realization, and move further to the point of actual realization.

The first way of comprehending is through logical understanding. Gampopa has explained that the second level of experiencing is something that has not yet transcended mind. It is like experiencing the sun on a day of occasional clouds: sometimes the sun is bright and clear, other times the sun hazy and obscured by clouds. It is like the temporary experiences of bliss, clarity, and non-thought. Sometimes these experiences are present and sometimes they are not. If we persist in this second way of passing experiences without becoming attached to them, we can transcend all doubt about the way in which the mind exists, and develop a definitive conviction of how the mind is. And this is realization.

B. THE VALIDITY OF THE FOUR YOGAS

1. THE FOUR YOGAS IN THE SUTRAS AND TANTRAS

[354] A number of authors have said that the four yogas are not part of the Buddhist dharma, but rather was made up by the Kagyu scholars. They say that there are many Buddhist texts which discuss the *five paths* and the ten *bodhisattva levels*, but do not mention the four yogas. However, Tashi Namgyal shows that the twelve yogas were mentioned in the mahayana *Lanksvatara Sutra,* and he cites passages from different tantras to illustrate that the four yogas weren't invented by the Kagyu scholars.

2. THE MEANING OF THE FOUR YOGAS

[358] There are four yogas: (1) one-pointedness, (2) freedom from elaboration, (3) one taste, and (4) non-meditation. Each of these has three internal divisions of small, middling, and great. Thus there is the smaller one-pointed yoga, the middling one-pointed yoga, and the great one-pointed yoga, making a total of twelve internal divisions for the four yogas. Moving through these twelve yogas, one arrives at the fruition of complete enlightenment.

More important is the meaning of these four yogas. First, one begins with shamatha and then joins this with Vipashyana, which creates a non-wandering mind; and one arrives at the first yoga, "one-pointed" yoga. One-pointedness principally indicates the stability of shamatha meditation. Shamatha initially is not very stable and the mind will not rest. However, when one's mind is brought to rest, that is "one-pointedness." Then through this resting, one sees mind clearly and superimpositions of mind are cut through. The complexities are resolved into simplicity.

Regarding the three aspects of one-pointedness, when one achieves the smaller level, one sees the nature of mind which is bliss, pleasure, or luminosity. However, one sees it in a somewhat rough manner. Still, having seen mind's nature, one becomes mostly free from anxiety and free from pain. At the second middle level of one-pointedness, one achieves power over this meditative stability, this samadhi, and begins to have some independence such that meditation is not difficult or hard work. At the greater level of one-pointedness, it is said that the experience of meditation surrounds one in every way, which is to say that meditation is continuous and one has it always.

When one develops a genuine, definite conviction and becomes free from elaboration and complexities, one arrives at the second yoga, which is "freedom from complexity," sometimes translated as "freedom from elaboration." This yoga involves recognizing luminosity on the one hand and emptiness on the other, and generating conviction about emptiness.

At the small level of freedom of complexity, one realizes the unborn nature of phenomena. At the middle level one understands that phenomena are not only unborn, but that they are actually rootless. Having understood the nature of internal mind, at the greater level the meditator understands that external appearances are not separate from reality or dharmata, so all superimpositions on external phenomena are completely severed.

As the experience of the second yoga intensifies, one arrives at the yoga of "one taste." This is the point at which one's meditation becomes more and more clear and one understands that samsara and nirvana are one taste. One understands that which is to be abandoned and that which is to be adopted as one taste.

Because one's realization of things as they are has become manifest, at the small level of one taste one sees that there is no difference between samsara and nirvana. At the middle level one cuts through the root of seeing a difference between the apprehended object and the apprehending subject so that they no longer appear to be separate. At the great level of one taste one sees that all phenomena whatsoever are truly of one taste and therefore, one no longer regards anything as dangerous and thus feels tremendous fearlessness.

By becoming ever more familiar with the realization of one taste, the meditator arrives at the point at which she or he does not need to engage in a formal structure of meditation. This is the level called non-meditation. The nature of mind has been resolved, and one does not need to practice any particular meditation to experience this.

At the small level of non-meditation, because mind itself and reality have become manifest, one no longer needs to meditate. There is no longer the sense of something meditated upon and someone meditating upon it. At the middle level one achieves spontaneous presence such that striving and effort are no longer required. Striving and effort were required to some extent at the small level of non-meditation, but at the middle level they are no longer necessary. It is said that at the great level, one has arrived at the bodhisattva level where one meets the dharmakaya, which is to say that the dharmakaya becomes fully manifest. The two clear lights mix at this point, that is, the clear light of ground and the clear light of the path.

There are many references to these levels in the sutras. However, they are not very important for our present purposes.

C. POSTMEDITATION AND THE FOUR YOGAS

[364] What is the postmeditation experience corresponding to each yoga? In the first yoga of one-pointedness, one is not very familiar with the deep nature of mind. The postmeditation experience is described as *ahteh* in Tibetan. At this stage in postmeditation one experiences various appearances and believes them to be real. However, one has few thoughts, perceptions, and little discursiveness.

In the postmeditation experience subsequent to the second yoga of freedom from complexity, the factor of clarity has gone further and one's understanding of the deep nature of mind has deepened. So in this yoga, as various phenomena appear, one understands them and regards them as being like illusions. One does not have much conceptuality.

The postmeditation experience subsequent to the third yoga of one taste involves understanding the union of appearance and emptiness. This union is not yet apprehended fully, and the experience of emptiness is stronger.

The fourth yoga of non-meditation is distinguished by the mixing of meditative equipoise and postmeditation. With this mixing one's compassion for all sentient beings becomes stronger. Having a great capacity for realizing the deep nature within meditative equipoise, there is a much greater force to one's compassion for sentient beings.

D. DETAILED DESCRIPTION OF THE FOUR YOGAS

1. INSTRUCTIONS FOR THE FIRST YOGA

[373] One-pointed yoga refers to one-pointedness of mind. Within that one-pointedness one understands gradually and clearly the nature of mind. As discussed earlier, the yoga of one-pointedness has three internal divisions, the lesser, average, and great (also called the small, middling, and great). Developing these requires some exertion. It is helpful to take a brief retreat of observing silence for perhaps one or two days since a lot of conversation tends to create confusion. When we are practicing this yoga of one-pointedness, we might experience the dullness or the wildness we discussed. It is important to clear away and abandon such states of mind using the methods already discussed, by applying concentration for the sinking state and relaxing for the wildness of mind. Or we might use the special method of mahamudra, of looking directly into the nature of mind and dispelling any obstacles in that way. Either way is fine at this point. What is necessary is that we clear away heavy and excited states of mind.

If we experience what is called a real darkness of stupidity, it is necessary to use methods for purifying ill deeds and obstructions, such as guru yoga. We receive various empowerments for meditative stabilization, we make offerings of various sorts, and we confess our ill deeds. Engaging in such methods reduces the severity of the obstacles we are experiencing. We can also speak with our guru or fellow meditators, asking them what they did when this obstacle came up and what would help in this particular case.

Finding that one has wrong views about points of dharma and meditation, one strives for the correct view. Sometimes one takes refuge and recites the liturgy for receiving refuge. One reflects on the way in which samsara has no essence whatsoever and that samsaric pursuits are entirely futile. This generates a genuine wish to become free from samsara, which furthers our devotion to the dharma and guru and helps generate compassion for sentient beings.

One may find that after practicing for a long period of time, one is just simply tired. If so it is appropriate to rest and just allow one's mind to become spacious. However, at all times mindfulness is important. There are two kinds of mindfulness at this point: an extremely concentrated, focused mindfulness, and mindfulness that is somewhat looser and is just not forgetting.

Sometimes when practicing, one may suddenly experience an extraordinarily good understanding of something and have genuine insight. In postmeditation whatever appearance takes place, the instruction is not to become involved with it; simply let it go. It has come; fine, let it go. Sometimes one may have the feeling that a certain meditation experience was good and at other times the meditation experience was bad. Whatever these experiences are, it doesn't matter. The important point is not to be concerned about them, but just to exert oneself at the practice of meditation. Those are the instructions for the one-pointed yoga.

2. Instructions for the Second Yoga

[373] The instructions for the second yoga of freedom from complexity is to go to an isolated place, remain alone, and practice meditation. Mainly one practices meditation. Between the two types of mindfulness just discussed, one relies upon the more relaxed type of mindfulness. When it seems beneficial for one's meditation, one makes offerings and supplicates the gurus of the lineage and engages in the methods for increasing devotion, pure appearances, and compassion for others.

When one is practicing this yoga of freedom from complexity, it is helpful to meet occasionally with one's guru or with companions who have had similar meditation experiences and converse with them about one's experience. This helps the experience to progress further and it helps to arouse more longing. Sometimes one also might read the spiritual songs of the siddhas, such as those of Marpa and Milarepa or the *Rain of Wisdom,* and think over their essential points or sing those songs to oneself.

When one's meditation is not progressing, one might practice the meditation upon one's own yidam. One imagines this deity vividly and clearly, and this will help one's meditation practice considerably.

3. INSTRUCTIONS FOR THE THIRD YOGA

[374] The third yoga is one taste. Sometimes one practices alone and sometimes one goes to a place with many people. By doing this one sees how one's mind and meditation are going. Is the meditation increasing or is it declining? Are afflictions being generated or not? Sometimes when one practices one relies upon strong mindfulness; sometimes one leaves the mindfulness very loose and then just observes to see how one's practice goes.

In the yoga of one taste the factor of realizing and ascertaining emptiness may become very strong and one might mistakenly believe that the relation between actions and their effects and the necessity to practice virtue and eliminate unvirtuous deeds are not really important. This is a serious mistake. If one begins to think that way, it is very important to understand why this is incorrect.

4. INSTRUCTIONS FOR THE FOURTH YOGA

[374] After the yoga of one taste comes the yoga of non-meditation. At this point one experiences more relaxation and spontaneity and experiences fewer afflictions. At this point one has reached Buddhahood. One realizes the nature of one's mind directly. One sees that there is no need to abandon certain things because one sees that they are natural and purified. On the other hand one realizes that there is something that needs to be realized. However, that is not strong and present either because one understands that the nature of one's mind is always there.

THE FOUR YOGAS AND THE FIVE PATHS

[402] If we correlate the four yogas of mahamudra with the five paths of the sutra path, the yoga of one-pointedness correlates to the first two paths of accumulation and unification. Even though one does not have direct realization of emptiness, nevertheless, meditation has been generated to some extent within one's continuum. The third path of seeing is the point at which emptiness is realized directly, non-conceptually. It correlates with the second yoga of freedom from complexity. The fourth path of meditation correlates with the third yoga of one taste. And the fifth path of no more learning correlates with the fourth yoga of nonmeditation.

The text and treatises speak extensively of the extraordinary qualities, such as the emanations, powers and clairvoyances, the thirty-two marks and the eighty signs of a buddha, that one develops on the paths and which are complete on the final path. When one has progressed through the four yogas and arrived at the final yoga, one does not have the qualities of emanation and clairvoyance and the physical signs of the Shakyamuni Buddha. What is the reason for that? There is really no difference in terms of the qualities of mind, in terms of what needs to be abandoned and what needs to be realized. However, the Buddha Shakyamuni spent incalculable lifetimes accumulating merit and wisdom so that when he took birth in India, he took birth not through the force of ordinary karma, but through the force of having accumulated vast collections of merit and wisdom. Milarepa, however, was born as a very ordinary person. Through the ripening of actions and afflictions that were accumulated on the basis of confusion, he was extremely fortunate to be able to meet with a fully qualified guru and receive profound instructions from that guru. He was able to exert himself ferociously at his practice so that he achieved enlightenment. Thus, the mind of Milarepa was no different from the mind of Shakyamuni Buddha in its abandonment and realization. However, not having progressed over the path in the same way, by accumulating such vast merits, Milarepa did not have the qualities of body and speech that Buddha Shakyamuni had.

Questions

Question: When I am sitting there are these bubbly little feelings going through me. I'm having a hard time knowing what to look at and not look at.

Rinpoche: There are two different issues there. One is the tightness in the body that can develop as one practices meditation. When one practices, it can be as if the flesh in our body intensifies, and the channels or nadis are very focused and intense. That can easily lead to all sorts of uncomfortable physical sensations. The point is to relax completely when one practices meditation. Mind relaxes and body relaxes also. The other issue is that perhaps there are some problems with the body that a doctor might be able to help with.

So there are things that have to do specifically with the practice of meditation and here the main point is to be very relaxed. Then if there are other sorts of things, they may have to do with the medical arena. It is good when you are practicing meditation to check in with your body from time to time, specifically to see if you are getting too tight. Check your whole body, hands, feet, etcetera just to see if the body is getting too tight, and then relax it. It can easily come about that as the awareness becomes concentrated, the body becomes concentrated and this concentration in the body is not helpful. So you just check the feeling throughout the body and just relax the whole body.

Question: Rinpoche, Trungpa Rinpoche once said that after enlightenment there is still pain. He added that it was no big deal, and of course neither was pleasure. I wonder if you might comment on this in the light of the teaching on one-pointedness, that there is no more pain at that point.

Rinpoche: I don't know that I understand precisely the measure of Trungpa Rinpoche's thought, but it strikes me that it was said from an extremely vast point of view. If one were to say that even a completely enlightened being still has pain, one might mean that perhaps it is reflecting on the fact that a buddha sees the pain and the frustration that all sentient beings throughout space are experiencing; and this buddha feels tremendous compassion for them, wishing to do something that would actually help. This buddha would also feel a sense of a great responsibility in that he or she has vowed to relieve all sentient beings of suffering and to establish them in a state of happiness, and is now at the point where he or she has the capacity to help all sentient beings.

Still, a buddha sees that all sentient beings have pain and that this pain can be dispelled and from that point of view there is no great danger. A buddha also has great pleasure in that a buddha has cleared away every last trace of samsara and is now completely free from the pain of samsara. For that reason a buddha is happy. At the same time that pleasure is empty of any nature of its own; that is something that is experienced manifestly and clearly and from that point of view, the pleasure is no big deal.

Chapter 18

How We Should Practice

I am delighted we have had this opportunity to study the text *Moonbeams of Mahamudra*. When you wonder what practice to do, practice mahamudra. Moreover, there are a great many oral instructions concerning mahamudra. Among them this text is very special. I explained in the beginning of our period of study that when Gyalwa Karmapa was asked which book if translated into English would be of the most benefit, the Karmapa said to translate *Moonbeams of Mahamudra*. This book was rendered into English. However, it is very long and many students who have been instructed to study this book, have responded saying it is a pretty big book. So I am glad that in this relatively brief period of time we have had a chance to look at it together as a group, to study what it has to say, to think about it in an environment of practice within a concentrated period of time. I am extremely happy about that.

There are a great many books concerned principally with knowledge that one might study. But when one tries to join them to experience, it is not easy to do so. Other books focus upon internal experience, but they are difficult to understand. As Tashi Namgyal said at the beginning, there are many laymen who have studied a lot, but they don't go on to practice and to gain experience of the meaning of what they have studied. And there are others who practice a lot, but because they are not skillful with the words they aren't able to explain things clearly. So, Tashi Namgyal composed this text with a lot of work combining the words, the meaning and the experience, producing a book useful both for study and practice.

Moonbeams of Mahamudra is quite a long book. When one reads it for the first time it is, of course, not that easy to understand. Who would expect it to be? However, if one reads it again carefully, one begins to understand that this is important, it is meaningful, and one develops some interest and enthusiasm for this book. By continually looking at the text and practicing the instructions given in it, the meaning of it will become clearer and clearer. In this way, tremendous benefit will occur.

I would like to say that the most important thing is to bring this experience and realization into greater clarity and stability. In particular, if you study and practice gradually, your understanding of the meaning and the character of the different teachings on selflessness and so forth will increase. The meaning presented in this text is profound, vivid, clear, practical, delightful and not very difficult. Please do not stop at understanding, but go further to the point of experience and further to realization until you have reached a complete perfect Buddhahood.

Some students have a lama who knows exactly what is going on in a student's mind. I am sorry, I have neither the compassion nor the blessings to impart this. I don't have that kind of clairvoyance. Nevertheless, I have given instructions on the practice of mahamudra. They are not my own instructions but the instructions that have been passed down through the Kagyu lineage. And I have been extremely fortunate in my life in that I have been able to receive many special and blessed oral instructions from many great teachers. I offer these to you who wish to practice the dharma, with my genuine confidence that if you practice these instructions they will unerringly lead to complete liberation. Some students might think, "Well, if he has no blessings or clairvoyance then probably he is on the wrong path." But you need not have any hesitation of that sort, these instructions are genuine. If you practice them, you will find that your practice will become perfected and you will achieve the result that was intended.

To arrive at realization in the tradition of the sutras one must practice and accumulate merit and wisdom for an incalculable number of eons. However, if one has been introduced to the oral instructions of mahamudra, then when one hears that all phenomena are emptiness, one might have the experience of prajna. Those who are fortunate will then see the experience directly. Others don't have such experience right away but will understand the meaning, and gradually this understanding will become experience. So you can see that you are in a fortunate situation and it should not to be wasted. Rather practice and meditate well.

When some begin to practice, they feel a very strong wish to renounce the world altogether. They think, "I am just going to practice the dharma, I don't need a place to live, I don't need to worry about my husband or my wife, I will just forget my children. I don't need to be concerned about food, I don't need to be concerned about clothing," and believe they can just throw everything else away. However, embracing into that sort of renunciation tends to not be very stable or enduring. In any case, one's family and one's parents are very important and it is important not to just throw them away. Instead one should continue with one's work in the world and with one's practice of the dharma. Because we are practitioners of the dharma, we should not be people who have no love or compassion, with our head just spinning all the time.

Because we have been fortunate enough to have experienced the dharma, we tend to be people who have love for others, compassion for others, and the wish to help people. Our mind does not continue to be distracted and be dragged along by anything that comes by. And when there is not much time to practice meditation, that is the time to practice mindfulness and awareness. When there is time to take a long or short retreat, it is beneficial to do so. What is crucial is that in all one's activities and at all times, one maintain mindfulness. If one can do that, it will help one's mind tremendously.

When you have the opportunity to practice meditation, that is extremely good fortune. We should also recognize that there are a great many people who have no faith in the dharma. They are not terrible or bad people, so there is no reason for becoming proud of your dharma accomplishments; it is just that they are temporarily unable to have an interest or confidence in the dharma so as to enter into it. So they should be recipients your love and compassion. To urge people to enter the dharma by saying the dharma is wonderful just pushes people away. It is a fruitless enterprise and not very skillful. There are simply some who have not yet generated faith in the dharma, but it is always possible for them to do so. If at the appropriate time you are able to help them find the path of dharma, then that is very good, but it is important to lead individuals to the path of dharma in a skillful way.

Some students are ready and others are not. Those who are not ready will gradually become ready. When the time is ripe the Buddha's activity will arise spontaneously and there will be an opportunity for them to enter into the door of the dharma. For those that are not ready, one must not push and urge them but wait for the right time when they are ready and able to enter into the dharma. Therefore, looking to see whether the person is ready or not ready is important.

If one has the good fortune to enter into practice and interest in doing so but contrary conditions come about, then that is the time for patience. Patience will facilitate the clearing away of such difficult and contrary conditions. And then, when the opportunity for practice again arises, do not waste it, but enter into practice again.

The Buddha said that taming one's mind is very important and the very essence of the dharma. Taming one's mind involves abandoning what is bad and cultivating what is good. One needs to abandon or pacify the afflictions such as desire, aggression, ignorance, pride, and jealousy. One needs to cultivate wisdom which leads to the good qualities and extraordinary attributes of a realized person. The principal method for abandoning what needs to be abandoned and developing what needs to be cultivated is through meditation. And having mindfulness and awareness is the proof of realization. When practicing meditation there is both the meditation session and the postmeditation session that arises from the meditation session. One maintains the continuum of mindfulness and awareness through both the meditation and postmeditation sessions. In that way they will benefit each other mutually. The important point is the continuity of mindfulness and the nonwandering of mind. That is what the Buddha meant about the very essence of the dharma being taming one's mind.

Notes

By Clark Johnson, Ph. D.

1. Tibetan texts don't have headings. We include headings to help the reader navigate this rather complex book. The headings with numbers follow the outline given on pages v to viii. The headings without numbers or letters are simply there to help the reader.
2. According to Reginald Ray in his book *Buddhist Saints,* since the time of the Buddha there have been practitioners who lived in the monasteries and upheld the Vinaya and there have been forest dwellers who also practiced Buddhism but did not follow the usual monastic code of taking several hundred vows and then trying to keep them. *Mahasiddhas* were later vajrayana practitioners who were greatly revered and achieved enlightenment in very unorthodox ways. There were undoubtedly thousands of them but the Tibetans collected these together into eighty-four stories, which is a sacred number, to describe their experience. Mahamudra practice, as we will learn later in this book, came directly from several of these mahasiddhas as the primary meditational practice of the Kagyu lineage, one of the four main lineages of Tibetan Buddhism.
3. The Tibetan is literally *chagchen* (mahamudra) *dawai* (of the moon) *özer* (light) and could be translated as "Moonlight of Mahamudra" or "moonlight of Mahamudra." We chose "moonlight" because it implies a more pervasive light than the more focused light of a moonbeam.
4. This book is the compilation of five different ten-day seminars which were given yearly at a mahamudra retreat at Big Bear Lake in California. Thrangu Rinpoche has also given Mahamudra retreats in England, Canada, and Germany. We combined the best of each topic in this manuscript and keyed it to the root text, *Mahamudra: the Quintessence of Mind and Meditation*.
5. His Holiness Karmapa has since been reborn and is now in his teens.
6. The numbers in brackets show the page number in the root text *Mahamudra:The Quentessence of Mind and Meditation* .
7. Buddhists have a different view of the world than our common sense would tell us. As ordinary people, we believe that the world is solid and real and that with our mind we can only fantasize about how it is. Buddhists would say that ordinary beings suffer in samsara because they do not actually see the true nature (Tib. *nge lug*) of phenomena or the true nature of their mind. Rather they see and become attached to outward appearances (Tib. *khrih lug*) which are actually empty of

inherent nature. In other words, according to the Buddhist view, the world is not real or solid and our mind is capable of realizing this.

A simple example of this is: if we hit a brick wall, it does indeed seem solid and hitting it hurts. This is the way it appears to us and our fellow human beings would agree with us. However, physicists tell us that the wall is actually composed of silicon and oxygen atoms and these atoms are moving at incredible speeds. The atoms are so far apart from each other that the wall is actually 99.99% space and the "red" that we see (but many other animals don't) is actually just a radiation of that particular wavelength. This view of the atomic structure is more like the true nature of the wall than its appearance as a solid object.

Thrangu Rinpoche also likes to say that highly realized individuals who have truly understood the emptiness of phenomena can, for example, put their hand through a rock. In Tsurphu outside Lhasa in Tibet there is a boulder with a palm print in it which was made less than a decade ago when the 17th Karmapa put his hand on it.

8. While the goal of all Buddhists is the same—to achieve enlightenment, the philosophical systems in the various schools of Buddhism do not always exactly agree. Thrangu Rinpoche in various teachings has explained phenomena using different systems or schools depending upon which one he felt explained the particular situation best. Throughout this book Thrangu Rinpoche takes the viewpoint of the *Chittamatra* school.

To give a very simplified review, the Hinayana schools of Buddhism hold the position that the self or ego is empty, but outer phenomena (called dharmas) such as trees and rocks are solid and real. In the first century of our era, Nagarjuna founded the Madhyamaka branch of the mahayana school. This school maintained that not only is self empty but external phenomena were empty as well. Finally, in the fourth century of our era, Asanga founded the Chittamatra school, which maintained both self and outer phenomena are empty and that outer phenomena are actually completely created by mind.

The Chittamatra view is more completely explained in Thrangu Rinpoche's *The Differentiation of Consciousness and Wisdom*.

Again to briefly summarize, there are eight consciousnesses and everything in our first six sensory consciousnesses (the visual, auditory, gustatory, olfactory, and tactile consciousnesses and the sixth mental consciousness) goes into the eighth storehouse consciousness. This has been going on for hundreds of lifetimes so when we see a tree, that visual impression of the tree goes into our mental consciousness with the thousands of latencies about trees from our eighth consciousness to give us an impression of a living, solid object made of wood—and we experience it as that. Every other human being has had similar latencies so they also experience the tree as roughly the same thing.

When we dream, the five sensory consciousnesses are turned off. We see these latencies coming out of the eighth consciousness, and the sixth mental consciousness believes them to be as real as anything experienced while awake.

When we reach some degree of enlightenment, these latencies are "purified" in that we see them to be latencies rather than real external objects. That is, we overcome our habitual patterns of perception gained over countless lifetimes. Then we can begin to do "miracles" such as putting our hand through solid objects, healing wounds with a touch, seeing and knowing things that occur hundreds of miles away and so on. All this is because we are no longer bound by these latencies (Tib. *chag pa*) that have bound our mind.

Understanding this perhaps we can see why enlightened masters tell us everything we experience in this worldly existence is created by our mind, not some outside force which we usually call "reality."

9. The Sanskrit word "klesha" literally means "afflictions," but was translated into Tibetan as *nyon mong,* which has more of a connotation of emotions that disturb the mind, such as intense passion or attachment, hatred or anger, confusion or bewilderment, pride, and jealousy. Since "afflictions" denote a permanent, almost innate, disability, we have chosen to translate this term as "disturbing emotions."
10. This practice is described in more detail later, but basically after the student has practiced a great deal, the teacher catches the student off guard with some surprising act and shows the student what the mind is really like, not how it appears conceptually. The experience has been described as being brilliant, an experience of great calm and bliss, a moment in which one understands everything, and unlike any other experience in life, the experience of mind as it really is, unpolluted and innately pure—completely unlike the mind we experience in daily life.
11. Everything in the world has the quality of emptiness. This emptiness is not, however, a complete voidness or "dead" emptiness because emptiness (Skt. *shunyata*) has an additional quality of *luminosity*. This quality is the quality of allowing everything to appear within it.

    In relation to mind, the mind is also completely empty, not having any solid existence, but mind obviously also has the quality of luminosity which is the knowing, aware quality of mind.
12. This theme will continue throughout this book. Basically the mind as we know it is full of thoughts, impulses, desires, and rigid conceptions and appears to us as a solid continuous stream that began when we were born. That is how the mind appears (Tib. *khrih lug*). However,

with the practice of mahamudra, the mind gradually relaxes, becomes more open, and begins to see the nature of reality clearly, without the dualism of "I" and "other." When this happens, we begin to see the true nature (Tib. *nge lug*) of the mind and see that the mind is really pure awareness, luminous, and clear. This original nature of mind is called in the Kagyu lineage "ordinary mind" which will be discussed later. Note that this word "ordinary mind" refers to an innately pure mind which we don't ordinarily experience.

13. Buddha-nature or Buddha-essence (Skt. *tathagatagarbha*) is one of the main teachings of the third wheel of the turning of the Dharma. This seed or essence is present in all sentient beings and it is what allows them to attain Buddhahood. All beings possess Buddha-essence to the same degree, so all have an equal capability to reach enlightenment.
14. One way to organize the Buddhist teachings is to divide them into three different major groups of teachings which are called the three turnings of the wheel of dharma (Skt. *dharmachakra*). The first turning began at Varanasi when the Buddha taught the four noble truths; these are basically the Hinayana (or Theravada) teachings. The second turning was given at Rajagriha and were the mahayana teachings, which were mainly about emptiness and compassion. The third turning (not recognized by all schools) were the teachings on Buddha-essence and luminosity.
15. This is described in the *One Hundred Thousand Songs of Milarepa*
16. When the Buddha taught that there was no creator and there was no permanent self, he then was asked, how did everything come about? His answer was everything came about by a natural process of cause and effect called interinterdependent origination. This process has twelve steps and begins with birth and goes through old age and decay, which in turn starts another cycle. This is more fully explained in Rinpoche's *The Twelve Links of Interinterdependent origination*.
17. Conventional truth (Tib. *kundzop*), also called conventional truth, is the world as it appears to us unenlightened beings who see the world in terms of duality. Ultimate truth (Tib. *dondam*), also called absolute truth, is the world as it really is, that is, as seen by an enlightened being.
18. Rinpoche gives the example of the image of the moon on the surface of a calm lake. The moon does not exist in the lake, yet because of the interdependence of night time, the moon, the calm water, and the person standing in the right place, the appearance of the moon will be seen by every one.
19. A detailed description of this argument can be found in Thrangu Rinpoche's *Open Door to Emptiness*. This argument comes from a

sutra of the Buddha called *The Questions for Melinda* which is said to be a dialogue between a Buddhist siddha and Alexander the Great.

20. The word is literally translated as "listening," but Thrangu Rinpoche has said that in more modern times this means "studying."
21. Hashang said that it doesn't matter if a black cloud or a white cloud covers the sun, it still darkens the world. Similarly, if one has a good or bad thought, it also doesn't matter because it is a thought. He was defeated by Kamalashila who said that the path of accumulation of merit was important (which, of course, involves cultivating good thoughts) and one couldn't simply just do mahamudra meditation of looking at thoughts directly. From that point on, Kamalashila's view was taught in Tibet.
22. This lecture actually came in the middle of the Fifth Bear Mahamudra retreat and is not part of Tashi Namgyal's book.
23. See Thrangu Rinpoche's *King of Samadhi* by Rangjung Yeshe Press for a fuller explanation.
24. These four uncommon preliminaries are discussed in detail in Thrangu Rinpoche's *The Four Foundations of Buddhist Practice* (Namo Buddha Publications).
25. This refers to a person putting his hands together at his heart as a sign of respect. So even if the person raises just one hand in respect it is beneficial and will help lead one to the dharma.
26. For more information on the eight consciousnesses see Thrangu Rinpoche's *Transcending Ego: Distinguishing Consciousness from Wisdom* (Boulder: Namo Buddha Publications, 2001).
27. In Tibetan medicine and meditation, the breath is said to possess some energy so one does, as described, breathing exercises to expel the "dead" or unenergized air and inhales the new air. This air is converted to life-giving energy or *prana* in the body and travels through channels or *nadi* which are not anatomical channels, but more like meridians in acupuncture.
28. "Emptiness of mind" differs from a complete blank which one might call voidness because it does indeed have the quality of knowing and remembering in spite of the fact that it does not have an origin or a place where it is which all material objects have. "Devoid of inherent existence" is simply another way of saying this because mind does have an existence—we all have minds. But this mind does not have an inherent existence which material objects have. "Lacking any nature of its own" also says this because mind doesn't have a nature like fire which is always hot and burning or a nature of liquid and flowing which is the nature of water because mind and so on.

29. Superimpositions means that one attributes something to a thing when it does not have that attribute. For example, we could say that sugar or salt in a food is a deadly poison.
30. Jay Garfield in *The Fundamental Wisdom of the Middle Way* Oxford: Oxford University Press, 1995, suggests that the translation of "dhatu" as "self-nature" is awkward and that this word really means "essence." The English "nature" comes from Aristotle. An example would be that water presents the outward appearances of a hot gas (steam), flowing and liquid (water), and hard and solid (ice). But its "true" nature or essence is "water" or in more modern terms two Hydrogen atoms combined with an Oxygen atom.
31. By "space" what is meant is the classical Aristotelian concept of "ether" which is the substance which pervades everything and gives it support.
32. See note 7.
33. Buddhists thought makes the distinction between how things appear in our world (Tib. *kundzop* meaning "fake" and often translated as "conventional truth") is not actually how they genuinely are (Tib. *dondam* translated as "ultimate truth"). For example, we see and experience a table as solid, composed of wood of different colors (the relative level), but a physicist would tell us the table is actually a swarm of moving atoms separated by great spaces of over 99%, emitting radiation that only human eyes see as these colors (the ultimate level).
34. See Thrangu Rinpoche's *The Four Dharmas of Gampopa* for more on this. Boulder: Namo Buddha Publications.
35. This type of attention has been called "awareness" but we prefer the translation of "attentiveness" because "awareness" is usually the translation for the Tibetan word "rigpa."
36. Zin is a Tibetan word that has two meanings. I've never been able to come up with one word that covers them both. It has the sense of holding or attaching and also view or identification of something present. The force of mindfulness at this occasions. I am merely identifying something saying it is such and such. So that kind of holding and at the same time emotional, attachment. It is *zin* in Tibetan. –Jules Levinson
37. For more detailed information on the bardo see Thrangu Rinpoche's *Journey of the Mind* (New Zealand: Zhyisil Chokyi Ghatsal Publications, 2000)
38. Thrangu Rinpoche deviates a little from the text and adds the next two sections because they are important.

The Glossary

Abhidharma (Tib. *chö ngön pa*) The Buddhist teachings are often divided into the Tripitaka: the sutras (teachings of the Buddha), the Vinaya (teachings on conduct), and the Abhidharma which are the analyses of phenomena that exist primarily as a commentarial tradition to the Buddhist teachings. There is not, in fact, an Abhidharma section within the Tibetan collection of the Buddhist teachings.

abhisheka See empowerment.

adventitious This means that the quality is not an inherent part of the object. The classical example is when dirt adheres to gold, the dirt is not an inherent part of the gold.

aggregates, five (Skt. *skandha*, Tib. *phung po nga*) Literally "heaps," These are the five basic transformations that perceptions undergo when an object is perceived. First is form which includes all sounds, smells, etc., everything that is not thought. The second and third are sensations (pleasant and unpleasant, etc.) and identification. Fourth is mental events which actually include the second and third aggregates. The fifth is ordinary consciousness such as the sensory and mental consciousnesses.

amrita (Tib. *dut tsi*) A blessed substance which can cause spiritual and physical healing.

analytical insight In the sutra tradition one begins by listening to the teachings which means studying the Dharma, then there is contemplation of this Dharma. Analytical insight is done by placing the mind in shamatha and putting the mind one-pointedly on these concepts. Third, there is actual meditation which is free from concept.

Animal realm. See realms, six

anuttara yoga tantra (Tib. *nal jor la na me pay jü*) There are four levels of the vajrayana and annutara tantra is the highest of these. It contains the Guhyasamaja, the Chakrasamvara, the Hevajra, and the Kalachakra tantras.

Asanga A fourth century Indian philosopher who founded the Chittamatra or Yogacara school and composed the five works of Maitreya which are important mahayana works. Also he was the brother of Vasubandu.

Atisha (982-1055 C.E.) Was a Buddhist scholar at Vikramashila University in India and came to Tibet at the invitation of the King to overcome the damage done by Langdarma. He helped found the Kadampa tradition.

atman Sanskrit for a permanent "self" which exists after death.

Avalokiteshvara (Tib. *Chenrezig*) Deity of compassion. Known as patron deity of Tibet and his mantra is OM MANI PADME HUM.

ayatana (Tib. *kye che*) These are the six sensory objects such as a sight, a sound, a smell, a taste, and body sensation; the six sense faculties such as the visual sensory faculty, the auditory sensory faculty, etc. and the six sensory consciousnesses such as the visual consciousness, the auditory consciousness, etc. They make up the eighteen constituents for perception.

bindu (Tib. *tiglé)* Vital essence drops or spheres of psychic energy which are often visualized in vajrayana practices.

blessing (Tib. *jinlap*) When an individual has great devotion, he or she is able to "tap into" or receive the blessings or energy created by the buddhas and bodhisattvas. The blessings of the lineage are always there, but can only be received if one makes oneself receptive to them so they are not something externally bestowed by more enlightened beings.

blessings (Tib. *chin lop*) The great practitioners in their meditation create blessings which literally means "waves of splendor" and the person who is open can receive this energy which will help their practice.

bodhichitta (Tib. *chang chup chi sem*) Literally, the mind of enlightenment. There are two kinds of bodhichitta: absolute bodhichitta, which is completely awakened mind that sees the emptiness of phenomena, and relative bodhichitta which is the aspiration to practice the six paramitas and free all beings from the suffering of samsara.

bodhisattva (Tib. *chang chup sem pa*) Literally, one who exhibits the mind of enlightenment. An individual who is committed to the mahayana path of practicing compassion and the six paramitas in order to achieve Buddhahood and free all beings from samsara. More specifically, those with a motivation to achieve liberation from samsara and are on one of the ten bodhisattva levels that culminates in Buddhahood.

bodhisattva (Tib. *chang chup sem pa*) Literally, one who exhibits the mind of enlightenment. Also an individual who has committed him or herself to the mahayana path of compassion and the practice of the six paramitas to achieve Buddhahood to free all beings from samsara.

bodhisattva levels (Skt. *bhumi,* Tib. *sa*) The levels or stages a bodhisattva goes through to reach enlightenment. These consist of ten levels in the sutra tradition and thirteen in the tantra tradition.

Buddha Shakyamuni The Shakyamuni Buddha, often called the Gautama Buddha, refers to the latest Buddha who lived between 563 and 483 B.C.E.

Buddha-dharma The teachings of the Buddha.

Buddha-essence(Skt. *tathagatagarbha*, Tib. *de shin shek pay nying po*) The original nature present in all beings which when realized leads to enlightenment. It is often called the essence of Buddhahood or Buddha-nature.

Buddha-nature See Buddha-essence.

Chakrasamvara (Tib. *korlo dompa*) A meditational deity which belongs to the annuttara tantra set of teachings.

caryatantra The second of the four tantras emphasizing meditation and external rituals.

Chenrezig (Skt. *Avalokiteshvara, Pron. Chenrayzee)* Deity of compassion. Known as patron deity of Tibet and his mantra is OM MANI PADME HUM.

Chittamatra school (Tib. *sem tsampa*) A school founded by Asanga in the fourth century and is usually translated as the Mind-only School. It is one of the four major schools in the mahayana tradition and its main tenet (to greatly simplify) is that all phenomena are mental events.

clarity (Tib. *salwa*) Also translated as luminosity. The nature of mind is that it is empty of inherent existence, but the mind is not just voidness, completely empty because it has this clarity which is awareness or the knowing of mind. So clarity is a characteristic of emptiness (*shunyata*) of mind.

clear light (Skt. *prabhasvara*, Tib. *ösel*) A subtle state of mind and according to tantric teachings is the state of mind wherein highest realization is attained.

coemergence (Tib. *lhen chik*). This means the coming together of two things such as the coming together of two rivers.

coemergent wisdom (Skt. *sahajajnana*, Tib. *lhen chik kye pay yeshe*) The advanced realization of the inseparability of samsara and nirvana and how these arise simultaneously and together.

completion stage (Tib. *dzo rim)* In the vajrayana there are two stages of meditation: the development and the completion stage. The completion stage is a method of tantric meditation in which one attains bliss, clarity, and non-thought by means of the subtle channels and energies within the body.

conditioned existence (Skt. *samsara*, Tib. *khor wa*) Ordinary existence which contains suffering because one still possesses attachment, aggression, and ignorance. It is contrasted to liberation or nirvana.

consciousnesses, eight (Skt. *vijnana*, Tib. *nam shé tsog gye*) These are the five sensory consciousnesses of sight, hearing, smell, taste, touch, and body sensation. Sixth is mental consciousness, seventh is afflicted consciousness, and eighth is ground consciousness.

consciousnesses, sensory These are the five sensory consciousnesses of sight, hearing, smell, taste, touch or body sensation. When a sense organ such as the eye registers an object, the eye consciousness is the information of this contact.

creation stage (Skt. *utpattikrama*, Tib. *che rim*) In the vajrayana there are two stages of meditation: the development and the completion stage. This is a method of tantric meditation which involves visualization and contemplating deities for the purpose of realizing the purity of all phenomena. In this stage visualization of the deity is established and maintained.

cyclic existence see samsara

dakini (Tib. *khandroma*) A yogini who has attained high realizations of the fully enlightened mind. She may be a human being who has achieved such attainments or a non-human manifestation of the enlightened mind of a meditational deity.

demon see mara.

dharma protector (Skt. *dharmapala*) Beings which are given the task to protect the dharma. Some were malevolent spirits who were converted by siddhas to dharma protectors.

dharmadhatu (Tib. *chö ying*) The all-encompassing space, unoriginated and without beginning, out of which all phenomena arises. The Sanskrit means "the essence of phenomena" and the Tibetan means "the expanse of phenomena" but usually it refers to the emptiness which is the essence of phenomena.

dharmakaya (Tib. *chö ku*) One of the three bodies of Buddha. It is enlightenment itself, that is wisdom beyond reference point. See kayas, three.

dharmata (Tib. *chö nyi*) Dharmata is often translated as "suchness" or "the true nature of things" or "things as they are." It is phenomena as it really is or as seen by a completely enlightened being without any distortion or obscuration so one can say it is "reality."

dhatu (Skt., Tib. *kham*) In Buddhism there are five elements of everything in the world in Buddhism: earth, water, fire, wind, and space (or ether). The internal elements are the same but have a property associated with them, so there is: earth (soldity), fluidity (water), fire (heat), wind (movement), and space (the vacuities within the body).

disturbing emotion (Skt. *klesha,* Tib. *nyön mong*) The emotional obscurations (in contrast to intellectual obscurations) which are also translated as "afflictions" or "poisons." The three main kleshas are (passion or attachment), (aggression or anger); and (ignorance or delusion). The five kleshas are the three above plus pride and (envy or jealousy).

Dusum Khyenpa (1110-1193 C.E.) The First Karmapa who was a student of Gampopa and founded the Karma Kagyu lineage. He is also known for founding the tulku system in Tibet.

Dzogchen (Skt. *mahasandhi*) This is known also as the "great perfection" or atiyoga. It is the highest of the nine yanas according to the Nyingma tradition.

egolessness (Tib. *dag me***)** Also called selflessness. There are two kinds of egolessness—the egolessness of other, that is, the emptiness of external phenomena and the egolessness of self, that is, the emptiness of a personal self.

egolesseness or selflessness of phenomena (Skt. *dharma-nairatmya*) This doctrine asserts than not only is there selflessness of person, but when one examines outer phenomena, one finds that this external phenomena is also empty, i.e. it does not have an independent or substantial nature. This position is not held by the Hinayana schools, but is put forth by the mahayana schools, particularly the Chittamatra school.

egolessness or selflessness of person (Skt. *pudgalanairatmya*) This doctrine asserts that when one examines or looks for the person, one finds that it is empty. The person does not possess a self (Skt. *atman*, Tib. *dagnyi*) as an independent or substantial self. This position is held by most Buddhist schools.

eight worldly dharmas (Tib. *jik ten chö gyé*) These keep one from the path; they are attachment to gain, attachment to pleasure, attachment to praise, attachment to fame, aversion to loss, aversion to pain, aversion to blame, and aversion to a bad reputation.

elements, five (Skt. *pancabhuta*, Tib. *jung wa nga*) These are earth, water, fire, wind, and space. These elements are both the constituents of external matter and the physical components of the body.

empowerment (Tib. *wang*, Skt. *abhisheka*) To do a vajrayana practice one must receive the empowerment from a qualified lama. One should also receive the practice instruction (Tib. *tri*) and the textual reading (Tib. *lung*).

empowerment vase. A vase which is used to hold the blessed substance in an empowerment. It is shaped with a narrow neck and a fat round bottom.

emptiness (Skt. *shunyata*, Tib. *tong pa nyi*) Also translated as voidness. The Buddha taught in the second turning of the wheel of dharma that external phenomena and the internal phenomena or concept of self or "I" have no real existence and therefore are "empty."

eye consciousness See consciousnesses, sensory.

father tantra (Tib. *pha gyu*) There are three kinds of tantras. The father tantra is concerned with transforming aggression, the mother tantra with transforming passion and the non-dual tantra with ignorance.

five paths (Tib. *lam nga*) Traditionally, a practitioner goes through five stages or paths to enlightenment. These are (1) The path of accumulation which emphasizes purifying one's obscurations and accumulating merit. (2) The path of junction or application in which the meditator develops profound understanding of the four noble truths and cuts the root to the desire realm. (3) The path of insight or seeing in which the meditator develops greater insight and enters the first bodhisattva level. (4) The path of meditation in which the meditator cultivates insight in the second through tenth bodhisattva levels. (5) The path of fulfillment which is the complete attainment of Buddhahood.

five wisdoms (Tib. *yeshe nga*) Upon reaching enlightenment, the eight consciousnesses are transformed into the five wisdoms: the mirror-like wisdom, discriminating wisdom, the wisdom of equality, the all-accomplishing wisdom, and the dharmadhatu wisdom.

form kayas (Skt. *rupakaya*, Tib. *zuk ku*) The sambhogakaya and the nirmanakaya. See the kayas, three.

form realm (Tib. *zuk kham*) These are seventeen heavenly realms in which beings have bodies of light. See the realms, three

formless realm (Tib. *zuk me kham*) The abode of an unenlightened being who has practiced the four absorptions. See the realms, three

four noble truths (Tib. *pak pay den pa shi*) The Buddha began teaching with a talk in India at Sarnath on the four noble truths. These are the truth of suffering, the truth of the cause of suffering, the cessation of suffering, and the path. These truths are the foundation of Buddhism, particularly the Theravadin path.

Gampopa (1079-1153 C.E.) One of the main lineage holders of the Kagyu lineage in Tibet. A student of Milarepa he established the first Kagyu monastic monastery and is known for writing the *Jewel Ornament of Liberation*.

Gerab Dorje also called Pramoda Vajra. The forefather of the Dzogchen lineage, who received the transmission of Dzogchen meditation from Vajrasattva.

geshe (Tib.) A scholar who has attained a doctorate in Buddhist studies. This usually takes fifteen to twenty years to attain.

Gomchung One of the major students of Gampopa. His name literally means "little meditator."

great bliss (Skt. *mahasukha*) This is a tremendous feeling of well-being which occurs when one's meditation goes very well. It is a result of the subtle energy entering the central channel.

guru (Tib. *lama*) A teacher in the Tibetan tradition who has reached realization.

guru yoga (Tib. *lamay naljor*) A practice of devotion to the guru culminating in receiving his blessing and blending indivisibly with his mind. Also the fourth practice of the preliminary practices of *ngöndro*.

healing nectar (Skt. *amrita* Tib. *dud tsi)* A blessed substance which can cause spiritual and physical healing.

Hinayana (Tib. *tek pa chung wa*) Literally, the "lesser vehicle." The term refers to the first teachings of the Buddha which emphasized the careful examination of mind and its confusion. Also known as the Theravadin path.

Indrabodhi An Indian king during the time of the Buddha who become an accomplished master.

insight meditation (Skt. *Vipashyana*, Tib. *lhak tong*) Meditation that develops insight into the nature of phenomena. In the Theravada tradition this involves observing every thought in daily life. In the vajrayana it involves more a close examination of the emptiness of phenomena. The other main meditation is shamatha meditation.

interinterdependent origination (Skt. *pratityasamutpada*, Tib. *ten drel*) Also called interdependent origination. The principal that nothing exists independently, but comes into existence only on dependency of various previous causes and conditions. There are twelve successive phases of this process that begins with ignorance and ends with old age and death.

Jamgön Kongtrul (1813-1899) Also known as Lodro Thaye. He was best known for founding the Rimay movement which is a non-sectarian, eclectic movement which preserved the various practice lineages that were on the verge of extinction. He also was a prolific writer of ninety volumes.

Kadampa (Tib.) A follower of one of the major schools in Tibet. It was founded by Atisha (993-1054 C.E.)

Kagyu (Tib.) One of the four major schools of Buddhism in Tibet. It was founded by Marpa and is headed by His Holiness Karmapa. The other three are the Nyingma, the Sakya, and the Gelugpa schools.

kalpa (Tib., Skt. *yuga*) An eon which lasts in the order of millions of years.

Karmapa The title of seventeen successive incarnations of Dusum Khyenpa who has headed the Karma Kagyu school of Tibetan Buddhism.

Karmapa The title of seventeen successive incarnations of Dusum Khyenpa who has headed the Karma Kagyu school of Tibetan Buddhism.

kayas, three (Tib. *ku sum*) There are three bodies of the Buddha: the nirmanakaya, sambhogakaya and dharmakaya. The dharmakaya, also called the "truth body," is the complete enlightenment or the complete wisdom of the Buddha which is unoriginated wisdom beyond form and manifests in the sambhogakaya and the nirmanakaya. The sambhogakaya, also called the "enjoyment body," manifests only to bodhisattvas. The nirmanakaya, also called the "emanation body," manifests in the world and in this context manifests as the Shakyamuni Buddha.

key instructions Sometimes called the quintessential instructions. These are instructions given directly from guru to student concerning meditation on the nature of mind. While some of these are written down, there are many passed on orally.

klesha (Tib. *nyön mong*) The emotional obscurations (in contrast to intellectual obscurations) which are also translated as "disturbing emotions" or "poisons." The three main kleshas are passion or attachment, aggression or anger, and ignorance or delusion. The five kleshas are the three above plus pride and envy or jealousy.

kleshas See disturbing emotions.

knowledge of how-it-is (Tib. *ji ta ba*) This is transcendent knowledge (Skt. *jnana*) of the true nature of reality, not as it appears to individuals in samsara.

knowledge of variety (Tib. *ji nye pa*) This is the transcendent knowledge (Skt. *jnana*) of the variety of phenomena.

kriya tantra (Tib. *ja way gyu*) One of the four tantras which emphasizes personal purity.

lama (Skt. *guru*) A spiritual teacher.

luminosity (Tib. *salwa*) In the third turning everything is void, but this voidness is not completely empty because it has luminosity. Luminosity or clarity allows all phenomena to appear and is a characteristic of emptiness (Skt. *shunyata*).

Madhyamaka (Tib. *u ma*) The most influential of the four schools of Indian Buddhism founded by Nagarjuna in the second century C.E. The name comes from the Sanskrit word meaning "the Middle-way" meaning it is the middle way between eternalism and nihilism. The main postulate of this school is that all phenomena—both internal mental events and external physical objects are empty of any true nature. The school uses extensive rational reasoning to establish the emptiness of phenomena. This school does, however, hold that phenomena do exist on the conventional level of reality.

mahamudra (Tib. *cha ja chen po*) Literally, "great seal" meaning that all phenomena are sealed by the primordially perfect true nature. This form of meditation is traced back to Saraha and was passed down in the Kagyu school through Marpa. This meditative transmission emphasizes perceiving mind directly rather than through rational analysis.

mahamudra (Tib. *cha ja chen po*) Literally, "great seal" meaning that all phenomena are sealed by the primordially perfect true nature. This form of meditation is traced back to Saraha (10th century) and was passed down in the Kagyu school through Marpa. This meditative transmission emphasizes perceiving mind directly rather than through rational analysis.

mahasiddha (Tib. *drup thop chen po)* A practitioner who has a great deal of realization. These were particularly vajrayana practitioners who lived in India between the eight and twelfth century and practiced tantra. The biography of some of the most famous is found in *The Eighty-four Mahasiddhas*.

mahayana (Tib. *tek pa chen po*) Literally, the "great vehicle." These are the teachings of the second turning of the wheel of dharma, which emphasize shunyata, compassion, and universal Buddha-essence

mantra (Tib. *ngak)* These are invocations to various meditation deities which are recited in Sanskrit. These Sanskrit syllables, representing various energies, are repeated in different vajrayana practices.

mantra tradition Another term for the vajrayana.

mara (Tib. *du*) Difficulties encountered by the practitioner. There are four kinds—skandha-mara which is incorrect view of self, klesha-mara which is being overpowered by negative emotions, mrityu-mara which is death and interrupts spiritual practice, and devaputra-mara which is becoming stuck in the bliss that comes from meditation.

Marpa (1012-1097 C. E.) Marpa was known for being a Tibetan who made three trips to India and brought back many tantric texts including the Six Yogas of Naropa, the Guhyasamaja, and the Chakrasamvara practices. His teacher was Tilopa and he founded the Kagyu lineage in Tibet.

mental consciousness (Tib. *yi kyi namshe*) The sixth consciousness responsible for analyzing the sensory perceptions of the five sensory consciousnesses. See consciousnesses, eight.

mental consciousness (Tib. *yid kyi namshe*) The sixth consciousness responsible for analyzing the sensory perceptions of the five sensory consciousnesses. See consciousnesses, eight.

mental factors (Tib. *sem yung*) Mental factors are contrasted to mind in that they are more long-term propensities of mind including eleven virtuous factors such as faith, detachment, and equanimity, and the six root defilements such as desire, anger, and pride, and the twenty secondary defilements such as resentment, dishonesty, harmfulness.

Middle-way (Tib. *u ma*) or Madhyamaka School. A philosophical school founded by Nagarjuna and based on the Prajnaparamita sutras of emptiness.

Milarepa (1040-1123 C.E.) Milarepa was a student of Marpa who attained enlightenment in one lifetime. His student Gampopa founded the (Dagpo) Kagyu lineage.

Mind-Only school. Also called Chittamatra school. This is one of the major schools in the mahayana tradition founded in the fourth century by Asanga who emphasized everything is mental events.

Mind-only school. See Chittamatra.

Mipham Rinpoche (1846-1914 C.E.) Great Nyingma master and writer of last century.

mother tantra (Tib. *ma gyu*) There are three kinds of tantras. The father tantra which is concerned with transforming aggression, the mother tantra which concerns transforming passion and the non-dual tantra which concerns ignorance.

nadi (Tib. *tsa*) Subtle channels through which the subtle energies (vayu) flow.

Nagarjuna (Tib. *ludrup)* An Indian scholar in the second century who founded the Madhyamaka philosophical school which emphasized emptiness.

ngöndro (Tib. and pronounced "nundro") Tibetan for preliminary practice. One usually begins the vajrayana path by doing the four preliminary practices which involve about 100,000 refuge prayers and prostrations, 100,000 Vajrasattva mantras 100,000 mandala offerings, and 100,000 guru yoga practices.

nirmanakaya (Tib. *tulku*) There are three bodies of the Buddha and the nirmanakaya or "emanation body" manifests in the world and in this context manifests as the Shakyamuni Buddha. See kayas, three.

nirvana (Tib. *nyangde)* Literally, "extinguished." Individuals live in samsara and with spiritual practice can attain a state of enlightenment in which all false ideas and conflicting emotions have been extinguished. This is called nirvana.

noble truths, four (Tib. *pak pay den pa zhi*) The Buddha founded Buddhism with a teaching at Sarnath, India on the four noble truths. These are the truth of suffering, the truth of the cause of suffering, the cessation of suffering, and the path. These are the foundation of Buddhism, particularly the Hinayana path.

nonself of dharmas see egolessness of phenomena

nonself of person see egolessness of person

ordinary mind (Tib. *thamel gyi shepa*) The mind as it was originally without being clouded over by disturbing emotions or ignorance.

phowa (Tib.) An advanced tantric practice concerned with the ejection of consciousness at death to a favorable realm.

prajna (Tib. *she rab*) In Sanskrit it means "perfect knowledge" and can mean wisdom, understanding, or discrimination. Usually it means the wisdom of seeing things from a high (e.g. non-dualistic) point of view.

Prajnaparamita (Tib. *sherab chi parol tu chin pa*) The Buddhist literature outlining the mahayana path and emptiness written mostly around the second century.

prana (Tib. *bindu*) Life supporting energy.

preliminary practices (Tib. *ngöndro*) The four preliminary practices which are done before doing yidam practice. See ngöndro.

quintessential instructions Sometimes called the key instructions. These are instructions given directly from guru to student concerning meditation on the nature of mind. While some of these are written down, there are many passed on orally.

Rangjung Dorje (1284-1339 C.E.) The Third Karmapa known for writing a series of texts widely used in the Kagyu school.

Rangtong School (Tib.) The Madhyamaka or Middle-way school is divided into two major schools: the Rangtong which maintains voidness is devoid of inherent existence and Shentong which maintains voidness is indivisible from luminosity.

conventional truth (Tib. *kun sop*) There are two truths: relative and absolute. Conventional truth is the perception of an ordinary (unenlightened) person who sees the world with all his or her projections based on the false belief in self.

root lama (Tib. *tsa way lama*) A teacher from whom one has received the instructions and empowerments that form the core of one's practice.

Sakya Pandita (1181-1251 C.E.) A hereditary head of the Shakya lineage. A great scholar who was an outspoken opponent of the Kagyu teachings. He also became head of the Tibetan state under the authority of the Mongol emperors.

samadhi (Tib. *tin ne zin*) Also called meditative absorption or one-pointed meditation, this is the highest form of meditation.

sambhogakaya (Tib. *long chö ku*) There are three bodies of the Buddha and the sambhogakaya, also called the "enjoyment body," is a realm of the dharmakaya which only manifests to bodhisattvas. See the three kayas.

samsara (Tib. *kor wa*) Conditioned existence of ordinary life in which suffering occurs because one still possesses attachment, aggression, and ignorance. It is contrasted to nirvana.

sangha (Tib. *gen dun*) These are the companions on the path. They may be all the persons on the path or the noble sangha, who are the realized ones.

Saraha One of the eighty-four mahasiddhas of India who was known for his spiritual songs on mahamudra.

secret mantra (Tib. *sang ngak*) A name for the vajrayana

sense fields see ayatana.

Shakyamuni Buddha (Tib. *shakya tubpa*) The Shakyamuni Buddha, often called the Gautama Buddha, refers to the latest Buddha who lived between 563 and 483 B.C.E.

shamatha or tranquility meditation (Tib. *shinay*) This is basic sitting meditation in which one usually follows the breath while observing the workings of the mind while sitting in the cross-legged posture. The main purpose of shamatha meditation is to settle or tame the mind so that it will stay where one places it.

Shantideva (675-725 C.E.) A great bodhisattva who lived in 7th and 8th century in India known for his two works on the conduct of a bodhisattva.

shastra (Tib. *tan chö*) The Buddhist teachings are divided into words of the Buddha (the sutras) and the commentaries of others on his works the (shastras).

Shavari A disciple of Saraha who was also the close disciple and heart son of Nagarjuna. Also called Lord of Hermits.

Shentong school (Tib.) The Madhyamaka or Middle-way school divided into two major schools: the Rangtong which maintains voidness is devoid of inherent existence and Shentong which maintains voidness is indivisible from luminosity.

siddha (Tib. *drup thop)* An accomplished Buddhist practitioner.

siddhi (Tib. *ngodrup*) Spiritual accomplishments of accomplished practitioners.

six realms of samsara (Tib. *rikdruk*) These are the possible types of rebirths for beings in samsara and are: the god realm in which gods have great pride, the asura realm in which the jealous gods try to maintain what they have, the human realm which is the best realm because one has the possibility of achieving enlightenment, the animal realm characterized by stupidity, the hungry ghost realm characterized by great craving, and the hell realm characterized by aggression.

skandha (Tib. *pung pa*) Literally "heaps." These are the five basic transformations that perceptions undergo when an object is perceived: form, feeling, perception, formation, and conscious-ness. First is form which includes all sounds, smells, etc. everything we usually think of as outside the mind. The second and third are sensations (pleasant and unpleasant, etc.) and identification. Fourth is mental events which actually include the second and third aggregates. The fifth is ordinary consciousness such as the sensory and mental consciousnesses.

skillful methods (Skt. *upaya,* Tib. *thab*) On the mahayana level, this is one of the ten paramitas and refers to dedicating the merits of all one's deeds to the benefit of all sentient beings. On the vajrayana level, it refers to practices of the internal yogas which manipulate the internal energies and channels.

stupa (Tib. *chö ten*) A dome shaped monument to the Buddha which often contains relics and remains of the Buddha or great bodhisattvas.

subtle channels (Skt. *nadi*, Tib. *tsa*) These refer to the subtle channels which are not anatomical ones but ones in which psychic energies or "winds" (Skt. *prana*, Tib. *lung*) travel.

supreme accomplishment This refers to attaining Buddhahood and this term is used almost exclusively in the Vajrayana.

supreme siddhi Another name for enlightenment.

sutra (Tib. *do*) These are the Hinayana and mahayana texts which are the words of the Buddha. These are often contrasted with the tantras which are the Buddha's vajrayana teachings and the shastras which are commentaries on the words of the Buddha.

sutra path The sutra approach to achieving enlightenment which includes the Hinayana and the mahayana.

sutrayana The sutra approach to achieving enlightenment which includes the Hinayana and the mahayana.

tantra (Tib. *gyü)* One can divide Tibetan Buddhism into the sutra tradition and the tantra tradition. The sutra tradition primarily involves the academic study of the mahayana sutras and the tantric path primarily involves practicing the vajrayana practices. The tantras are primarily the texts of the vajrayana practices.

Tashi Namgyal (1512-1587 C.E.) A famous teacher who wrote many texts and acted as Gampopa's regent and presided over Gampopa's Dakla Gampo monastery in later years.

temporary experiences (Tib. *nyam*) Experiences of bliss, of great clarity, of nonthought. In contrast to the experience of ordinary mind, these experiences come and go so the meditator should not become attach to them.

Tilopa (928-1009 C.E.) One of the eighty-four mahasiddhas who became the guru of Naropa who transmitted his teachings to the Kagyu lineage in Tibet.

tranquillity meditation (Skt. *shamatha*, Tib. *shinay)* A basic meditation practice aimed at taming and sharpening the mind. It is also called basic sitting meditation.

transcendent knowledge (Skt. *Prajnaparamita***,** Tib. *sherab chi parol tu chin pa*) The Buddhist literature outlining the mahayana path and emptiness written mostly around the second century.

Tushita (Tib. *gan dan*) This is one of the heaven fields of the Buddha. Tushita is in the sambhogakaya and therefore is not located in any place or time.

Vairocana (Tib. *nam par nang dze*) The sambhogakaya buddha of the buddha family.

Vajrasattva (Tib. *Dorje Sempa*) The Buddha of purification. Vajrasattva practice is part of four preliminary practices.

vajrayana (Tib. *dorje tek pa*) There are three major traditions of Buddhism (Hinayana, mahayana, vajrayana) The vajrayana is based on the tantras and emphasizes the clarity aspect of phenomena and is mainly practiced in Tibet.

vase breathing An advanced breathing practice which has to be learned under the supervision of an experience teacher and involves the retention of the breath in the abdomen which is thus like an air filled vase.

Vasubandu A great fourth century Indian scholar who was brother of Asanga and wrote the Hinayana work, the *Abhidharmakosha* explaining the Abhidharma.

Vipashyana meditation (Tib. *lha tong*) Sanskrit for "insight meditation" This meditation develops insight into the nature of reality (Skt. *dharmata*). The other main meditation is shamatha meditation.

Wangchuk Dorje The Ninth Karmapa (1556-1603 C.E.) He is known for writing the Kagyu ngondro text, *Pointing Out the Dharmakaya*, *Mahamudra: Dispelling the Darkness* and *The Ocean of Definitive Meaning*.

wheel of dharma (Skt. *dharmacakra*) The Buddha's teachings correspond to three levels: the Hinayana, the mahayana and the vajrayana with each level being one turning of the wheel.

wisdom of multiplicity or variety (Tib. *ji nye pa*) This is the transcendent knowledge (jnana) of the variety of phenomena.

wisdom of nature of phenomena (Tib. *ji ta ba*) This is transcendent knowledge (jnana) of the true nature of reality, not as it appears to individuals in samsara.

yidam (Tib.) A tantric deity that embodies qualities of Buddhahood and is practice in the vajrayana. Also called a tutelary deity.

yogi or yogin (Tib. *naljorpa*) A Buddhist practitioner who has chosen an unconventional path of practicing.

Glossary of Tibetan Words

Pronounced	Spelled	English
bem strong	bem strong	dead space
cha ja chen po	phyag rgya chen po	mahamudra
chag pa	chags pa	attachment
chak ja chenpo	phyag rgya chen po	mahamudra
chang chup chi sem pa	byang chub sems pa	bodhisattva
chang chup chi sem	byang chub kyi sems	bodhichitta
che rim	bskyed rim	creation stage
Chenrezig	span ras gzigs	Chenrezig
chin lap	byin brlab	blessings
chin lop	byin brlap	blessings
ching wa	bying ba	sinking
chö ku	choŝ sku	dharmakaya
chö ngön pa	chos mngon pa	Abhidharma
chö nyi	chos nyid	dharmata
chö ten	mchod rten	stupa
chö ying	chos byings	dharmadhatu
dag me	bdag med	egolessness
dag nyi	bdag nyid	a self
de shin shek pay nyingpo	de bzhin gshegs pa'i nyingpo	Buddha-essence
do	mdo	sutra
dön	gdon	harmful deities
dondam	don dam pai' bden pa	absolute truth
dorje sempa	rdo rje sems dpa'	Vajrasattva
dorje tek pa	rdo rje theg pa	vajrayana
drup thop chen po	grub thob chen po	mahasiddha
drup thop	grub thob	siddha
du	bdud	mara
dud tsi	bdud rtsi	amrita
duje	adu byed	composite
dzo rim	rdzogs rim	completion stage
Dzogchen	rdzogs pa chen po	Dzogchen
gan dan	dga' ldan	Tushita heaven
gen dun	dge 'dun	sangha
göpa	rgod pa	excited mind
gya	phyag rgya	mudra
gyöpa	'gyod pa	regret or sadness
gyu	rgyud	tantra

ja way gyu	bya ba'i rgyud	kriya tantra
ji nye ba	ji shyed pa	know. of variety
ji ta ba	ji lta ba	know. how it is
kham	khams	dhatu
khandroma	mkha' 'gro ma	dakini
khom	sgom	habituate
khor wa	'khor ba	samsara
kor wa	'khor ba	samsara
korlo dompa	'khor lo sdom pa	Chakrasamvara
ku sum	sku gsum	3 kayas
kun sop	kun rdzob	conventional truth
kundzop	kun rdzob	conventional truth
kye che	skye mched	ayatanas
kyerim	bskyed rim	completion stage
lam nga	lam lnga	5 paths
lama	bla ma	guru
lamay naljor	bla ma'I rnal 'byor	guru yoga
lhag tong	lhag mthong	Vipashyana
lhen chik kye pay yeshe	lhan chik kyes pa'I ye shes	coemergent wis.
lhen chik	lhan chig	coemergence
long chö ku	longs spyod sku	sambhogakaya
lung	lung	text transmission
mögu	mos gus	devotion
mukpa	rmugs pa	dullness
nal jor la na me pay ju	rnal 'byor bla ma med pa'i	anuttara-yoga
naljorpa	rnal 'byor pa	yogin
nam par tog me yeshe	rnam par rtog pa ye shes	thor. Nonconcept.
ngak	sngags	mantra
nge luk	gnas lugs	true nature
ngelug	gnas lugs	true nature
ngo drup	dngos grub	siddhi
ngo wo	ngo bo	essence or nature
ngondro	sngon 'gro	preliminary pract.
nyangde	myang 'das	nirvana
nyangde	myang 'das	nirvana
nyingthig	snying thig	heart essence
nyön mong	nyon mongs	disturbing emot.
nyön mong	nyon mongs	klesha
ösel	'od gsal	clear light
pak pay den pa zhi	'phags pa'I bden pa bzhi	4 noble truths
phowa	'pho ba	consc. transfer
phung po nga	phung po lnga	five skandhas

phung po	phung po	aggregates
pyam ne pa	phyam gnas pa	smoothly-evenly
rangzhin	rang bzhin	nature
rigpa	rig pa	knowledge
sa	sa	bodhisattva level
salwa	gsal ba	luminosity
sem jung	sems byung	mental factors
sem ne	(sems nge)	mind itself
sem tri	sems sdi	pointing out
sem tsampa	sems tsam pa	Chittamatra
sem yung	sems byung	mental factors
sem	sems	mind
seshin	shes bzhin	vigilance
she rab	shes rab	prajna
shentong	gzhan strong	Shentong school
sherab chi parol tu chin pa	shes rab pha rol tu phyin	Prajnaparamita
sherab	shes rab	prajna
shinay	zhi gnas	shamatha
soso rang dge yeshe	so so rang dge ye shes	discrim awaren w
tan chö	bstan bcos	commentary
tek pa chen po	theg pa chen po	mahayana
ten drel	rten 'brel	interdependent or.
tigle	thig le	bindu
tin ne zin	ting nge 'dzin	samadhi
tong pa nyi	strog pa nyid	emptiness
trenpa	dran pa	memory
tsa way lama	rtsa ba'i bla ma	root guru
tsa	rtsa	nadi
tulku	sprul sku	nirmanakaya
u ma	dbu ma	Madhyamaka
wang	dbang	empowerment
yeshe nga	ye shes	five wisdoms
yidam	yi dam	tantric deity
ying	dbyings	element
zuk kham	gzuks khams	form realm
zuk ku	gzugs sku	form kayas
zuk me kham	gzuks med khams	formless realm

Bibliography

Sutras

The King of Meditation. (Skt. *Samadhi raja sutra)* This is one of the few teachings of the Buddha that discusses mahamudra meditation. The first four chapters of this sutra have been translated by John Rockwell at Naropa Institute and the eleventh chapter was translated by Mark Tatz in his Ph.D. thesis at the University of Washington. Thrangu Rinpoche has given an extensive commentary on this sutra in the *King of Meditation*. Boudhanath, Nepal: Rangjung Yeshe Publications, 1994.

The King of Meditation. (Skt. *Samadhi-raja sutra).* This is one of the few teachings of the Buddha that discusses mahamudra meditation. The first four chapters of this sutra has been translated by John Rockwell at Naropa Institute and the eleventh chapter was translated by Mark Tatz in his Ph.D. thesis at the University of Washington. Thrangu Rinpoche has given an extensive commentary on this sutra in the *King of Meditation*. Boudhanath, Nepal: Rangjung Yeshe Publications, 1994.

The Heart Sutra. (Skt. *Prajnaparamita-hridaya-sutra,* Tib. *shes rab snying po'i mdo,* Pron. "sherab nyinpo dho*") Translated by Conze (1959) as Hridya-mahayana-sutra.* One of the most important mahayana sutras which is often chanted each morning in dharma centers. It is a short sutra of the Buddha of several hundred words summarizing the Prajnaparamita teaching on the meditation on emptiness.

The Heart Sutra. (Skt. *Maha-prajnaparamita-mitahriidaya sutra*, Tib. *bcom ldan 'das ma shes rab kyi pha rol tu phyin pa'i snying po'i mdo*). This is a sutra by the Buddha which is a condensation of the Prajnaparamita sutra. This sutra is chanted daily in almost all mahayana Buddhist centers.

The Lankavatara Sutra. In English "The Sutra on the Descent to Sri Lanka." This famous mahayana sutra in ten chapters explains the concept of tathatagarbha and other Chittamatra concepts. It can be found in the Kangjur. Has been translated by D. T. Suzuki The Lankavatara Sutra. London: Routledge and kegan, 1932.

Sagaramatiparipriccha Sutra. (Tib. *bumo rinchen gyi shupai dho*) This sutra is by the Buddha and is found in the Kangyur. It has not been translated into English.

Samadhinirmocana Sutra. An important mahayana sutra which has been translated by John Powers as *Wisdom of Buddha*. Berkeley: Dharma Publishing, 1995.

Manifest Purification of Vairocana(Skt. Vairocana-bhisambodhi, Tib.

Sutra of Great Compassion (Skt. Maitreya-paripriccha sutra, Pron. Jamzhukyi Dho)

Perfection of Wisdom Literature by the Buddha. There is a prajna-paramita text of 100,000 verses, a text of 25,000 verses, a text of 8,000 verses, the Heart sutra of only a few verses right on down to a single seed syllable AH. The *Perfection of Wisdom* in 8,000 verses (Skt. *ashtasahasrika-prajna-paramita* sutra, Tib. *'phag pa shes rab kyi pha rol tu phyin pa brgyad stron pa'i mdo*) has been translated by Edward Conze. *The Large Sutra on Perfect Wisdom*. Berkeley: University of California Press, 1975.

Lankavatara Sutra. This is a mahayana sutra of the Buddha which has been translated into English by D. T. Suzuki.

Tantras

Glorious Unblemished tantra. (Skt. *Sri-anavila*, Tib. *dpal rnyogs pa med pa*, Pron. Pel Nyokpa Mepa). This tantra has not been translated into English.

Kalacakra tantra (Tib. *dus kyi 'khor lo,* Pro. Tukhor khorlo) This is one of the most famous tantras which is an explanation of light and dark time with a practice which allows one to be reborn in Shambhala in the future. It was introduced into Tibet in 1033. Tibetans try to receive at least one Kalacakra initiation in their lifetime.

Mahamudra Subtle Drop tantra (Skt. *Mahamudra-tilaka*, Tib. *phyag chen thig le*, Pro. *Chakchen Thigle.*) This tantra has not been translated into English.

Samputa-tantra (Tib. *sambuti sam ti*) This tantra appears in the Tengyur and has not been translated into English.

Thoroughly Abiding tantra (Tib. *rab tu mi gnas pa'i rgyud*, Pron. Raptu Minepe Gyu). Has not been translated into English.

Others

An Aspirational Prayer for Mahamudra (Pron. "tsarchen menla"). Boulder, Colorado: Namo Buddha Publications. This prayer for achieving mahamudra was written by the Third Karmapa and gives a brief outline of the path. The text includes the translation of root verses and a commentary by Thrangu Rinpoche.

A Guide to the Bodhisattva's Way of Life by Shantideva and translated by Steven Batchelor. Archives of Tibetan Works. Also see Thrangu Rinpoche's *A Guide to the Bodhisattva's Way of Life* which includes a translation of the root text as well as his commentary on this valuable text on how to behave on the mahayana path.

Buddhist Saints in India by Reginald Ray. New York: Oxford University Press, 1994. This book presents a lot of evidence that there were two traditions in Buddhism—the monasteries who carried on the Vinaya and the saints who lived in the forest and lead unconventional lives but had a great deal of realization.

Clear Ornament of Liberation (Skt. *Mahayana-sutra-lamkara)* by Maitreya and Asanga. One of the five works of Maitreya which is identified as one of the main sources of interpretation of emptiness by the Chittamatra and Shentong schools. It was written in twenty-one chapters in verse. See Thrangu Rinpoche's *Ornament of Clear Realization* Boulder, Colorado: Namo Buddha Publications for a commentary on this

Differentiating Consciousness and Wisdom (Tib. *rnam shes ye shes 'byed pa*, Pron. "namshe yeshe gepa") by the Third Karmapa.

This text is a text in Buddhist psychology and was written to describe the eight consciousnesses and how these translate into the five wisdoms upon attaining enlightenment. The text and a commentary is available in Thrangu Rinpoche's *The Treatise Differentiating Consciousness and Wisdom*. Boulder: Namo Buddha Publications.

Entrance Into the Middle Way by Chandrakirti or the *Madhyamaka-vatara*.

The Four Dharmas of Gampopa by Thrangu Rinpoche. Boulder: Namo Buddha Publications.

The Four Foundations of Buddhist Practice by Thrangu Rinpoche. Boulder: Namo Buddha Publications.

Great Tibetan Dictionary (pron. "tik zdö chenmo") This is a Tibetan-Tibetan dictionary which has excellent definitions of dharma terms. It is presently being translated into English.

The Karma Nyingthig This work has not been translated into English.

Knowledge of the Middle Way (Skt. *Mula-madhyamaka*, Tib. *dbgu ma rtsa ba'i shes rab*) by Nagarjuna.

Legends of the Eighty-four Mahasiddhas (Tib. *grub thob bryad bcu trs bzhi'I*) by Abhayadatta. Translated by Keith Downman as ***Masters of Mahamudra*** (Albany, NY: State University of New York, 1985).

Mahamudra: Eliminating the Darkness of Ignorance (Tib. *phyag chen ma rig mun sel*, Pron. "chag chen marig munsel") by Wangchuk Dorje, The Ninth Karmapa (1556-1603). Alexander Berzin (trans.) Dharamsala, India: Library of Tibetan Works and Archives, 1978.

Mahamudra: The Quintessence of Mind and Meditation by Takpo Tashi Namgyal (Tib. *phyag rgya chen mo*, Pron. "chakgya chenpo"). Translated by Lobsang Lhalungpa. Boston: Shambhala Publications, 1986.

An extremely detailed description of mahamudra meditation. This text was used by Thrangu Rinpoche in his five mahamudra retreats at Big Bear Lake.

***The Ocean of Definitive Meaning** (Pron. nedon jamso)* by Ninth Karmapa, Wangjung Dorje.

The ninth Karmpa wrote three main treatises on mahamudra. The longest was the *Ocean of Definitive Meaning*, the middle length was *Mahamudra: Eliminating the Darkness of Ignorance* and the shortest was *Pointing Out the Dharmakaya*. The *Ocean of Definitive Meaning* has been recently translated into English and is soon to be published. Thrangu Rinpoche has given commentaries on all three of these works.

Perfection of Wisdom (or Prajnaparamita). There are many versions of this text beginning with the Prajnaparamita text of 100,000 verses, a text of 25,000 verses, a text of 8,000 verses, to the familiar Heart sutra of only a few verses. The *Perfection of Wisdom* in 8,000 verses (Skt. *ashtasahasrika-prajna-paramita-sutra*, Tib. *'phag pa shes rab kyi pha rol tu phyin pa brgyad stron pa'i mdo*) has been translated by Edward Conze. *The Large Sutra on Perfect Wisdom*. Berkeley: University of California Press, 1975.

The Practice of Tranquillity and Insight by Thrangu Rinpoche. Ithaca, New York: Snow Lion Publications, 1993. This is a detailed teaching on shamatha and Vipashyana meditation and their union.

Pointing Out the Dharmakaya by Thrangu Rinpoche. Boulder: Namo Buddha Publications.

The Rain of Wisdom (Tib. *bka' brgyud mgur mtsho*, Pron. "kagyu gurtso") by Nalanda Translation Committee. Boston: Shambhala Publications, 1980.

This is a compilation of spiritual songs of the Kagyu lineage holders.

Royal Song of Saraha by Herbert Guenther. Seattle: University of Washington Press, 1969. This is one of the few translations of the works of Saraha who was one of the earliest masters of mahamudra. There is another translation in Edward Conze: *Buddhist Texts through the Ages*. Oxford: Bruno Cassirer, 1954.

Seven Yogas of Maitripa (Skt. yogasapta, Tib sbyor ba bdun pa, Pro. jorwa dunpa). Has not been translated into English.

The Stages of Meditation by Kamalashila (Skt. *bhavanakrama*, Tib. *sgom pa'i rim pa,* Pron. "gomrim"). A text in three volumes was written by Kamalashila (8th century C.E.) and laid the foundation for teaching the gradual path in Tibetan Buddhism. The first book was translated by Giuseppe Tucci in *Minor Buddhist Texts*, Part II. Serie Orientale Roma, IX. 2. Rome: Is. M. E. O., 1958.

Ten Teachings from the Hundred Thousand Songs of Milarepa by Thrangu Rinpoche. This text takes ten spiritual songs and summarizes them with a commentary on their meaning for practice. Boulder: Namo Buddha Publications, 1995.

Treasury of the Abhidharma by Vasubandhu *(Skt. abhidharmakosha*, Tib. *mngon pa mdzod*, Pron. *ngönpa dzö)*
This is a summary of the vast Abhidharma literature by the brother of Asanga. This text is studied in Tibet more than the original texts.

Treasury of Oral Instruction (Tib. *gdams ngag ndzod*, Pron. "damngak dzö") by Jamgon Kongtrul the First. This is a collection of thirteen volumes of the oral instructions of the eight practice lineages. Jamgon Kongtrul collected these so that they would not be lost. This collection is one of this "Five Treasures."

Treatise Differentiating Consciousness and Wisdom (Tib. *rnam shes ye shes 'byed pa*, Pron. "namshe yeshe gepa") by Rangjung Dorje. This text by the Third Karmapa is a summary of the eight consciousnesses and how these are transformed into the five wisdoms. The original root verses and a commentary by Thrangu Rinpoche are given. Boulder, Colorado: Namo Buddha Publications, 1996.

Uttara Tantra by Asanga and Maitreya (Skt. *ratnagotravibhaga*, Tib. *rgyud bla ma*, Pron. "gyu lama") This text was written by Asanga who received the transmission from the bodhisattva Maitreya in Sanskrit in about the fourth century. The complete Tibetan text has been translated by Obermiller (E. Obermiller, Acta Orientalia, IX, 1931, pp. 81-306) and has been reprinted more recently in a book edited by H. S. Prasad (*The Uttaratantra of Maitreya*. Delhi, India: Sri Satguru Publications, 1991). Thrangu Rinpoche has also written a commentary on this text called *The Uttara Tantra: A Treatise on Buddha Nature*. Boulder, Colorado: Namo Buddha Publications, 1994. This book also includes a translation of the 404 root verses and Rinpoche's commentary.

Four Dharmas of Gampopa. by Thrangu Rinpoche. Boulder: Namo Buddha Publications, 1999.

Kagyu Lineage Chant (Pronounced Dorje Tungma). This chant in Tibetan and it English translation and a commentary by Thrangu Rinpoche is available in *Showing the Path to Liberation.*

Looking Directly at Mind: An Overview of Mahamudra Meditation by Thrangu Rinpoche. This book is an overview of Tashi Namgyal's Moonlight of Mahamudra. Boulder: Namo Buddha Publications, 1999.

Mahamudra: The Quintessence of Mind and Meditation by Tashi Namgyal and translated by Lobsang Lhalungpa. Boston: Shambhala Publications, 1986.

Masters of Mahamudra. by Keith Dowman. Albany, New York. Keith Dowman translated a work by Abhayadatta who collected the stories of eighty-four mahasiddhas, although there were many more than this.

The Practice of Tranquillity and Insight by Thrangu Rinpoche. Ithaca, New York: Snow Lion Publications, 1993.

The Rain of Wisdom. Translated by the Nalanda Translation Committee. This is a collection of spiritual songs of the Kagyu Lineage. Boston: Shambhala Publications, 1980.

The Three Distinctive Commitments to the Precepts. (Tib. *domsum rabya*) by the Sakya Pandita. This text has not been translated into the United States.

Index